# WOMEN AND RELIGION

## Contemporary and future challenges in the Global Era

Edited by Elisabetta Ruspini, Glenda Tibe Bonifacio
and Consuelo Corradi

First published in Great Britain in 2019 by

Policy Press
University of Bristol
1-9 Old Park Hill
Bristol
BS2 8BB
UK
t: +44 (0)117 954 5940
pp-info@bristol.ac.uk
www.policypress.co.uk

North America office:
Policy Press
c/o The University of Chicago Press
1427 East 60th Street
Chicago, IL 60637, USA
t: +1 773 702 7700
f: +1 773-702-9756
sales@press.uchicago.edu
www.press.uchicago.edu

British Library Cataloguing in Publication Data
A catalogue record for this book is available from the British Library

Library of Congress Cataloging-in-Publication Data
A catalog record for this book has been requested

ISBN 978-1-4473-3640-2 paperback
ISBN 978-1-4473-3635-8 hardcover
ISBN 978-1-4473-3637-2 ePub
ISBN 978-1-4473-3638-9 Mobi
ISBN 978-1-4473-3636-5 epdf

The right of Elisabetta Ruspini, Glenda Tibe Bonifacio and Consuelo Corradi to be
identified as editors of this work has been asserted by them in accordance with the Copyright,
Designs and Patents Act 1988.

The statements and opinions contained within this publication are solely those of the editors
and contributors and not of the University of Bristol or Policy Press. The University of
Bristol and Policy Press disclaim responsibility for any injury to persons or property resulting
from any material published in this publication.

Policy Press works to counter discrimination on grounds of gender, race,
disability, age and sexuality.

Cover design by Dave Rogers
Front cover image: shutterstock
Printed and bound in Great Britain by CPI Group (UK) Ltd,
Croydon, CR0 4YY
Policy Press uses environmentally responsible print partners

# Contents

# List of figures, tables and appendices

## Figures

## Tables

## Appendices

# Notes on contributors

**Francesco Antonelli** is Research Fellow of Sociology at the University of Roma Tre (Italy). Since 2016 he has been Secretary of the Research Section 'Studi di Genere' (Gender Studies), part of the AIS (Associazione Italiana di Sociologia-Italian Sociological Association). He was Visiting Professor at EHESS (Paris), Universidade de São Paulo (Brazil), Universidade do Minho (Portugal), GESIS Leibniz Institute (Germany), La Trobe University (Australia). He has published a number of books and articles and contributed papers to many conferences.

**Marziyeh Bakhshizadeh** is a Lecturer with special responsibilities for Social Sciences, Faculty of Society and Economics at the Rhein-Waal University of Applied Sciences (Germany). She did her PhD in the field of Social Sciences at the Ruhr University Bochum. Her dissertation is about women's rights in the main interpretations of Islam in Iran after the 1979 revolution. She obtained an MA in Sociology from Tehran University in Iran and an MA in 'Roads to Democracy(ies)', an international Master's Programme in History, Political Science and Sociology at the University of Siegen (Germany) in cooperation with the University of Coimbra (Portugal) and the University of Uppsala (Sweden).

**Glenda Tibe Bonifacio** is Associate Professor in Women and Gender Studies at the University of Lethbridge, Canada. She is the author of *Pinay on the Prairies: Filipino Women and Transnational Identities* (University of British Columbia Press, 2013) and has edited books on various topics related to gender and migration. Glenda is a research affiliate of the Prentice Institute for Global Population and Economy.

**Consuelo Corradi** is Professor of Sociology and Vice-Rector for research and international relations at Lumsa University, Rome, Italy. She served as co-Chair of the COST Action IS1206 on Femicide across Europe. She was Vice-President of the European Sociological Association from 2007 to 2009. Her research interests include violence against women, femicide, and the cross-national comparison of gender policy regimes across Europe. Her most recent book is *The concept and measurement of violence against women and men* (Policy Press, 2017), co-authored with S. Walby and others.

**Shannon N. Davis** is Associate Professor of Sociology at George Mason University, USA. Her research focuses on the reproduction of gender inequality in institutions, in particular within families and higher education, as well as the construction and maintenance of beliefs about gender (gender ideologies). In addition to numerous publications in scholarly journals such as *Journal of Family Issues*, *Marriage & Family Review*, and *Community, Work, & Family*, she is co-editor (with Sarah Winslow and David J. Maume) of *Gender in the Twenty-First Century, The Stalled Revolution and the Road to Equality* (University of California Press, 2017) and co-author (with Theodore N. Greenstein) of *Methods of Family Research* (3rd edition, Sage, 2012).

**Mari-Sol García Somoza** is a PhD candidate in Social Sciences at the University of Buenos Aires. Since 2010 she has been a member of the editorial board for the CEIL-CONICET journal, *Sociedad y Religión*. She is also a member of CEIL-CONICET's Society, Culture and Religion Programme and of the Centre for Cultural Anthropology (CANTHEL-Paris 5). She is part of the Steering Committee of the MERCOSUR Association of Social Scientists of Religion (ACSRM) for the period 2015–18.

**Kemal Kızılca** is a Lecturer at the Economics Department of Ankara University (Turkey). He has published several papers and delivered conference presentations in the areas of gender economics, labour economics, and post-Keynesian economics. His most recent contribution was published in *Feminist Economics*.

**Chia Longman** is Associate Professor in Gender Studies at the Department of Languages and Cultures and Director of the Research Centre for Culture and Gender (CRCG) at Ghent University, Belgium. She is also Programme Director of the Flemish Inter University Master Programme in Gender and Diversity. Her work focuses on women's identity and agency within different religious communities and movements including Orthodox, Judaism and the new spirituality. Her publications include: *Interrogating Harmful Cultural Practices: Gender, Culture and Coercion* (Routledge, 2015, with T. Bradley); *Féminisme et multiculturalisme: Les paradoxes du debat* (Peter Lang, 2010, with G. Coene) and various book chapters and articles in international journals.

**Angela M. Moe** is a Professor of Sociology at Western Michigan University, USA, with affiliated faculty status in Gender and Women's Studies as well as Global and International Studies. Her work focuses on women's health, the family and child welfare. She has published over 30 articles, taught myriad classes, and devoted countless hours to community service. She currently serves on the board of Trauma Recovery Associates, an international non-profit serving adult survivors of childhood trauma.

**Stefania Palmisano** is Associate Professor in the Sociology of Religion at the University of Turin, Italy, where she teaches courses in Sociology of Religion and Religious Organizational Cultures. She is Visiting Research Fellow, Department of Politics, Philosophy and Religion at Lancaster University, UK. She is a member of the editorial board of *Etnografia e Ricerca Qualitativa* (Il Mulino). In addition, she is coordinator of the research centre CRAFT (Contemporary Religions and Faiths in Transition), Department of Culture, Politics and Society of the University of Turin.

**Roberta Pibiri** (PhD) is a Researcher and Lecturer at the University of Turin, Italy. She is a member of the research centre CRAFT (Contemporary Religions and Faiths in Transition), Department of Culture, Politics and Society of the University of Turin. Among her research interests are: gender and religion; alternative spirituality and religious transformations; cultural and religious diversity; religious experience, self transformation and emotions; and ritual performance. Her recent publications include: 'Re-membering the Goddess: the Avalon Sacred Path in Italy between Tradition and Innovation', in S. Palmisano and N. Pannofino (eds), *Invention of Tradition and Syncretism in Contemporary Religion: Sacred Creativity* (Palgrave Macmillan, 2017).

**Ladan Rahbari** is a Researcher and part-time Lecturer at Ghent University, Belgium. She has a PhD in Sociology, and a Master's degree in Anthropology. She is currently conducting a joint doctorate research project funded by FWO in Ghent University and Vrije Universiteit Brussels. Rahbari has teaching and research experience on gender studies and social sciences in several universities. Her research interests include gender politics, sexuality, space, body, harmful practices and feminist theory. She is currently affiliated with the Centre for Research on Culture and Gender (UGent) and Centre of Expertise on Gender, Diversity and Intersectionality (VUB).

**Elisabetta Ruspini** is Associate Professor of Sociology at the University of Milano-Bicocca, Italy. Since 2012 she has coordinated the Research Section 'Studi di Genere' (Gender Studies), part of the AIS

(Associazione Italiana di Sociologia/Italian Sociological Association). She is a board member of the ESA Research Network 33 'Women's and Gender Studies' and has extensive teaching and research experience on gender issues. She has published a number of books and articles in peer-reviewed journals and has contributed papers to many conferences.

**Manu Sharma** is Associate Professor of History at Lovely Professional University, India. Since 2011, she has also taken the responsibility of Academic Operation coordinator. Her research interests include Gender/Women-related issues, Yoga-Ayurveda, and Cross-Cultural issues. She also has extensive teaching and research experience on gender issues. She has published a number of research papers and articles and contributed papers to many conferences.

**Joshua D. Tuttle** is a Doctoral Candidate of Sociology at George Mason University, USA and a research consultant. His research focuses on religious change, gender and political economy, with a concentration on the contemporary United States. Joshua has published his work in peer-reviewed journals, such as the *Journal of Divorce and Remarriage*, and edited volumes, including *Gender in the Twenty-First Century, The Stalled Revolution and the Road to Equality*. His dissertation research addresses the role that American Evangelicals have played in the rise of neoliberalism during the late 20th century.

**Mayra Soledad Valcarcel** is a graduate in Anthropological Sciences from the University of Buenos Aires (UBA), Argentina. She is currently a PhD student of the National Scientific and Technical Research Council (CONICET) at the Interdisciplinary Institute of Gender Studies (IIEGE-FFyL)-UBA, working on the project *Muslim Women: Intersections, Tensions and Identitarian Trajectories of Women Professing Islam in Argentina*.

**Nella van den Brandt** has a PhD from Ghent University, Belgium and is currently a postdoctoral Researcher at the Philosophy and Religious Studies Department at Utrecht University, the Netherlands. She has published in peer-reviewed journals such as *Culture and Religion, Social Compass, Women's Studies International Forum*, and *Social Movement Studies*. Her current research focuses on religion/secularity, religious conversion, media and culture, and the production of difference. She additionally is the manager assistant of the online open access journal *Religion and Gender*, https://www.religionandgender.org/.

**Masoumeh Velayati** is Associate Professor at Al-Maktoum College of Higher Education in Dundee, Scotland. Currently, she is on sabbatical leave at the Sociology Department, University of Warwick. She has a multi-disciplinary educational background in Islamic studies and comparative religions as well as social science, with particular focus on development, gender and Islamic feminism. She has published a book, several articles and chapters in peer-reviewed journals and edited books, and has contributed papers to many conferences.

# Women and religion: contemporary and future challenges: editors' introduction

*Elisabetta Ruspini, Glenda Tibe Bonifacio and Consuelo Corradi*

## Women and religion: an invisible story

This book aims to discuss some aspects of the relationship between social change, religion and women's lives and self-definition in the contemporary world. Using international and interdisciplinary perspectives reflective of different religious traditions, this collection pays attention to the specific experiences and positions of women, or particular groups of women, to understand current patterns of religiosity and religious change.

Women have played and are playing an active role, albeit underexplored and underestimated, in the construction and consolidation of religion. All religions depend heavily on the contributions of women to maintain and transmit religious values and tradition, even if these are largely invisible from the perspective of its officially credentialed leaders: priests, ministers, teachers and organizational authorities (Keller and Ruether, 2006). However, as pointed out by different scholars (see for example King and Beattie, 2004; Woodhead, 2007 and 2008), dominant theoretical frameworks within the sociology of religion often remain gender blind. The reasons for this are manifold, such as: androcentrism; the fact that women's studies in the field of religion have been slow to develop (King, 2005) and that their development have been restricted to a limited number of themes; and the vexed relationship between feminism and religion.

Due to the patriarchal dispositions of societies in which religions emerged, women scholars of religion were faced with the problem posed by the pervasive influence of androcentrism on all religious cultures. Androcentrism originates from a male monopoly on cultural leadership and on the transmission of culture: androcentric scholarship proceeds as if women do not exist, or as if they are passive actors, objects rather than subjects, and the voice of women is rarely heard.

Men have monopolized priestly and teaching roles of religion and excluded women both from the exercise of these roles and from the education that such roles require (Gross, 1977; Ruether, 1987). A number of scholars underline that, prior to the advent of women's studies (which emerged as a new field of inquiry across a number of academic disciplines in the late 1960s and early 1970s) the study of religions and historical religious development was primarily the study of men's religion and of the elite males who had shaped religions (see for example Gross, 1977): it was the religious experience of men that was being recorded for posterity, through religious texts and traditions, themselves largely the products of male authorship and systematization (Kinsley, 2002).

Another reason for the lack of attention to women's issues in the sociology of religion has to do with the fact that feminist studies have arrived rather later in the study of religion than in most other fields (King, 2005). Religion's central role in consolidating gender difference and inequality was initially recognized, explored and critiqued by 19th-century feminists (Woodhead, 2007; Schwartz, 2013): one well-known example is Elizabeth Cady Stanton and her revising committee in The Woman's Bible. In the late 1880s Stanton began a study of the Bible and sought to establish a committee of academic and church women to contribute to the project (it is believed, however, that much of the work was done by Stanton alone). The book was controversial since it attacked not only the Bible's use as an authority on which to base women's subordination, but also its divine inspiration. Stanton's work failed to be accepted as a major work of biblical scholarship and for many years the book was forgotten; with the revival of feminism in the late 1960s, interest in the book as a historical document was refreshed[1] (Davis, 2010).

In the 1960s and 1970s many European and North American women researchers began to focus on the analysis of female religious experience (Clague, 2005; Giorgi, 2016). Mary Daly's book *The Church and the Second Sex,* published in 1968, inaugurated a new era of feminist theological reflection marked by the systematic critique and reformulation of Christian doctrine from the perspective of women's experience. According to June O'Connor (1989, pp 101–2), the following concerns characterized work in the field during this period: androcentrism and misogyny of the Christian and, to a lesser extent, the Jewish traditions (Ruether, 1974; Saiving, 1976; Plaskow, 1990); the need to identify women as active agents of religious practice and religious innovators; the exploration of new forms of female-centred religiosity (Goddess Movement), a trend that is not necessarily aimed at rejecting religion, but rather at acknowledging the value of forms of religiosity promoted by women in order to empower women regardless of ethnicity, origin, age, belief, and sexual orientation (King, 1989; Plaskow and Christ, 1989; Woodhead, 2001; Giorgi, 2016); and the development of epistemological and methodological tools in order to challenge the androcentric bias of mainstream scholarship in theology and religious studies (Hawthorne, 2005; Woodhead, 2007).

However, Ursula King (1990) has noted the invisibility of religious studies within feminist and women's studies curricula and anthologies, and this can be attributed to the prevalent assumption among feminists that religion had little to offer women. The controversial relationship between feminism and religion often springs from the common assumption that feminism can only emerge and flourish when religion is removed from the public space. The fields of women's and religious studies have often been criticized for neglecting to engage with one another. On the one hand, when dealing with women's rights, equality and the deconstruction of women's traditional roles, religion is often perceived as an obstacle. For many feminists, religion is a tool of patriarchy that is still used to oppress and exclude women and to deny them the opportunity to make their own decisions (Kawahashi, Komatsu, Kuroki, 2013). On the other hand, many religious agents involved in the public debate take a firm stand against issues at the core of feminist engagement (such as divorce and abortion) and against the concept of gender itself (Gemzöe, Keinänen, Maddrell, 2016; Giorgi, 2016). Research on gender inequality and religion (Seguino, 2011; Klingorová and Havlíček, 2015) shows that even if most major religions agree on the respect for women and their crucial role in family life, especially with emphasis on women as mothers and wives, they do not, however, advocate emancipation in the sense of total equality with men (see for example Holm, 1994; Nyhagen and Halsaa, 2016). However, religious institutions are susceptible to change, albeit slow, and internal groups, within which women's groups can operate, may promote gender equality. But changes can occur in the opposite direction as well, due to the rise of religious fundamentalism wherein women's rights are deeply undermined (see for example Howland, 1999; Sturm, 2013).

## Contemporary challenges

The tendencies we have just described can be summarized as follows: all religions are characterized by male dominance (Young, 1994); the roles of women in the religious sphere tended to be marginal; women as researchers and subjects of research in the social scientific study of religion had long been in the minority up until the last couple of decades (King, 1995; Woodhead, 2001; Clague, 2005).

Today, contemporary challenges and changes are reshaping the landscape of studies in religion. Even if there is clear empirical support for the claim that women are more likely to be religious than men, women today are leaving the churches at a faster rate than men (Woodhead, 2008, Matteo, 2012; Berzano and Palmisano 2013; Crespi, 2014). Women also outnumber men in those forms of alternative spirituality which have developed since the late 1980s. This trend cannot be explained by the secularization theory alone: as Woodhead notes (2007), although intensifying secularization is positively correlated with growing gender equality, religion's continuing ability to consolidate gender inequality remains evident in contemporary societies.

Recent studies have shown that there is a strong connection between processes of change – such as the impact of globalization, increased intercultural and transcultural interaction and exchange, migration flows, and Information and Communication Technologies (ICTs) – and religious identities. Overall, recent literature has revealed a great complexity and often contradiction in late modern negotiations of religion and secularism by girls and boys, women and men, and a range of possibilities for change (see for example Corradi, 2007; Gross, Davies and Diab, 2013; Crespi and Ruspini, 2014; Nyhagen and Halsaa, 2016). Women's identities are rapidly changing and so, consequently, are the relations between women and men, and between women's identities and institutions. Women's identities have undergone the most intense transformations since the 20th century, for example women's increasing investment in education; their growing aspirations for self-achievement in work; a greater involvement in working life; the possibility to decide regarding reproduction choices; and the free expression of their sexualities. Some interesting changes can be observed among the younger male generations which contribute to new religious modalities. The number of men willing to question the stereotyped model of masculinity is growing, along with the emergence of critical and reflexive studies on men that historicized and analysed dominant constructions of masculinity and were attentive to the differences among men (see for example Connell, 1995; Kimmel, 1996; Hearn, 2010).

Changes in the status and roles of women and men are also being accelerated by the emergence of ICTs. Because of these new technologies, new forms of culture are emerging: for example, central to Web 2.0 is the requirement for interactive systems to enable the participation of users in production and social interaction (Anderson, 2012). The 'bottom-up', self-organizing of the social networking within information-sharing sites has been described as challenging the power of elite hierarchies to determine and organize knowledge and practice (Kolbitsch and Maurer, 2006). The interpersonal interaction between individuals in Web 2.0, for example, has been specifically valued for its capacity to empower users culturally, socially and politically (Pascu et al, 2007; for an overview, see Jarrett, 2008). Following Messina-Dysert and Ruether (2014), where women's participation in religious traditions has generally been suppressed because of patriarchy, the digital world has offered tools of liberation, solidarity and empowerment (see also Llewellyn, 2015).

Other crucial challenges for religious studies have to do with the complex interplay between women, religion and globalization: will increasing cross-national exchange and communication lead to improvements in women's status, empowerment and equality also within religion? Following a trend started in the 1990s – when feminist and gender studies have been increasingly influenced by poststructural, postcolonial and queer theories – there is a growing interest today in the connection between women and religion in a global perspective, especially when compared with non-Christian religious traditions and in the context of migration. More recent studies (for example King and Beattie, 2004) have shed light on the plurality of religious experiences, both within traditional religions and in non-mainstream forms of religiosity that overturn gender hierarchy (see for example King and Beattie, 2004).

How women (and men) experience their religious identity in a new context or country is also a theme now gaining more attention: religiosity is one key factor for determining the attitudes of different generations of migrants on gender roles and gender egalitarianism (Bonifacio and Angeles, 2010; Röder, 2011). A further, crucial challenge is to understand how Muslim women negotiate religious and cultural norms and values and if/where/how Islam, as a religion, can foster gender equality. This implies the exploration of different issues: Muslim women's experiences while seeking gender equality via an Islamic theological framework; Islamic feminism discourses and practices (see for example Mernissi, 1991, 2003); the links and tensions between Islamic feminist movements, institutions and social change.

The Muslim world is wide and highly heterogeneous; not only are the national contexts very different, but the history of Islamic movements in these contexts, their relationship with the state and their interplay with other political and social movements also differs widely (Baden, 1992). Therefore, as Gray (2015) notes, an attempt should be made to move beyond the simple bifurcation of 'feminist' and 'Islamist' to look at the many facets of internal gender discourse within Muslim countries, allowing for a more nuanced understanding of the discussion on women's rights in the Muslim world. Within this context, the focus on interfaith dialogue – as both a way to deconstruct gender stereotypes and to support the ability of women from different religious traditions to bond and develop interfaith understanding through their relationships with other women – is challenging previous paradigms and creating new fields of study. Interfaith dialogue is today particularly crucial; there is a need to stimulate communication, to correct stereotypes, to explore similarities and differences, and to facilitate cooperation, particularly among the three monotheistic religions (that is, Judaism, Christianity, Islam), and especially between Christians and Muslims, who comprise almost half the world's population. The way in which these three religions' worlds relate is bound to have profound consequences for both communities and for the entire world (Kimball, 2017).

## Form and contents of the book

Based on these premises, this book aims to fill existing gaps by adding new knowledge to the existing body of literature on academic research on the dynamic relationship between women and religion, and on the contemporary and future challenges posed by women's changes to religion – in different parts of the world and among different religious traditions and practices.

The 12 chapters included in this book – written by senior and junior leading scholars from different continents – Asia, North and South America, and Europe – present unique studies to explore tensions and opportunities in the intersection of the different concepts: gender, gender equality, religion, activism, feminism and social change. By using a variety of 'qualitative' and 'quantitative' methods, the authors address a number of questions: What are the present attitudes of different religions to gender equality? How do women construct their identity through religious activity? Is there a way to reconcile faith and feminism? Do these processes change within different religious traditions? How are contemporary processes of change affecting religious identities and practices for women and men in different contexts?

In order to answer these questions, the book develops along three lines. The first part of the book focuses on today's attitudes of different religions to gender equality (Part 1: Women, gender equality and religion between past and present, Chapters 1–4). Secondly, the book sheds light on how women negotiate their personal identities within religion, considering women active social actors (Part 2: Identities, women's movements and religion, Chapters 5–8). Thirdly, a focus is given on contemporary women's religious experiences in order to contribute to the understanding of the rich global diversity and complexity of women's religious choices and practices (Part 3: Contemporary women's religious experiences, Chapters 9–12). In most of the chapters, the notion of gender is used to describe the culturally and socially constructed difference between women and men. This does not mean that authors and editors view gender as a binary concept: gender is a spectrum, and not limited to just two possibilities. It simply means that when it comes to analysing the different position of women in traditional and contemporary religious views of the world, the relationship between women and men is extremely relevant.

Part 1 of the book opens with the chapter by Marziyeh Bakhshizadeh 'Gender equality in different readings of Islam in post-revolutionary Iran'. This chapter provides an understanding of women's rights and gender equality based on three interpretations of Islam within the context of post-revolutionary Iran. The debate among different interpretations of Islam provides a foundation for the investigation of women's rights and gender equality in various readings of Islam beyond the regional dimensions of Iran, but also in the Islamic world. Recognizing various interpretations of Islam is of utmost importance to the study of gender equality in the Islamic context. While some studies and academic discussions tend to use the term fundamentalism to refer to religious revival movements, particularly within Islamic traditions, such discussions often fail to distinguish reformist and other movements within Islam, therefore identifying all Islamic revival movements as fundamentalist or as part of fundamentalist movements. Accordingly, they make certain assumptions about Islam and its incompatibility with modern ideas such as gender equality.

The second chapter, 'Religion and gender equality in Catholic Philippines: discourses and practices in the 21st century' by Glenda Tibe Bonifacio, aims to present Catholic religious discourses and practices of gender equality in the contemporary Philippines. The Philippines is the only Catholic-dominated country in Asia and this chapter looks at particular practices among Catholic women and examines the role of religion in the movement towards gender equality. Through ethnographic data in small communities in Eastern Visayas, participant observation, and a case study of two women from Leyte, this chapter provides insight into how religiosity is enmeshed with the aims of local women to improve their status in society. The chapter shows that, even if the Catholic Church retains its prominent presence in the social fabric, and is very much a part of the rituals of life, the symbolism of its moral power, particularly in the lives of women, has been contested by lived experiences quite different from what is prescribed.

Chapter 3, 'A slow march forward: the impact of religious change on gender ideology in the contemporary United States' by Joshua D. Tuttle and Shannon N. Davis, refers to the substantial decline of Mainline Protestantism and the tremendous growth of the religiously unaffiliated population. In this chapter the authors ask how these cultural changes are related to the trends in gender ideology since the late 1970s, with a specific focus on the reversal in the trend towards gender egalitarianism in the mid-1990s, and the slow growth of gender egalitarianism throughout the 2000s. A constrained age–period–cohort model to several decades of data from the GSS-General Social Survey is applied to evaluate the effect that religious change has had on gender ideology in the US. The results suggest that shifts in the religious composition of the US population over time are significantly related to the observed trends in gender ideology. The decline of Mainline Protestantism has undermined progress towards gender egalitarianism, while the rise of the religiously unaffiliated seems not significantly related to trends in gender ideology.

Chapter 4, 'Divine shadows: Indian Devadasis between religious beliefs and sexual exploitation' by Manu Sharma, aims to understand the origin and growth of the Devadasi system and highlights the present status of Devadasis in Indian society. The term Devadasi is a Sanskrit word, which literally translates to 'female slave of God'. In contemporary times, for various socio-historical reasons, the Devadasi tradition appears to have lost its status and is equated synonymously with prostitution and slavery in India. Devadasi practice today is a challenge to both NGOs and the government. This chapter questions the importance of the religious factor in explaining the logic of the Devadasis' institution. Conversely, the element of caste and socio-economic background are two fundamental aspects that should be taken into account. These factors, strictly interwoven, contribute to keeping this practice alive. The Devadasi's consecration is deeply embedded both in the rural social structure and religious beliefs and represents a form of dominance and social control of upper castes over lower ones.

Part 2 of the book opens with Chapter 5 by Masoumeh Velayati 'Formation of "religious" identity among British Muslim women'. In the UK, Muslim women are generally disadvantaged, which is reflected in their high unemployment and inactivity rates compared to their male counterparts and other ethnic minority women. This is despite policies to reduce the diversity gap in the UK labour market based on gender and religious affiliations. Applying feminist theory and questioning Muslim women's place as a marginalized group at the centre of social inquiry, this chapter aims to explore the ways in which Muslim women negotiate religious and cultural norms and values. The study is grounded in empirical data between 2012 and 2013, drawing from personal narratives collected through 53 semi-structured interviews and 64 questionnaires from different ethnic and cultural groups of Muslim women in the UK. Findings indicate a feminist consciousness tapping into the Islamic framework as an enabling means for personal empowering in a rapidly changing world that challenges traditional gender issues. For Muslim women, the search for a distinctive social identity means exercising their 'religious' manifestations in a way in which they ensure that they look to be both modern and Muslim simultaneously.

Chapter 6 by Nella van den Brandt, 'Christian women's movements in secularizing and diversifying contexts: a case study from Belgium' focuses on the case of Flanders, In Flanders, Christian women's movements belonging to Catholic civil society (the 'Catholic pillar') used to draw a large following and were able to contribute to the political, religious and social emancipation of Catholic women throughout Belgium. Today, these Christian women's movements face declining membership and the need to 'reinvent' themselves according to contemporary times and women's needs. This chapter explores, against the background of various facets of social change, how Femma, a large Christian women's movement uniting 65,000 members, reinvented its self-presentation and self-positioning in order to maintain its religious, social and cultural relevance. Looking at how a movement that is constitutive of Christian women's history in Flanders rethinks its self-presentation and self-positioning, this chapter aims to generate important insights, both descriptive and normative, into the role and place of Christian feminism and Christian women's movements in the face of social changes that take place, in both similar and different ways, across Western Europe. The chapter also maps feminist approaches to the secular emerging in Western European contexts and argues for the importance of bridging divides across disciplines, methodological approaches and political-analytical priorities.

Chapter 7, 'Muslim women in contemporary Argentina' by Mari-Sol García Somoza and Mayra Soledad Valcarcel, deepens and develops the discourses, practices, identity constructions, performance and modes of socialization among Muslim women in contemporary Argentinean society. The main aim is to describe, understand and explain the process of identity building among women professing Islam in Argentina by analysing the ways they articulate and reconstruct their different loci of identity belongings (sex/gender, Arab, Argentinean and Muslim identities). This chapter inquiries into the specific modes of religious identity building in Muslim women through the development of careers, enabling comparisons to be drawn between the religious careers of women occupying different positions in the social field; analyses the discourses and counter-discourses generated by the actors both at the core and on the periphery of the membership group; and tries to understand and describe how Muslim women experience (embodiment) and externalize (performance) their religiosity and religious identity, while paying attention to the different types of female agency and the relation they establish between their reinterpretation of Islamic principles during their self-constitution and the definition of their presence in the world (being-in-the-world).

The aim of Chapter 8, 'The impact of religious unorthodoxy on family choices and women's well-being in Turkey' by F. Kemal Kızılca, is to provide evidence from Turkey, a Muslim-majority country, on how religious unorthodoxy is related to the number of children and generations living in a household, both of which strongly link to women's time burden and, consequently, their well-being. In this chapter the author uses data from Turkish Household Consumption Surveys, which contain rich information regarding household-level consumption, household characteristics and individual characteristics. This study both contributes to and moves beyond the literature that establishes a link between secularization and women's agency. The evidence from Turkish Household Budget Surveys supports the idea that women who live in 'sinful' households, that is households which do not follow Sunni dogmas in their consumption patterns, are faced with lesser burdens of childcare and elder-care responsibilities.

Part 3 of the book is composed of four chapters. Chapter 9, '"Between me and my God": a life story narrative of conciliating cultural discourses and personalization of Islam' by Ladan Rahbari and Chia Longman, aims to contribute to a better understanding of the relation between gender and Islam by portraying and exploring a subjective account of conciliating religiosity and modern individualism. The study is conducted based on a life story narrative of a Muslim migrant woman from Iran, living in Belgium. Her life story and experiences prior to and after migration are analysed to reveal how she has built and made sense of her religiosity in the European context. Muslim migrants in Europe have faced challenges defining their identity and fighting against Islamophobia since 11 September 2001. While emancipating themselves from representations purely based on their religious affiliation, Muslim migrants in Europe have remained attached to their countries of origin and their religious and cultural background. By adopting a life story method, this chapter aims to investigate dynamics of conciliating supposedly contradicting cultural and religious discourses, and to explore religious belonging and personalization of faith.

Chapter 10, '"We are all Goddesses": female sacred paths in Italy' by Roberta Pibiri and Stefania Palmisano, aims to reflect on the relations between gender and religion, by analysing a new form of spirituality coming from the Anglophone world, Goddess Spirituality, which has arrived in Italy in the new millennium. The analysis moves from secondary data on alternative spiritualities in Italy and is based on ethnographic research carried out in 2013–14 by one of the authors in the Turin Goddess Spirituality group. Goddess Spirituality is one of the most important – and in some ways challenging – forms, where the movement of rediscovering paths of the sacred female are evident. As some studies demonstrate, while an ever-increasing proportion of women leave the Catholic Church, the majority do not redirect their spiritual seeking outside the Catholic milieu by approaching the world of so-called alternative spiritualities. Goddess Spirituality's contemporaneous spiritual/secular orientation is a source of empowerment for its adherents because it is capable of integrating into its symbolic, axiological universe a gender concept with a sacred dimension. This opens up the possibility of a radical change in the construction of male/female relationships according to the principles of Goddess Spirituality.

Chapter 11 by Angela M. Moe, 'Explorations of spiritual embodiment in belly dance', examines how US belly dancers view the practice as a spiritual endeavour, particularly in light of the negative perceptions surrounding it. The author discusses findings from a decade-long ethnographic study (2003–13) involving several data collection methods: observations; journal entries; online statements; and qualitative interviews, a mixed methods design needed due to the lack of research on this topic and the complexity involved in understanding it. Findings suggest that belly dance holds much potential as an embodied spiritual practice, particularly when premised on holistic health (integration of body, mind and spirit). As such, the chapter contributes to this critical examination of women's spirituality within contemporary contexts. This chapter adds to a growing body of research on alternative spiritual practices – that is, finding spiritual salience in social contexts that are not traditionally viewed as spiritual in nature.

The purpose of Chapter 12 by Francesco Antonelli and Elisabetta Ruspini, 'From exclusion to inclusion: women and interfaith dialogue in the Mediterranean area', is to discuss women's contribution to interfaith dialogue in the Mediterranean. This area is often referred to as a uniform region and usually depicted as highly problematic (where conflicts and migration flows pose considerable risks to the security of the entire region). The Mediterranean is not a single society, instead it is a multipolar world; the Mediterranean basin offers a mosaic of societies and cultures that have influenced one another (and continue to do so). Moreover, the Mediterranean is not only an area of crisis and conflict, but also a space for opportunities and dialogue. Interreligious dialogue is a powerful tool for achieving peace and stability. Today, institutions for intercultural dialogue and cooperation, religious representatives and interfaith organizations are working together to build mutual understanding in the region. What is the role played by Mediterranean women in this process? This chapter shows that the inter-religious dialogue has been changing its nature through a two-fold enlargement centred on the gender dimension: vertical, by women belonging to intellectual elites; and horizontal, through a growing involvement of civil society. This chapter also discusses the role played by Millennial women in advancing intercultural and interfaith dialogue.

## Conclusion

This book uses comparative perspectives to explore the relationship between women, religion and gender change. Women are social actors active in reforming and changing existing social institutions, such as religion. However, the active role of women in the religious sphere has rarely received the attention it deserves. This book provides an opportunity to both explore women's contribution to religious change and to promote women's empowerment and equality within religious traditions in a globalized environment. In the scientific study of religion (and specifically within the sociology of religion), paying attention to the contribution of women is an essential corrective to the gender-blindness which has, until recently, restricted the discipline's field of vision. From the methodological point of view, the chapters collected in this book use different approaches. If a predilection for the qualitative approach has been consolidated among feminist scholars, while the logic of quantitative research has long been considered a gender-blind practice of male domination, we also argue that quantitative research may greatly contribute to address the intersection of *gender* and *religion*, and that an effort should be made to overcome the quality–quantity dualism in order to be able to grasp the complexity of the issues involved (Decataldo and Ruspini, 2014). Insights gained from using these approaches serve to advance our understanding of what has been invisible for centuries.

## Note

[1]  'The Woman's Bible', Form and Content, Masterpieces of Women's Literature, ed. Frank Northern Magill, eNotes.com, Inc. 1995. Available at: http://www. enotes.com/topics/womans-bible/in-depth#in-depth-form-and-content.

## References

Anderson, P. (2012) *Web 2.0 and Beyond: Principles and Technologies*, London: Chapman & Hall/CRC Textbooks in Computing.

Baden, S. (1992) *The Position of Women in Islamic Countries: Possibilities, Constraints and Strategies for Change. Briefing on Development and Gender, Report No. 4*, Brighton, UK: Institute of Development Studies. Available at: http://www.bridge.ids.ac.uk/reports/re4c.pdf.

Berzano, L. and Palmisano, S. (2013) 'Prospettive di genere nella sociologia della religione italiana', in Consiglio Scientifico della Sezione AIS Studi di Genere (ed) *Sotto la lente del genere. La sociologia italiana si racconta*, Milan: FrancoAngeli, pp 119–29.

Clague, J. (2005) 'Women's Studies in Religion', in Encyclopedia of Religion, Encyclopedia.com. Available at: http://www.encyclopedia. com/environment/encyclopedias-almanacs-transcripts-and-maps/ womens-studies-religion.

Connell, R.W. (1995) *Masculinities*, Berkeley: University of California Press.

Corradi, C. (2007) 'La conoscenza del limite. Il dialogo tra fede e ragione in un'età post-secolare', in L. Leuzzi (ed) *La carità intellettuale. Percorsi culturali per un nuovo umanesimo*, Rome: LEV, pp 67–73.

Crespi. I. (2014) 'Religiosità e differenze di genere in Italia: credenze, pratiche e cambiamenti generazionali', in I. Crespi and E. Ruspini (eds) *Genere e religioni in Italia: voci a confronto*, Milan: FrancoAngeli, pp 83–132.

Crespi, I. and Ruspini, E. (eds) (2014) *Genere e religioni in Italia: voci a confronto (Gender and Religions in Italy)*, Milan: FrancoAngeli.

Davis, S. (2010) *The Political Thought of Elizabeth Cady Stanton: Women's Rights* and the American Political Traditions, New York: New York University Press.

Decataldo, A. and Ruspini, E. (2014) *La ricerca di genere (Gender-sensitive Research)*, Rome: Carocci.

Giorgi, A. (2016) 'Gender, Religion, and Political Agency: Mapping the Field', *Revista Crítica de Ciências Sociais*, no 110, pp 51–72. Available at: http://dx.doi.org/10.4000/rccs.6371.

Gray, D.H. (2015) *Beyond Feminism and Islamism: Gender and Equality in North Africa*, London and New York: I.B. Tauris.

Gross, R.M. (ed) (1977) *Beyond Androcentrism: New Essays on Women and Religion*, Missoula, MT.: Scholars Press.

Gross, Z., Davies, L. and Diab, Al-K. (eds) (2013) *Gender, Religion and Education in a Chaotic Postmodern World*, New York: Springer.

Hawthorne, S. (2005) 'Gender and Religion: History of Study', in Encyclopedia of Religion, Encyclopedia.com: http://www.encyclopedia.com/environment/encyclopedias-almanacs-transcripts-and-maps/gender-and-religion-history-study.

Hearn, J. (2010) 'The Implications of Critical Studies on Men', *NORA-Nordic Journal of Feminist and Gender Research*, vol 5, no 1, pp 48–60.

Holm, J. (1994) 'Introduction: Raising the Issues', in J. Holm and J. Bowker (eds) *Women in Religion*, New York: Continuum, pp 12–22.

Howland, C.W. (1999), *Religious Fundamentalisms and the Human Rights of Women*, New York: Palgrave Macmillan.

Jarrett, K. (2008) 'Interactivity is Evil! A Critical Investigation of Web 2.0', *First Monday*, vol 13, no 3, March. Available at: http://firstmonday.org/htbin/cgiwrap/bin/ojs/index.php/fm/article/view/2140/1947.

Kawahashi, N., Komatsu, K. and Kuroki, M. (2013) 'Gendering Religious Studies: Reconstructing Religion and Gender Studies in Japan', in Z. Gross, L. Davies and Al-K. Diab (eds) *Gender, Religion and Education in a Chaotic Postmodern World*, New York: Springer, pp 111–23. Available at: https://link.springer.com/chapter/10.1007/978-94-007-5270-2_8.

Keller, R.S. and Ruether, R.R. (2006) 'Introduction: Integrating the Worlds of Women's Religious Experience in North America', in R.S. Keller and R.R. Ruether (eds) *Encyclopedia of Women and Religion in North America*, vol 1, Bloomington and Indianapolis: Indiana University Press, pp xxv–xlvii.

Kimball, C.A. (2017) 'Muslim-Christian dialogue', in *The Oxford Encyclopedia of the Islamic World. Oxford Islamic Studies Online.* Available at: http://www.oxfordislamicstudies.com/article/opr/t236/e0567.

Kimmel, M.S. (1996) *Manhood in America. A Cultural History*, New York: Free Press.

King, U. (1989) *Women and Spirituality: Voices of Protest and Promise*, Basingstoke: Macmillan.

King, U. (1990) 'Religion and gender', in U. King (ed) *Turning Points in Religious Studies*, London, Oxford, New York: Bloomsbury Publishing, pp 275–86.

King, U. (1995) (ed) *Religion and Gender*, Oxford and Cambridge, MA: Blackwell.

King, U. (2005) 'Gender and religion: an overview', in *Encyclopedia of Religion*, Encyclopedia.com. Available at: http://www.encyclopedia.com/environment/encyclopedias-almanacs-transcripts-and-maps/gender-and-religion-overview.

King, U. and Beattie T. (eds) (2004) *Gender, Religion, and Diversity: Cross-Cultural Perspectives*, London and New York: Continuum.

Kinsley, D. (2002) 'Women's Studies in the History of Religions', in A. Sharma (ed) *Methodology in Religious Studies: The Interface with Women's Studies*, New York: SUNY Press, pp 1–15. Available at: http://www.sunypress.edu/pdf/60553.pdf.

Klingorová, K. and Havlíček, T. (2015) 'Religion and gender inequality: the status of women in the societies of world religions', *Moravian Geographical Reports*, vol 23, no 2, pp 2–11, doi:10.1515/mgr-2015-0006.

Kolbitsch, J. and Maurer, H. (2006) 'The transformation of the web: how emerging communities shape the information we consume', *Journal of Universal Computer Science*, vol 12, no 2, pp 187–213.

Llewellyn, D. (2015) *Reading, Feminism, and Spirituality: Troubling the Waves*, New York: Palgrave Macmillan.

Matteo, A. (2012) *La fuga delle quarantenni. Il difficile rapporto delle donne con la Chiesa*, Soveria Mannelli: Rubbettino.

Mernissi, F. (1991) *Women and Islam: An Historical and Theological Enquiry*, Oxford: Blackwell Publishers.

Mernissi, F. (2003) *Beyond the Veil: Male–female Dynamics in Muslim Society*, London: Saqi Books.

Messina-Dysert, G. and Ruether, R.R. (2014) *Feminism and Religion in the 21st Century: Technology, Dialogue, and Expanding Borders*, 1st edition, London: Routledge.

Nyhagen, L. and Halsaa, B. (2016) *Religion, Gender and Citizenship: Women of Faith, Gender Equality and Feminism*, New York: Palgrave Macmillan.

O'Connor, J. (1989) 'Rereading, Reconceiving, and Reconstructing Traditions: Feminist Research in Religion', *Women's Studies*, vol 17, no 1, pp 101–23.

Pascu, C., Osimo, D., Ulbrich, M., Turlea, G. and Burgelman, J.C. (2007) 'The Potential Disruptive Impact of Internet 2 Based Technologies', First Monday, vol 12, no 3. Available at: http://journals.uic.edu/fm/article/view/1630/1545.

Plaskow, J. (1990) *Standing Again at Sinai: Judaism from a Feminist Perspective*, San Francisco: Harper & Row.

Plaskow, J. and Christ, C.P. (eds) (1989) *Weaving the Visions: New Patterns in Feminist Spirituality*, San Francisco, Harper & Row.

Ruether, R.R. (ed) (1974) *Religion and Sexism: Images of Women in the Jewish and Christian Traditions*, New York: Simon & Schuster.

Ruether, R.R. (1987) 'Androcentrism', in M. Eliade (ed) *The Encyclopedia of Religion*, 2nd edition, New York and London, pp 334–37, available at: http://www.iupui.edu/~womrel/REL301%20Women/Ruether_Androcentrism.pdf.

Röder, A. (2011) *Gender Role Attitudes of Migrants: The Impact of Religion and Origin Country Context*, Trinity College Dublin.

Saiving Goldstein, V. (1960) 'The human situation: a feminine view', *The Journal of Religion*, vol 40, no 2, pp 100–12.

Saiving, V. (1976) 'Androcentrism in Religious Studies', *The Journal of Religion*, vol 56, no 2, pp 177–97.

Schwartz, L. (2013) *Infidel Feminism: Secularism, Religion and Women's Emancipation, England 1830–1914*, Manchester and New York: Manchester University Press.

Seguino, S. (2011) 'Help or hindrance? Religion's impact on gender inequality in attitudes and outcomes', *World Development*, vol 39, no 8, pp 1308–21.

Sturm, T. (2013) 'The future of religious geopolitics: towards a research and theory agenda', *Area*, vol 45, no 2, pp 134–40.

Woodhead, L. (2001) 'Feminism and the sociology of religion: from gender-blindness to gendered difference', in R.K. Fenn (ed) *The Blackwell Companion to Sociology of Religion*, Maldon, MA: Blackwell, pp 67–84, doi:10.1002/9780470998571.ch4.

Woodhead, L. (2007) 'Gender differences in religious practice and significance', in J. Beckford and N.J. Demerath III (eds) *The Sage Handbook of the Sociology of Religion*, Los Angeles, London, New Delhi, Singapore: Sage, pp 550–70.

Woodhead, L. (2008) 'Gendering secularization theory', *Social Compass*, vol 55, no 2, pp 187–93.

Young, K. (1994) 'Introduction', in A. Sharma (ed) *Today's Women in World Religions*, Albany, NY: State University of New York Press, pp 1–36.

# Part 1
# Women, gender equality and religion between past and present

# ONE

# Gender equality in different readings of Islam in post-revolutionary Iran[*]

*Marziyeh Bakhshizadeh*

## Introduction

In recent years, the study of the relationship between religion and social change as well as the relationship between religion and women's rights has been the subject of many studies and literature. In the context of Islam, there have been many debates on this topic since, in such communities and countries, Islamic laws directly affect women's lives. Women's movements in Islamic countries, despite having a long history, have not achieved much progress in their quest for gender equality (Abu Zayd, 1999, pp 106–9). For instance, an overview of the history of Iranian women's struggles to gain basic human rights illustrates that today, after more than 100 years of efforts, women are still striving to make polygamy illegal, to have unconditional rights to education, to work, to travel outside the country, to transfer their Iranian nationality to their non-Iranian husbands and their children, to have the right of custody of their children, and to be recognized as citizens with equal rights. Throughout their struggles, they have been faced with opposition that argues that women rights must be 'in conformity with Islamic criteria', which is demonstrated in several articles of the Constitution of the Islamic Republic of Iran[1].

The question that arises here is whether Islam legitimates a discriminatory perspective and laws against women. Accordingly this chapter intends to investigate women's rights in the main currents of Islam and how women's rights and self-agency of women in various interpretations of Islam are affected by social changes in Iran. To enter into this discussion, it is important to take into account that Islam is not a monolithic and homogeneous religious tradition (Mojtahed

---

[*]   This chapter is a synopsis of my dissertation published by Barbara Budrich Publishers and titled *Changing Gender Norms in Islam between Reason and Revelation*.

Shabestari, 1384/2006). There are different interpretations of Islam which are categorized in this research in three schools of thought based on their understanding of how compatible Islamic laws are with a specific time and space. Accordingly, this chapter considers different interpretations of Islam within a spectrum; on the far right are fundamentalists, in the middle are reformists, and on the far left are secular; each having diverse views on the legitimacy and applicability of all Islamic laws in modern times, and thus having various perspectives on justice and women's rights.

For this purpose, the chapter focuses on different interpretations of Islam within the context of post-revolutionary Iran, where an Islamic government has been established since the 1979 revolution, and claims that all articles of the Constitution, as well as all other laws and regulations, are based on Islamic criteria. This led to a discourse among different interpretations of Islam in Iran. Gender equality and women's rights in modern society have been one of the most important subjects in the debate among various readings of Islam. Accordingly, this discourse in Iran presents a foundation for the investigation of women's rights in the main currents of Islam, which surpasses the regional dimensions of Iran and represents the discourse in the Islamic world. Therefore, Iran not only represents different interpretations of Islam, but also reflects the discourse and debate on women's rights among different interpretations of Islam in the Islamic world and provides an understanding of how social changes affect the interpretations of Islam and, in general, the religiosity of women's lives and self-agency in the contemporary world. Therefore, to gain a better understanding of different interpretations of Islam and their view of women's rights, this chapter focuses on the current discourse among various readings of Islam in Iran.

This chapter, after presenting a literature review on women's issues in different interpretations of Islam in some Islamic countries, proceeds to a theoretical discussion of the relationship between structure and individual based on Giddens' Structuration Theory (Giddens, 1991a) to analyse the main currents of Islamic thought through a sociological perspective. To achieve this purpose, the chapter employs a comparative method as a tool of analysis to attain a 'concept-formation' by focusing on similarities and contrasts among cases (Collier, 1993, p 105). This chapter intends to compare the perspectives of the main currents of Islamic thought on women's rights and equality in order to explore similarities and differences of these perspectives, as well as to achieve a typology towards a better understanding and explanation of women's rights in various interpretations of Islam. Finally, this chapter concludes with a comparison of women's equality and self-agency in various readings of Islam.

## Literature review

Gender equality, interpreted as equal access to resources and opportunities for everyone regardless of gender, is recognized as crucial in the global concept of justice. In relation to religion, gender equality is often rejected because of local cultural value systems; therefore, the subject of Islam and gender equality has become a popular issue in several fields of human sciences. Studies relating to women's rights and gender equality are generally based on three interpretations of Islam: fundamentalist, reformist and secularist. This section briefly introduces literature on women's issues in some Islamic societies in Asia based on these three interpretations. Restricted to no single region, this section considers women's positions in different Islamic societies; however, it is not meant to take a reductive perspective on women's status in Islamic societies or to reduce other variables of nationality, ethnicity, economics, geography and culture to only one variable of religion. This section focuses more on how women in some Islamic societies relate their self-agencies and self-definition to their interpretations of Islam. In this way, we can achieve a better understanding of the impact of social changes on the interpretation of Islam, religiosity and self-agency of women.

### Studies on women's issues in fundamentalist interpretations

Islamic fundamentalism seeks a worldview based on a golden age and 'utopian and past-oriented' perspective (Eisenstadt, 1996, cited in Moghissi, 1999, p 71) through fulfilment of Islamic laws in a contemporary society without any adjustment to the contemporary needs of human beings. Despite significant regional and political differences among Islamic fundamentalist movements, they have certain similar features. Fundamentalist movements are considered as opposed to modern, secular values, anti-democracy and anti-feminist; however, they are not against modern living conditions (Moghissi, 1999, p 76). They follow certain policies concerning matters of family and gender relations by trying to turn women to practise more traditional roles. These methods include encouraging procreation, veiling of women, segregation of the sexes, control over female sexuality, and submission to patriarchal values (Afary, 1997).

One remarkable point that must be considered regarding fundamentalism is that Muslim women in different countries have also participated in reconstruction of fundamentalism, and it is not solely imposed on women by men (Afary, 1997). Women are attracted to fundamentalism for several reasons, including the emphasis on family and the priority of raising children (Afary, 1997). Some women might have more interest in traditional culture and show a willingness to accept the apparently secure patriarchal values to gain the husband's loyalty and economic support, including support for their children (Kandiyoti, 1988). This willingness can be related to the insecurities of the structure of society, such as unemployment, the low status of jobs for women, lack of childcare, and responsibility for household services for children and the elderly (Ruthven, 2007).

However, women's positions in a fundamentalist community are in a transitional phase, so that women are no longer largely confined to the home, but gradually undertake active roles and participate in public and business lives (Ruthven, 2007). In this transitional period, women apply fundamentalist norms to achieve some personal autonomy and subjectivity in building the Islamic society, which is another reason that women support the fundamentalist movement. An example is subjectivity of women and their personal choice for veiling (Mahmood, 2005). Accordingly, some argue that veiling of women, although it restricts women's individual freedom, provides women with more opportunities to access education and employment, to work as members of political organizations, and to participate in public spaces (Bahramitash and Esfahani, 2011). Furthermore, veiled women in Muslim countries face less sexual harassment in society. The veil can protect women from sexual harassment in various forms, such as touching, fondling, stalking and derogatory comments on the streets, in buses and in work places, for which women not only have no recourse by law, but also are accused of having seduced the men (Abu Odeh, 1993). The policy of segregation and compulsory veiling of women in Iran on the one hand imposed restrictions on social and economic activities of women; on the other hand, such policies reassured conservative religious families that education of their women would not cause religious degradation (Bahramitash and Esfahani, 2011, p 99). In this way, the education of women became an accepted norm, so that two decades after the revolution there was a 23% increase in the number of women taking nationwide university entrance exams, with 65% of girls passing the test. Education gave young women proper justification to postpone their marriage (Bahramitash and Esfahani, 2011, p 100) as well as enabling them to become much more involved in employment and even civil society and gradually gain self-agency and more control over their lives, despite the prevalence of traditional roles for women based on fundamentalist interpretation of Islamic texts.

## Studies on women's issues in reformist interpretations

Although fundamentalism imposed patriarchal authority on women, women have gradually attained individual autonomy and agency to rethink religious traditions, to reject gender relations and to challenge the patriarchal tradition in Islam. A new consciousness about women's discourse emerged and is known as 'Islamic feminism'. Islamic feminists reclaim an ethical vision of the Quran that liberates women and insistently enjoins equality and justice. This new strategy is aimed at a rereading of the Quran outside of the traditional, patriarchal interpretation for the advancement and empowerment of Muslim women. Badran (2005) identifies Islamic feminism as a new discourse within feminism. In her point of view, religion is not monolithic and static and there is the possibility for change within an Islamic framework. Moghadam (2002) further argues how Islamic feminism could be regarded as part of a broader religious reformation within the Islamic world.

Islamic feminism articulates the Quran-based idea of the equality of all human beings, irrespective of gender, race or ethnicity. In this view, the Quran does not mention specific gender roles, but it instead emphasizes the notion of mutuality of the conjugal relationship, in the way that spouses are regarded as each other's protectors or mutual helpers. This idea holds further that specific gender roles and the hierarchical order for women and men in the family are social and cultural constructions in the name of Islam (Badran, 2005).

Islamic feminism is not restricted to a definite region, but it is particularly evident where fundamentalism was strongest (Badran, 2005, p 7). By the end of the 1990s in Iran, the debate on Islamic feminism was especially prevalent among scholars who recognized the potential within Islamic discourse and the Islamic Republic of Iran to develop and improve women's positions (Najmabadi, 1998). Islamic feminism presented a vision of an 'ideal Islamic society' and women's roles within that society, which enabled them to criticize the past, present and traditional Islam (Paidar, 1996).

Political conditions after the presidency of Akbar Hashemi Rafsanjani (1989–97), particularly during the era of the presidency of Seyed Mohammad Khatami (1997–2005), were characterized by a more moderate interpretation of Islamic texts regarding women's rights and provided a platform for Islamic feminism which ultimately caused a few amendments in laws in favour of women in Iran. In this era, more journals and magazines (including those for women) emerged and brought different women's issues into public discourse, despite the censorship and threat of losing publication licences (Sadeghi, 2010).

Civil society prospered in Khatami's era with more freedom of the press, the closer coordination of all women activists, and the opening of the Centre for Women's Participation. The centre had the task of empowering women to run non-governmental organizations in order to reinforce women's participation in the sociopolitical, economic and cultural process of civil society and to provide women with more freedom in the public sphere (Sadeghi, 2010). Many women's groups sought to participate in various international meetings and conferences, particularly in Asia. These opportunities allowed Iranian women to share their experiences with other women activists, to gain new insights about women's issues in other regions, and to enter the global women's movement (Tohidi, 2002). Khatami also promoted women's rights by appointing women to significant political positions. Masoumeh Ebtakar, the first female vice-president of Iran, was appointed as head of the Department of Environment, and Zahra Shojaee was appointed as the director of the Centre for Women's Participation. These appointments led to a change in public attitudes and behaviour to take women's work more seriously (Tohidi, 2002).

However, only a small number of legal reforms were passed during Khatami's presidency. These limited reforms are especially surprising, as the sixth Parliament had 13 female representatives, who aimed to remove the obstacles hindering women's progress. The minimum age of marriage and the age of penal responsibility for girls were increased from nine to 13 years, although girls as young as nine could be married with the permission of the court. Another reform lifted the ban on unaccompanied single women studying abroad on government scholarships. Divorced women were granted custody of boys and girls up to seven years of age (the previous law entitled mothers to have custody of boys up to two years and girls up to seven). Decisions about custody of children after the age of seven were given to the court; however, other articles and reforms that promoted women's rights provided by the sixth Parliament were rejected by the Council of Guardians[2] (Koolaee, 2012). Another reform included the 'law on insurance for women', which was passed by the sixth Parliament and ratified by the seventh. The law aimed to entitle women to family property at the time of divorce and it was particularly important for many women who did not work in the formal sector of the economy.

The seventh Parliament also passed the 'equality in blood money insurance law', which stipulates that insurance companies are obligated to pay equal blood money to men and women in the event that payment of blood money is required (Koolaee, 2012). Iran's abortion law was also amended in 2005 and stipulates:

> performing abortion by physicians is permitted with definite diagnosis of retardation or malformation of the fetus that is unbearable for the mother or life-threatening disease of mother by three specialist medical doctors and verification of Legal Medicine Organization (LMO). This act allows therapeutic abortion (TA) with mother's consent, only before ensoulment that is considered 4 months after conception. In addition, the list of maternal and fetal problems that legally justify TA is open and the LMO holds the authority to verify such diseases (Shamsi Gooshki et al, 2014, p 77).

However, according to this law, if a woman is pregnant as a result of rape, she still does not have the right to an abortion.

Many of Khatami's reformist efforts were blocked by fundamentalists so that he 'declared publicly that he lacks sufficient powers to implement the Constitution and the rule of law' (Moghissi and Rahnema, 2001). The conservative and fundamentalist thought remained rooted in the ideology that women must stay at home, perform household duties and raise children, while men work to earn money and manage the family (Koolaee, 2012).

One notable unsuccessful effort in Khatami's era was the Convention on the Elimination of All Forms of Discrimination against Women (CEDAW). CEDAW was ratified by the reformist government and approved by Parliament. However, the Guardian Council ultimately rejected it, arguing that it was incompatible with Islam. The Guardian Council then disqualified most reformist candidates from participating in the seventh and eighth Parliament elections, which enabled the fundamentalists to regain control of the Parliament. However, the reformists in the seventh Parliament (2004–08) proposed two conditions on CEDAW, that 'international institutions should not have the right to violate Islamic laws and that international courts should not intervene in the internal affairs of Iran' (Koolaee, 2012, p 147). The proposal was rejected by the Parliament, even the female representatives, after identifying 70 cases where CEDAW violated Islamic laws. The conservative female representatives argued that CEDAW was based on the Western definition of women's rights, which was not acceptable in Iranian society. Some even claimed CEDAW created a more difficult economic situation for women since it would have banned polygamy.

Accordingly, Muslim women in Iran tried to renegotiate roles and codes in order to 'find a path of compromise and creative synthesis' (Tohidi, 1997, cited in Moghadam 2002, pp 1146–7). In other words, women are 'bargaining with patriarchy' (Kandiyoti, 1988), but also undermining patriarchal principles (Moghadam, 2002). According to Najmabadi (1998), Islamic feminism also creates a dialogue between religious and secular feminism in Islamic countries, including Iran; hence it provides a common ground and platform for cooperation with secular feminists in order to improve women's legal status and social positions.

Mir-Hosseini (2007) argues that new discourses on gender relations and debate on Islamic family laws have raised a new consciousness. Mir-Hosseini (2007) also emphasizes the necessity of developing religion, law and gender within the Muslim context and how women's rights and gender equality is a 'newly created issue'. One of the most controversial concepts is *qiwama*, which refers to male guardianship over women and caused obstacles in realizing equality before the law (Mir-Hosseini et al, 2015). The idea is derived from verse 4:34 of the Quran[3] and is therefore considered the basis for all laws concerning family relations. Although women may achieve some improved positions in the economic, political and social dimensions in society, the area of family laws rarely changes. Kabaskal Arat (2003) refers to barriers in Islamic laws in the implementation of equality; this equality cannot be fully realized even in Islamic societies that are to some degree secular, because family laws are still largely based on Islamic laws.

### Studies on women's issues in the secular stream

Secular feminism entered into the Muslim world even before the rise of Islamic feminism. As Badran explains, 'the foundational moment of women's "secular feminism" may be traced to the late nineteenth century while the emergence of Islamic feminism became evident in the late twentieth century' (Badran, 2005, p 6). During the 1970s and 1980s, secular feminism was in opposition to Islamists and their patriarchal definition of religion. According to Badran, 'Women's secular feminist movements in the Middle East for many decades in the twentieth century struggled with considerable success within the framework of the nation-state to make its institutions fully open and responsive to the needs of women and men alike as citizens' (Badran, 2005, p 11).

The secular-oriented tendencies, as Al-Ali (2000, p 130) describes, accepts the separation between religion and politics, although it does not denote an anti-religious or anti-Islamic position. Secular women do not recognize Islamic laws as the main source of legislation; rather, 'they also refer to civil law and resolution of human rights conventions adopted by the United Nations, as frames of reference for their struggle' (Al-Ali, 2000, p 130). Therefore, according to this approach, legislation and government are separated from faith and religious laws. One can be Muslim and still be committed to equality and universal human rights as a basis for legislation, even when these may conflict with certain Islamic traditions and values. Hence, secular feminism is neither about hostility to religion, nor about negating religion in the lives of people. Rather, it is about separating state and religion and about the necessity of respecting human rights and gender equality, and not violating these rights in favour of religious traditions and values. However, secular feminism in the Islamic world is often considered to be a Western imposition that belittles and marginalizes not just religions, but also local cultural and moral values particularly in respect of the family (Ahmed-Ghosh, 2008, pp 106−7).

Secular feminists criticize arguments in support of veiling of women as a tool for empowerment of women and for ignoring the element of coercion in different forms of using brutal force or social, cultural and political pressure in different Islamic countries such as Iran, Algeria, Sudan, Iraq and Jordan. Some women in several countries have adopted veiling for political or spiritual reasons; however, a large number of women have experienced losing the chance of employment by refusing to wear a veil (Moghissi, 1999, pp 42−4).

Some secular feminists like Moghissi (1999) believe that Islam and feminism are essentially incompatible because Islamic teaching and scripture are based on a gender hierarchy and therefore not devised to develop a programme for equal rights for women (Moghissi, 1999, p 126). According to Moghissi (1999), there is a legal and political Islam in Iran which is incompatible with individual choice. In these struggles, secular feminism reproaches Islamic feminists for delegitimizing secular trends and strengthening 'the legitimacy of the Islamic system in Iran and weakening the struggle of women inside Iran' (as cited in Moghadam, 2002, p 1148). Mojab (2005) criticizes Islamic feminism: 'what Iran's Islamic feminists have achieved is, at any rate, quite limited in content and consequence. Real change − real democratization − will come about outside of the religious framework'. Some other secular feminists consider Islamic feminism to be a valuable addition and believe that feminists should challenge the politics of patriarchs in the region. Ahmed-Ghosh (2008) states: 'If the current appropriate framework of social empowerment is Islam, feminists have to work with it to empower women. It is then for women in these situations to exercise their agency to bring the changes to their lives that matches their aspirations' (Ahmed-Ghosh, 2008, pp 106–7).

In a cooperation of Islamic and secular feminism, Islamic feminism provides a new edge for feminism in Islamic countries by offering new tools, while secular feminists provide the Islamic feminist progressive religious discourse (Badran, 2005, pp 13–14). An-Na'im (1995) refers to the dichotomy between religious and secular views about the rights of women in Islamic societies and suggests reconciling and integrating the two types of discourse and minimizing the differences between them. One discourse arises from the authority of scripture, and another is derived from human reason and experiences. Both discourses interact and overlap, which overshadows the sharp dichotomy between them. In other words, as An-Na'im explains, 'it is conceptually misleading to speak of "purely" religious or secular discourse about the rights of women' (An-Na'im, 1995, p 56). However, it does not mean to disclaim their distinction, but to advocate for women's right to 'fully engage in religious as well as secular discourse relevant to the matter' (An-Na'im, 1995, pp 51–4). Only a partnering of these discourses 'might avoid the schism and stalemate that may exist in the discourse on women's rights in the Islamic regions and help bring about at least some changes in women's rights and positions in the Islamic countries' (Ahmed-Ghosh, 2008, p 113).

This section has introduced studies on women's position in Islamic countries, beginning with fundamentalism, to reformist perspectives, and ultimately to a combination of reformist and secularist discourses to improve women's rights and situations. The objective and aim of the change from fundamentalist insight to reformist/secular perspectives can be summarized as strengthening women's rights in Islamic schools of thought so that the reformist view is moving from merely rereading the scripture in order to present an egalitarian interpretation to a critique on the scripture (Rahman (d. 1988), Arkoun (d. 2010), and Abu Zayd (d. 2010)). They applied scientific methods of textual critiques from linguistics and literary critics for interpretation of Quran; in this way, they insisted on the possibility of different interpretations of the Quran (Mirza, 2005, p 310). As a result, the foundations for a secular perspective have been provided, which acknowledge human rights as a requirement of human dignity.

According to An-Na'im (1995), partnering secular and reformist views implies the union of revelation and human reason and experience. This requires a theoretical discourse to investigate the relations between revelation and human reason in various schools of Islamic thought, and the importance of improving women's positions in Islamic societies. The relationship between revelation and human reason is examined in the following section using structuration theory.

## Structuration theory: Islam and the individual

According to Anthony Giddens' structuration theory there is a dialectical relationship between individual and social systems. This relationship is discussed under the concept of duality of structure in Giddens's structuration theory. The theory investigates 'the nature of human action, social institutions and interrelations between action and institutions' (Giddens, 1991b, p 201). The dialectical relationship between individual and social systems accentuates the role of agency of the individual in creating social institutions and, at the same time, the role of social systems in constitution of the individual.

Based on Giddens' definition of structure, religion can be considered an element of structure, in which 'religious cosmologies provide moral and practical interpretations of personal and social life, as well as of the natural world, which represent an environment of security for the believer' (Giddens, 1991b, p 103). Therefore, religion, providing rules and resources through its moral and practical interpretations of personal and social life as well as its obligations and sanctions, defines a framework for interaction that can be considered an element of structure. The dialectical relation between individual and structure can also be recognized as a dialectical relationship between the individual and religion.

Individual agents might adopt a schema of meaning and interpretations as well as a system of sanction for their daily interactions. In this regard, moral rules legitimize the power of religion as a resource of meaning and interpretations. However, the individual agents play an essential role in producing and reproducing rules and resources through reflecting and monitoring interactions. Human agents are characterized as knowledgeable and capable of reasoning their action and also that of others (Cloke et al, 1991, pp 97–9). The human agents examine what they receive from structure and religion and underline their reason, and influence the rules and resources that are considered as the basis of structure and religion. Therefore, while the human agents adopt the patterns of interaction offered by structure and religion and, thereby, legitimate the power of religion and structure, at the same time, they influence and reproduce the rules and resources. To have the dialectic relationships between religion and the individual, religion must recognize self-agency of the individual. At the same time, religion provides the individual with a meaningful system and strategy to overcome the major concerns of human life (Roberts and Yamane, 2012, p 7). The individual affects religion and the value system offered by religion in order to cope with new concerns of individuals in modern time. Hence, the value system offered by religion must be compatible with individual concerns and values raised by social changes. In this way, Muslim women, as knowledgeable and reasonable individuals, demand that religion considers 'the wishes of their members' (Berger and Luckmann, 1995, p 46) as well as new globalized values and new concepts such as individual rights and gender equality, which are considered cosmopolitan norms of justice. Woodhead and Heelas (2001, p 51) describe these as non-negotiable values of human life which are mediated and globalized through cultural exchanges that spread uniquely modern universalism of humanitarian ethics and legislation.

In the following sections, the potential of a dialectic relationship between religion and the individual in the main currents of Islamic thought will be discussed. For this purpose, first a general introduction of every stream will be presented. Then, employing the comparative method, this chapter will compare the similarities and differences of the main currents of Islam in their perceptions of the dialectic relationship between religion and individual and the concept of self-agency of women. Accordingly, a typology will be achieved towards a better understanding and explanation of women's rights in various interpretations of Islam. These sections are based on the documentary research method, which involves the analysis of literature that contains information about the topic. Despite the similarity of arguments of these main streams in the Islamic world, these sections are mainly restricted to investigation of the representatives' opinions of main currents of Islamic thought in Iran after the revolution 1979 as a Shiite Islamic country in order to gain an integrated perception.

## Fundamentalist-oriented thought stream

Fundamentalists aim to put all Islamic laws into practice regardless of the modern circumstances in society. In their view, Islamic laws are consistent and eternal, and cannot be interpreted. Any interpretation of the Quran and *sunna* results in the modification of and changes in

Islamic laws, which is regarded as innovation in religion and, hence, is unacceptable. Since God's will is ipso facto just, obedience of his commands embodied in Islamic laws leads to fulfilment of perfect justice (Mesbah Yazdi, 1386/2007). They emphasize that Islamic laws are 'the divinely revealed path, it is not the law that must change or modernize, they say, but society that must conform to God's will' (Esposito, 2011, p 257).

Accordingly, religion has only its own value system, regardless of individuals' new needs and concerns. Individuals are expected to execute God's will and agency; hence, self-agency of the individual does not have any place in this perspective. New concepts, such as human rights and gender equality beyond the revelation's framework, are not acceptable in this stream of thought.

## Reformist-oriented thought stream

Reformists aim to present an interpretation of Islam in which Islamic laws are compatible with modern concepts, such as human and women's rights. In this perspective, the Islamic legal system is divided into non-worldly and worldly aspects. The sacred aspect of the Islamic legal system refers to the non-worldly and eternal factor. This aspect refers to essential, non-worldly precepts concerning matters of faith, ethics and devotion, such as praying, fasting, belief in the afterworld, and prophecy, which are immutable and fixed. The second group of precepts – non-essential – deals with the worldly aspects presented in human interactions and sociopolitical affairs which are time- and space-bounded. This realm is allocated to the realm of appraisal of reason in the reformist perspective; thus, the collective reason of humanity is the yardstick of such precepts in Islam (Yousefi Eshkevari, 2013). It must be noted, however, that reformists do not present a definite criterion for distinguishing the essential from non-essential precepts. Therefore, they accept the authority of human reason conditionally, but the range of acceptance is related to their position on the spectrum. Reformists consider laws related to women's rights to be part of the realm of non-essential precepts. It means that 'when we are absolutely sure that the Lawgiver has not forbidden it, our rational ruling can be counted as a shri'a ruling' (Kadivar, 2013, p 217). Therefore, they recognize individual agency conditionally, but the range of acceptance is related to their position on the spectrum.

Reformists have successfully opened a potential for debating and accepting human and women's rights in society through their efforts to offer an interpretation of Islam based on an egalitarian notion of justice, which is not only compatible with human and women's rights in general, but also recognizes that human and women's rights are essential for Muslim society. This perspective has changed some discriminatory Islamic laws in favour of women's rights in Iran, though it was not completely successful in changing patronizing perspectives on women. Reformist perspectives need more debate and should be challenged in the public sphere in order to attain a better understanding of human rights, justice and equality.

## Secular-oriented thought stream

The secular thought stream emerged from the reformist view. It seems that reformists are gradually leaning towards secularist thought in that they do not stand on a fixed position on the spectrum. Instead they have been moving towards more recognition of individual agency. According to this view, all people living in the modern era have different ideas and worldviews from people in traditional societies (Malekian, 1381/2002).

Mojtahed Shabestari (1389/2010), criticizing the text-based interpretation of religion, defines religion as a transcendental experience from the issues of daily life and emphasizes faith, spirituality and unitary experience of the world. In this experience, the individual has an important determining role, for the individual determines their own unitary experience and the sources for the experience of transcendence. Individuals choose their life and thought style by applying reason and rationality rather than imitating institutionalized traditions. This turn from life lived according to external expectations to life lived according to individuals' own inner experience is similar to what Heelas and Woodhead (2005) call 'subjectivization', which refers to a shift from external authority offered by institutionalized traditional religions to the authority 'rooted in individual experience and subjective validations'.

On this matter, human beings are regarded as subjective agents who recognize their identities as Muslims. In this way, the Muslim is not a passive believer who simply accepts a historical definition of being Muslim. The historical definition means that everything in history that has been understood as Islam and all historical events which have occurred in the name of Islam provide and determine a definition of being Muslim. Being Muslim means a commitment to following the definite set of rituals and precepts provided in the course of history (Mojtahed Shabestari, 1389/2010). The secular view challenges this notion of religion as closed, defined solely by a text-based interpretation.

Similar to reformists, seculars are critical of the fundamentalist view of women's rights. For instance, Malekian (1387/2008) explains that fundamentalists are only concerned about the ritualistic aspects of Islam and cannot see the spirit and the core message of the religion. This reading of Islam is also superficially juridical and posits that this is the only way to be a real Muslim. Fundamentalists define the whole religion with the juridical aspect of Islam, namely the *fiqh*. Malekian sees this reading of Islam as patriarchal, based on natural order with three main characteristics: inferiority of women to men, lawful and juristic privileges for men, and the right to establish parentage for men in the family (Malekian 1387/2008, p 323). For attaining religious and spiritual experience, a healthy society where social and political arrangements provide human beings with individual freedom and self-determination is required; accordingly, equality between men and women is the essential means for living based on faith and spirituality (Mojtahed Shabestari, 1382/2003, p 37; Malekian, 1387/2008).

## Conclusion

Gender equality is not conceivable in the fundamentalist interpretation of Islam. Nonetheless, this perspective and its followers and representatives should be challenged in the public sphere in order to show how such insights are unsacred and originate from patriarchal interpretations of Islam. It is also necessary to discuss more secular interpretations of Islam in the public sphere so that they gradually find their place among various interpretations of Islam. In addition, the reformist view should be further challenged and debated in the public sphere in order to attain various interpretations of Islam that are compatible with human rights and gender equality, which are non-reducible to local, cultural and religious life-world.

Acknowledging a subjective definition of religion in which women determine their life and thoughts style based on reason and rationality, consequently based on an egalitarian definition of justice and gender equality, is not in contrast to the concept of being Muslim. Challenging institutionalized traditional religions as well as patronizing perspectives of women presented by every interpretation of Islam, including reformist, is necessary for subjective Muslim women in Iran and elsewhere. Therefore, Muslim women's efforts to achieve gender equality are not restricted to rereading and reinterpreting the Quran and *sunna* in order to provide an interpretation of Islam compatible with gender equality, but they emphasize self-agency of women to affect religion in the way that religion extends its value system regarding Muslim women's concerns today.

## Notes

[1] For instance, Article 4 of the Constitution states, 'all civil, penal financial, economic, administrative, cultural, military, political, and other laws and regulations must be based on Islamic criteria.' Also, Article 20 of the Constitution states that both men and women equally enjoy the protection of the law, as well as all human, political, economic, social and cultural rights. However, this article does not recognize unconditional equal protection, but rather makes the protection of equal rights conditional to be in conformity with Islamic criteria (Preamble of the Constitution of the Islamic Republic of Iran).

[2] Article 91 of the Constitution introduces the Guardian Council with the following terms: 'With a view to safeguarding Islamic commands and the Constitution, so that the legislation of the Islamic Assembly are not in contravention with them, a council named the Guardian Council shall be established composed of the following: 1) Six clerics, just and acquainted with the needs of the time and problems of the day. These individuals will be appointed by the Leader or the Council of Leadership; 2) Six jurists who are qualified in various branches of law, from among Muslim jurists, introduced to the Islamic Assembly by the Head of the Judiciary and appointed with the approval of the Assembly.' Also according to Article 96, the majority of the clerics of the Guardian Council will decide whether the legislation passed by the Majlis is in conformity with the precepts of Islam, while the decision with regard to the conformity of the acts with the Constitution comes from the majority of all members. A Bill is passed into law after it is passed by the Majlis, approved by the Guardian Council, and signed by the president (Kar, 2010, p 44).

[3] 'Men are in charge of women by [right of] what Allah has given one over the other and what they spend [for maintenance] from their wealth. So righteous women are devoutly obedient, guarding in [the husband's] absence what Allah would have them guard. But those [wives] from whom you fear arrogance – [first] advise them; [then if they persist], forsake them in bed; and [finally], strike them. But if they obey you [once more], seek no means against them. Indeed, Allah is ever Exalted and Grand' (Quran 4:34), https://quran.com/4/34 (15.02.2017).

## References

Abu Odeh, L. (1993) 'Post-colonial feminism and the veil: thinking the difference', *Feminist Review*, no 43, pp 26–37. Available at: http://www.jstor.org/stable/1395067.

Abu Zayd, N.H. (1999) *Dawair al-Khawf: Qira'ah fi Khitab al-Mar'ah (Circles of Fear: Analysis of the Discourse about Women)*, Beirut and Casablanca: al-Markaz al-Thaqafi al- Arabi.

Afary, J. (1997) 'The war against feminism in the name of the almighty: making sense of gender and Muslim fundamentalism', in B. Reed (ed) *Nothing Sacred: Women Respond to Religious Fundamentalism and Terror*, New York: Thunder's mouth Press/Nation Books, pp 45–74.

Ahmed-Ghosh, H. (2008) 'Dilemmas of Islamic and secular feminists and feminisms', *Journal of International Women's Studies*, vol 9, no 3, pp 99–116. Available at: http://vc.bridgew.edu/jiws/vol9/iss3/7.

Al-Ali, N.S. (2000) *Secularism, Gender and the State in the Middle East: The Egyptian Women's Movement*, Cambridge: Cambridge University Press.

An-Na'im, A.A. (1995) 'The dichotomy between religious and secular discourse in Islamic societies', in M. Afkhami (ed) *Faith & Freedom: Women's Human Rights in the Muslim World*, Syracuse: Syracuse University Press, pp 51–60.

Badran, M. (2005) 'Between secular and Islamic feminism/s: reflections on the Middle East and beyond', *Journal of Middle East Women's Studies*, vol 1, no 1, pp 6–28. Available at: http://www.jstor.org/stable/40326847.

Bahramitash, R. and Salehi Esfahani, H. (2011) *Veiled Employment: Islamism and the Political Economy of Women's Employment in Iran*, Syracuse: Syracuse University Press.

Berger, P.L. and Luckmann, T. (1995) *Modernity, Pluralism and the Crisis of Meaning, the Orientation of Modern Man*, Gütersloh: Bertelsmann Foundation Publishers.

Cloke, P., Sadler, D.J. and Philo, Ch. (1991) *Approaching Human Geography: An Introduction to Contemporary Theoretical Debates*, London: SAGE Publications Ltd.

Collier, D. (1993) 'The comparative method', in A.W. Finifter (ed) *Political Science: The State of the Discipline II*, Washington D.C.: American Political Science Association, pp 105–19.

Esposito, J.L. (2011) *Islam, the Straight Path*, Oxford: Oxford University Press.

Giddens, A. (1991a) 'Structuration theory: past, present and future', in C.G.A. Bryant and D. Jary (eds) *Giddens' Theory of Structuration: a Critical Appreciation*, London: Routledge.

Giddens, A. (1991b) *The Consequence of Modernity*, Cambridge: Polity Press.

Heelas, P. and Woodhead, L. (2005) *The Spiritual Revolution: Why Religion is Giving Way to Spirituality*, Oxford: Blackwell.

Kabaskal Arat, Z.F. (2003) 'Promoting women's rights against patriarchal cultural claims: the women's convention and reservations by Muslim states', in D. Forsythe and P. McMahon (eds) *Global Human Rights Norms: Area Studies Revisited*, Nebraska: Nebraska University Press, pp 231–51.

Kadivar, M. (2013) 'Revisiting Women's Rights in Islam: "Egalitarian Justice" in Lieu of "Deserts-based Justice"', in Z. Mir-Hosseini, K. Vogt, L. Larson and C. Moe (eds) *Gender Equality in Muslim Family Law: Justice and Ethics in Islamic Legal Tradition*, London: I.B. Tauris, pp 213–34.

Kandiyoti, D. (1988) 'Bargaining with Patriarchy', *Gender and Society*, vol 2, no 3, pp 274–90.

Kar, M. (2010) *Constitutional Obstacles: Human Rights and Democracy in Iran*, Iran Human Rights Documentation Center (IHRDC). Available at: http://tinyurl.com/qa9th5u (accessed 16 June 2015).

Koolaee, E. (2012) 'Women in the Parliament', in T. Povey and E. Rostami-Povey (eds) *Women, Power and Politics in 21st Century Iran*, London: Ashgate, pp 137–51.

Mahmood, S. (2005) *Politics of Piety: The Islamic Revival and the Feminist Subject*, Princeton: Princeton University Press.

Malekian, M. (1381/2002) 'Ma'naviyat: Gohar-e Adiyan (1)', in M. Malekian et al (eds) *Sonnat wa Sekoularism (Tradition and Secularism)*, Tehran: Serat, pp 267–306.

Malekian, M. (1387/2008) *Moshtaqi wa Mahjouri: Goftegou dar bab-e Farhang va Siyasat*, Tehran: Negah-e Moa´ser.

Mesbah Yazdi, M.T. (1386/2007) *Andisheha-ye Bonyadin-e Eslami (The Fundamental Thoughts of Islam)*, Qom: Moassese-ye Emam Khomeini.

Mir-Hosseini, Z. (2007) 'Islam and Gender Justice', in V. Cornell, O. Safi and V. Gray Henry (eds) *Voices of Islam: Voices of Change*, London: Praeger Publishers, pp 85–113.

Mir-Hosseini, Z., Al-Sharmani, M. and Rumminger, J. (eds) (2015) *Men in Charge? Rethinking Authority in Muslim Legal Tradition*, London: Oneworld Publications.

Mirza, Q. (2005) 'Islamic Feminism, Possibilities and Limitations', in H. Moghissi (ed) *Women and Islam: Critical Concepts in Sociology: Women's Movements in Muslim Societies*, New York: Routledge, pp 300–19.

Moghadam, V.M. (2002) 'Islamic Feminism and Its Discontents: Toward a Resolution of the Debate', *Signs*, vol 27, no 4, pp 1135–71. Available at: http://www.jstor.org/stable/3175948.

Moghissi, H. (1999) *Feminism and Islamic Fundamentalism: The Limits of Postmodern Analysis*, London: Zed Books.

Moghissi, H. and Rahnema, S. (2001) *Clerical Oligarchy and the Question of 'Democracy' in Iran*, Iran Chamber Society. Available at http://tinyurl.com/pm4chmo.

Mojab, S. (2005) 'Islamic Feminism: Alternative or Contradiction?', in H. Moghissi (ed) *Women and Islam: Critical Concepts in Sociology, Vol. 3: Women's Movements in Muslim Societies,*USA and Canada: Routledge, pp 320–25.

Mojtahed Shabestari, M. (1382/2003) *Iman wa Azadi (Faith and Freedom)*, Tehran: Tarh-e No.

Mojtahed Shabestari, M. (1384/2006) *Naqdi bar Qera'at-e Rasmi az Din (A Critique of The Official Reading of Religion)*, Tehran: Tarh-e No.

Mojtahed Shabestari, M. (1389/2010) Masael-e Asasi-ye Noandishi-ye Dini dar Iran-e Mo`aser (The Main Issues of Religious Intellectualism in Contemporary Iran), A speech at the Knowledge and Research Institution.

Najmabadi, A. (1998) 'Feminism in an Islamic Republic: Years of Hardship, Years of Growth', in Y. Haddad and J. Esposito (eds) *Islam, Gender, and Social Change in the Muslim World*, New York: Oxford University Press, pp 59–84.

Paidar, P. (1996) 'Feminism and Islam in Iran', in D. Kandiyoti (ed) *Gendering the Middle East: Emerging Perspectives*, London: I.B. Tauris, pp 51–68.

Roberts, K.A. and Yamane. D. (2012), *Religion in Sociological Perspective*, 5th ed., Los Angeles: Sage.

Ruthven, M. (2007) *Fundamentalism: A Very Short Introduction*, Oxford: Oxford University Press.

Sadeghi, F. (2010) 'Bypassing Islamism and Feminism: Women's Resistance and Rebellion in Post-Revolutionary Iran', *Revue des mondes musulmans et de la Méditerranée (Remmm)* no 128, pp 209–28. Available at: http://remmm.revues.org/6936.

Shamsi Gooshki, E., Abbasi, M. and Allahbedashti, N. (2014) 'Abortion in Iranian Legal System', *Iranian Journal of Allergy, Asthma and Immunology*, vol 13, no 1, pp 71–84.

Tohidi, N. (2002) 'International Connection of the Iranian Women's Movement', in N.R. Keddie and R.P. Matthee (eds) *Iran and the Surrounding World: Interactions in Culture and Cultural Politics*, London: University of Washington Press, pp 205–31.

Woodhead, L. and Heelas, P. (2001) 'Homeless Minds Today?, in L. Woodhead, P. Heelas and D. Martin (eds) *Peter Berger and the Study of Religion*, New York: Routledge, pp 43–72.

Yousefi Eshkevari, H. (2013) 'Rethinking Men's Authority over Women: Qiwama, Wilaya and their Underlying Assumptions', in Z. Mir-Hosseini, et al (eds), *Gender and Equality in Muslim Family Law: Justice and Ethics in the Islamic Legal Tradition*, London: I.B. Tauris, pp 191–211.

# TWO

# Religion and gender equality in Catholic Philippines: discourses and practices in the 21st century

*Glenda Tibe Bonifacio*

## Introduction

The Philippines is the only predominantly Catholic country in Asia, with over 92 million adherents in 2010 or over 86% of the population (Philippine Statistics Authority [PSA], 2015; Miller, 2017). Evangelicals, Protestants and nationalist Christian churches form another variant to make Christianity the dominant religion in the archipelago. Since the introduction of Catholicism in the 16th century under the colonial rule of Spain, the Philippines have offered a unique perspective of gender roles and equality with the intersections of indigenous, colonial and modern overtures that remains visible today. In the 21st century, these intersections are significant aspects to examine the role of religion in the lives of women, and how it is negotiated under present social and economic conditions where Filipino women are said to be living in the most gender-equal country in Asia.

The Philippines has lain at the crux of imperialism and globalization of American influence in Asia since the beginning of the 20th century, and the introduction of popular education and the labour market economy facilitated a certain push towards gender equality. By 2015, the Philippines ranked seventh in the world based on the gender gap index measured in terms of economic participation, educational attainment, health and survival, and political empowerment by the World Economic Forum (2015); the only Asian country on the top list and even beating the United States (ranked 28), Canada (ranked 30), Australia (ranked 36), and Japan (ranked 101) of 145 countries. This top ranking of gender equality in an economically poor country in the South East Asia region offers a 'puzzle' (Quimbo, 2014), and rightly so relative to the index ranking of economically richer countries. It would seem that the Philippines is a paradox, having both high religiosity and gender equality at the same time. Consistent with the theme of this book, the situated realities of women in the Philippines provide a lens to examine the ways in which Catholicism retains its hold in society yet those who embrace it find new ways to negotiate their subjective identities. Its global ranking of closing the gender gap, or leaning towards gender equality, is a compelling factor to understand the intersections of gender and religion in the Philippines.

This chapter aims to present Catholic religious discourses and practices of gender equality in the Philippines based on island ethnography, participant observation, and a case study of two women from Leyte. It is divided into four sections: Review of studies, Island ethnography, Constructs and contestations of women in Philippines Catholicism, and Practices towards gender equality. A concluding section provides insight into the dynamics of religion and gender in the lives of Catholic Filipino women.

## Review of studies

Recent studies on gender in South East Asian contexts, including the Philippines, Thailand, Malaysia, Indonesia, Vietnam, Cambodia, Myanmar and Brunei, are very rich in scope and breadth (Peletz, 2006; Andaya, 2007). Gender is a critical factor to examine relations of power and its manifestations in politics, development, education, access to reproductive health and others. In the Philippines, an earlier compendium of scholarly sources on sex and gender in society included the ideological and cultural practice of a sexist ideology, social construction of sexuality, family household, and sexual division of labour (Eviota, 1994). Feliciano (1994) traced the development of legal equalities of Filipino women until the 1986 Philippine Constitution. Since the 1990s gender issues have remained significant in a number of scholarly works and policies (Sobritchea, 2005; Asian Development Bank, 2013).

In terms of combining gender with religion in the Philippine context, the scholarly materials available in the English language also speak of its scope since pre-colonial times. These include, among others, the high valuing of indigenous women before Spanish colonialism ensued in 1521 compared to the subordination of women under the Spanish Catholic regime (Brewer, 2001; 2004); the struggles for equality, resistance and negotiation in the Catholic fold and in society (Blanc-Szanton, 1989; Claussen, 2001; Roces, 2008); sexual agency of young Filipino women and Catholic mores (Delgado-Infante and Ofreneo, 2014); women's political participation and Catholic fundamentalism

(Aguiling-Pangalangan, 2010); and reproductive politics and religion (Natividad, 2012). I am convinced that there are still a number of significant studies that fuse gender and religion in the Philippines to which this section cannot do justice, and I follow in their path to traverse a more nuanced examination of religious discourses vis-a-vis practices towards gender equality in the country. Perhaps what this chapter offers is the positive framing of gender equality as opposed to gender inequality to begin with. Because the Philippines belongs to the top 10 countries in the world with a 'lesser' gender gap index compared to most developed economies, I opt for a reframing to equality with the caveat that the numbers 'don't tell the full story' (Strother, 2013).

## Island ethnography

The Philippines has over 7,000 islands with diverse ethnolinguistic groupings. These islands are divided into three major groups: Luzon, Visayas and Mindanao. Each island grouping comprises different political jurisdictions and administration into provinces, municipalities, towns and barangays. While this chapter refers to the Philippines, the data is based on fieldwork in the islands of Leyte and Samar in the Visayas in 2012 and 2015. These islands are chosen because of the convenience in understanding the local language, Waray. There are over 100 languages in the Philippines, including Waray, and the ease of conversing in this language made Leyte and Samar the best locale to study under financial constraints. As well, I have my family roots in Leyte and am familiar with the local terrain, history and changing social practices.

Ethnography provides the best tool to examine religious discourse and practices of Filipino women in the Philippines as it deals with knowing the 'lived experiences, daily activities, and social context … of those being studied' (Buch and Staller, 2007, pp 187–8). As a feminist researcher, I enjoy the privilege of being both an 'insider and outsider' (Naples, 2003, p 46) of the topic to be explored and of the place to be studied. This 'insider/outsider' status is said to construct 'power differentials and experiential differences' (Naples, 2004, p 373) between me and the subject of study. Although my familial linguistic roots are in Leyte, I have been away for the last 16 years and have recently reconnected with its language and people due to certain circumstances such as death and natural disaster. The 'insider' and 'outsider' positions in the research process – a Filipino heritage and a Canadian citizenship – proved beneficial. Being Filipino enabled access to local knowledge and cultural appreciation of Filipino women's lives, and being Canadian provided the resources and status to undertake travel and connect with the community.

I conducted participant observation, the 'cornerstone' of ethnographic practice (Buch and Staller, 2007, p 189), into the daily rudiments of life in the Leyte-Samar islands: economy, politics, religion and rituals. In the hot days of June and July in both summers of 2012 and 2015, I attended local events such as weddings, parties, baptisms and fiestas in various towns in which I was introduced as a scholar from a Canadian university. Because familial connections and kinship associations are highly regarded in Filipino culture, I was able to establish a good rapport among those who were at these events. In particular, I observed two wedding ceremonies and took notes of the discourse of officiating priests. These field notes provided the bases for analysing the Catholic stance on the role of women in the family and in society.

Through the lens of lived experiences of two women in Leyte, I provide some insights into the discourses and practices in relation to gender equality among Catholic women in the Philippines. These two women, one in the rural area and one in the urban area, were selected because of close familiarity with their situation; coming to know them more during the field work when I frequented these areas many times in the course of the two summers. Their identities were known by personal associates who facilitated their introduction to me in the process. Writing formal agreements of consent with local individuals for research is not the norm, and, when these were presented to these two women, they declined to affix their signature but gave their consent nonetheless. My positionality as fellow Filipino and Canadian scholar gave me the privilege to hear their stories, with the promise of keeping their identities confidential. They were also uncomfortable with the use of recording devices, and I took down notes during times of informal interviews about being a Catholic woman in the Philippines. These interviews were done during visits to their local residences coinciding with a social event such as a baptism and fiesta.

Lived experiences, as Carlson (2016, p 22) notes, provide the fourth pillar of 'Christian ethical reflection' in examining women's role in Catholicism alongside teaching, scriptural studies and natural law. Women's experiences, from a feminist standpoint, also reflect their situated location that produces knowledge about the world they live in (Hesse-Biber and Leavy, 2007). The stories of these two women become the vantage point to examine the particular ways Filipino women make meanings of their Catholic identity in the 21st century.

According to official government statistics, of the total Philippine population of 92.3 million in 2010, females comprised 45.7 million

(PSA, 2016). The sex ratio for the same year was 102 males for every 100 females; those between 18 years and 64 years old represented 62.4% of the total population. By 2030, the population is projected to reach 125.3 million, and the female population to increase to 62.1 million, at an annual growth rate of 1.27% (PSA, 2016). In terms of education, the Philippines has one of the highest rates among economically developing countries in the world with a female simple literacy rate of 97.6% and a female functional literacy rate of 88.7% in 2010 (Villegas, 2001; PSA, 2016). As of October 2015, the employment rate was 63.3% and the unemployment rate 94.4%. Filipino women have a life expectancy of 76 years, while that of men is 71 years (PSA, 2016).

The Leyte-Samar islands form part of the Eastern Visayas region in the Philippines, or Region VIII. In 2010, the population of the region reached over 4 million, and most of its inhabitants are called Waray-Waray and speak their own Waray dialect – the fourth largest ethnolinguistic group in the country (National Statistical Coordination Board, n.d.). The Leyte-Samar islands are mainly agricultural based and produce mostly rice, coconut, corn and sugarcane. There were 106 males for every 100 females in the 2007 census (Phillippine Statistics Office, 2010), which could mainly be attributed to migration by the latter.

Leyte is important in the spread of Catholicism in the Philippines, where the first mass was held in the southern island of Limasawa in 1521 (Guillermo, 2012) and in the same area where the leader of the Bankaw Revolt came from in 1622 for a return to native beliefs (Halili, 2004). To this day, the Eastern Visayas region remains predominantly Catholic, with other Christian groups forming the rest, and a small number of Muslims from Mindanao. The Waray people are also known in Tagalog popular culture as *matapang* (brave), and the women generally characterized in the vernacular language as *maisog* (strong/bold). It is within this context of religiosity and resistance that this chapter looks into the religious discourse and practice towards gender equality as gleaned from those in the islands in Eastern Visayas.

## Women and Philippine Catholicism: constructs and contestations

Religious discourse refers to the statements and pronouncements made by authorities in the Catholic clergy about a topic. Discourse produces meaning in a Foucauldian sense (McHoul and Grace, 2015) within systems of power relations (Mills, 1997), and creates and produces hegemonic constructs about groups in society. The entrenchment of Catholicism since the 16th century in the Philippines, and the continued strong influence of the Philippine Catholic clergy, perpetuate ideal constructs and relations between women and men in society. In this section, I draw on discourses on women – wives, mothers and daughters – espoused by Catholic priests during weddings and in their sermons during mass, and the contestations of these constructs in lived experiences.

By and large, the construct of ideal womanhood in Catholicism is the Virgin Mary – mother and wife. As mother of Jesus Christ, Mary represents the virtues of purity, patience, perseverance, modesty, humility, hope, obedience, charity and many more (Lanzoni, 2012). The iconography of Mary in Catholic Philippines is central to worship and devotion among Filipinos: for example, La Immaculada in Intramuros, Lady of Peñafrancia in Naga, Lady of Manaoag in Pangasinan, Lady of Candles in Jaro, and the month-long *Flores de Mayo* (Flowers of May) every summer throughout the country.

The Marian devotion, however, is at odds with the doctrinal teaching as issued in a pastoral letter by the Catholic Bishops Conference of the Philippines (CBCP) that Mary is not a god; she is venerated but not worshipped (De la Rosa, 2016). Christian critics regard the popular devotions like Mother Mary expressed through festivals as idolatry and paganism. But for millions of Marian devotees in the Philippines, scattered in many islands like Eastern Visayas, Mary sits at the right place in heaven with personal scapulars and rosaries to ward off harm. *Cofradias* (confraternities) about her remain strong in local communities, for example, the *Birhen sa Lourdes* (Our Lady of Lourdes), *Inahan sa Kanunayng Panabang* (Our Lady of Perpetual Help) in Sogod, and the Cofradia of Our Lady of Refuge in Dulag – both towns in the province of Leyte.

## Ideals and realities

The ideal wife in Catholic parlance is someone who obeys her husband in the sacred sacrament of marriage, whose purpose is the creation of a heterosexual family. This is an indissoluble union ended by death of one spouse. There are two popular references in the Bible related to this ideal construct pronounced during wedding ceremonies:

- Mark 10:9: 'Therefore what God has joined together, let no one separate.'
- Matthew 19:6: 'So they are no longer two, but one flesh.'

Catholic marriages are church-held marriages where the priest officiates at the ceremony in front of the gathered community (Williams and Guest, 2005; Lauser, 2008). During this ceremony the priest reminds the bride and groom about the extolled virtues of loyalty, obedience and harmony in the family. The popular biblical references include:

- Ephesians 5:22: 'Wives, follow the lead of your husbands as you follow the Lord.'
- Ecclesiastes 4:9: 'Two are better than one, because they have a good reward for their toil.'

Marital union is blessed by God and remains sacred until one of them is called to the afterlife. These messages resonate in all church weddings I have observed in the Leyte-Samar islands.

The indissolubility of marriage is bolstered by the fact that there is no divorce in the Philippines, the only Christian country outside the Vatican where this is the case (Emery, 2013, p 971). Instead, the Family Code of the Philippines provides 10 grounds for legal separation in Article 55 but does not dissolve the marriage:

a) Repeated physical violence or grossly abusive conduct directed against the petitioner, a common child, or a child of the petitioner;
b) Physical violence or moral pressure to compel the petitioner to change religious or political affiliation;
c) Attempt of respondent to corrupt or induce the petitioner, a common child, or a child of the petitioner, to engage in prostitution, or connivance in such corruption or inducement;
d) Final judgment sentencing the respondent to imprisonment of more than six years, even if pardoned;
e) Drug addiction or habitual alcoholism of the respondent;
f) Lesbianism or homosexuality of the respondent;
g) Contracting by the respondent of a subsequent bigamous marriage, whether in or outside the Philippines;
h) Sexual infidelity or perversion of the respondent;
i) Attempt on the life of petitioner by the respondent; or
j) Abandonment of petitioner by respondent without justifiable cause for more than one year (Robles, 2017).

Further, Article 45 provides six grounds to petition the court to annul a marriage with prescriptive periods:

1. absence of parental consent;
2. mental illness;
3. fraud;
4. that the consent of either party was obtained by force, intimidation or undue influence;
5. one or the other party was physically incapable of consummating the marriage, and such incapacity continues and appears to be incurable;
6. either party was at the time of marriage afflicted with a sexually transmitted disease (STD) found to be serious and that seems to be incurable (BC Philippines Lawyers, 2009).

Those who wish to remarry in the Catholic Church must also have an ecclesiastical annulment of their previous marriage, which is also costly and arduous like the civil annulment.

The wedding symbolizes a woman's entry into motherhood, of waiting to this day to consummate sexual relations. In the 21st century the construct of the ideal virgin bride remains in island Philippines. In preparing for a monogamous marriage, women's sexuality and reproduction are discursive areas to instil the image of a sexually moral Filipino woman. In many pronouncements during sermons, priests enjoin women to practise natural sex and avoid artificial methods of contraception. The Catholic hierarchy in the Philippines are strong opponents of family planning and reproductive health legislation (Lema, 2012; Vincent, 2012).

Respect for parents is the primary virtue pronounced to daughters. As instilled in the Ten Commandments, it is religiously ingrained in children to honour their father and mother at all times. The most common of parental teachings directed to unmarried daughters is to remain chaste. Purity in spirit and body are reflected in the white wedding dress. Chastity takes some biblical significance in the following:

1. Corinthians 6:18: 'Flee from sexual immorality. All other sins a person commits are outside the body, but whoever sins sexually, sins against their own body.'
2. Thessalonians 4:3: 'For this is the will of God, your sanctification, that you should abstain from fornication.'

The 'unitive and procreative' purpose of marriage (Catholic Bishops Conference of the Philippines, 1990) exacts sexual relations only with the husband and not to commit adultery as expressed in Exodus 20:14.

Religious admonitions of sexual purity for unmarried women appear contrary to social realities. There is a looming 'national teenage pregnancy crisis' in the Philippines where 24 babies are born every hour to teenagers (Van der Hor, 2014). The Philippines is the only country in the Asia-Pacific region with rising teenage birth rates in over a decade (Fernandez, 2016). But the Eastern Visayas region does not belong to the top 10 regions with high numbers of teenage pregnancies in the country (Leyte Samar Daily News, 2014). The contraceptive prevalence rates of the Philippines in 2013 were: 17.5% traditional contraceptive methods, 37.6% modern methods, and 44.9% no methods (PSA, 2016).

These ideal constructs of wife and daughter based on religious discourse appear rooted in time and unchanging, which highlights the essential notions of womanhood and that Filipino women in these discursive lens are static with no capacity for agency. In a country with high basic literacy rates at about 96% (Philippine Education for All 2015 Review Report), these ideal constructs somehow preclude the exercise of rationality and practicality among the subject women and youth to define their lives. I ask this: In what ways do they subvert religious discourses of womanhood? The next section presents the practices towards gender equality based on ethnographic data from Eastern Visayas.

## Practices towards gender equality

The Philippines has a strong indigenous tradition of egalitarianism, which regards highly the roles and contribution of women, from the *babaylan* (priestess) to daughters, with no apparent system of exclusion in affairs in the community (University Center for Women's Studies, 2001). In contrast to gender-restrictive cultural practices in traditional societies in other parts of Asia, such as *purdah* (seclusion) and arranged marriages, Filipino women have long enjoyed the freedom to engage in the public sphere, for example in the market economy to sell agricultural by-products like delicacies, and in grassroots politics as participants, advocates, organizers, or combatants in resistance movements (Lanzona, 2009), for example. The Spanish colonial ideal of womanhood mainly rested with elite women whose lives were affected by the social decorum of the colonial administrators, with whom their families interact. The majority of Filipino women today belong to the economic middle class and lower classes, which seem undeterred by the limiting precepts of Catholicism.

In contemporary Philippines, according to the Magna Carta of Women or the Republic Act No. 9710, gender equality refers to

> the principle asserting the equality of men and women and their right to enjoy equal conditions realizing their full human potentials to contribute to and benefit from the results of development, and with the State recognizing that all human beings are free and equal in dignity and rights (Republic of the Philippines, 2009).

This legislation attempts to embolden the principle of equality between women and men, but not other genders yet, with the same enjoyment and privileges. Like the religious discourse, this legislative fiat did not create the reality of equality between them. Rather, the grounded practices in the daily lives of people, particularly women, give insights into how equality has been made possible since the pre-Spanish era. I present two women in different ethnographic scenarios in which the practice of gender equality subverts the religious discourse of women: Ludy, the farmer, and Nelia, the government employee. As discussed earlier, these two women were selected because of established familiarity with personal associates during the course of field work in these areas in Leyte. While not representative of the Catholic Filipino women in the Philippines, these two women reflect the particular negotiations of religion in their lives today.

## Ludy

An hour away from Tacloban City, the capital of the province of Leyte, lies a rural town where Ludy lives with her family of five. Together with her husband, Ludy farms a piece of land owned by a distant relative. Her children help them during planting and harvesting season, often skipping school when more hands are needed. On certain Sundays when the weather permits and when a ride is available, they go to town to attend mass in the local church located near the market. Ludy's family sits near the back door of the church to get more fresh air as the electric fans to cool the parishioners are mostly found in front pews. Ludy understands the sermon of the parish priest if said in the vernacular; although she is literate her knowledge of English is limited. She takes the words of the priest as a guide to daily living but does not take the sermon as a dictate on what to do. Ludy believes she has gained enough knowledge to farm the land on her own without being supervised by her husband. She considers her husband as partner, not her master.

Since the Spanish period, the spatial arrangement of the town centre reflects the 'plaza complex' (Halili, 2004, 86) where the rectangular plaza has the church alongside the government buildings and houses of the town elites. Nothing much has changed with this architectural placement of powerholders in the community today. In democratic Philippines, there is already the principle of separation of church and state enshrined in the constitution but the visible presence of the local priest in civil affairs remains: inauguration of buildings where a mass is held, opening prayers in school programmes, and the like. But at this time the priest is busier with fundraising drives to repair the church, or joining other priests in other areas for bigger celebrations in the province. This means that the pastoral work of priests in rural areas appears less than in previous years. Ludy remembers that the town priest regularly used to go out of town to encourage people to attend mass and contribute to church projects. She rarely sees the town priest now going into the rural hinterlands.

As a farmer, Ludy has no time to venture out except during the time between the planting and harvesting seasons. While in town, Ludy and her family are exposed to new technology, commodities and information that keeps them busy. She goes to the health centre to obtain free medicines and sometimes participate in reproductive health programmes. She knows her body and does not want another child. Her youngest child, the fifth, is 10 years old.

### Nelia

Tacloban City is the economic hub and centre of education in Eastern Visayas. Nelia works as a government employee and lives in the city with her parents and two children. Nelia is a single mother who provides not only for her children, but also for her aging parents. Her parents help watch over the children when Nelia is away on official trips. She commutes using the public transportation available in her area: the jeepney. As long as she can remember, her parents have always gone to church to hear Sunday mass. Nelia also joins them or attends with her children at different mass times; her parents prefer the early morning mass while the children prefer a mid-morning mass, which often leads to lunch at a favourite fast food outlet afterwards.

While society generally frowns on single mothers, their numbers are increasing, brought about by de facto separation from abusive husbands, or for reasons such as incompatibility, infidelity and abandonment.

Nelia separated from her husband after learning of him having another family while he was employed in Saudi Arabia. While her husband gives little financial support for their children, Nelia earns a sufficient income to live independently. She lives in her natal home with no mortgage payments to consider, with her main outgoings being for food, school and public transportation. However, Nelia plans to seek employment overseas when her children go to college.

In Nelia's view, marriage is better dissolved in peace than continued in pain. Since she and husband had not acquired properties as a married couple to divide, de facto separation was their best option. Nelia and her estranged husband are still considered married in the eyes of the law and the Church but they consider their fate as a reality in a changing world. In 2007, there was a 71% increase in the number of applications for annulment and legal separation filed in court from 2001 (Sabangan, 2008). Many Filipinos like Nelia choose not to file this type of application because it is simply impractical to pursue. Couples in lower socioeconomic classes have no money to pay for legal costs nor the luxury of time to take part in a lengthy court process. Nelia and others in the same situation found much relief in 2000 when the government enacted the Solo Parent's Welfare Act or Republic Act No. 8972, providing certain benefits and accommodation in the workplace.

Furthermore, since the 1980s the migration of Filipino women has highlighted a new form of mothering – transnational (Parreñas, 2001). Of 2.4 million overseas Filipino workers (OFWs) between April and September 2015, women comprised 51% (PSA, 2016a). Like Nelia, these women aspire to better opportunities not only for themselves, but for their families left behind. In a country with no defined and secure system of social welfare, Filipino migrant workers provide the steady support for health, education and living expenses (Bonifacio, 2014). The realities of migration create alternative forms of parenting, family dynamics and roles of women in the family and society. With an ever-increasing number of female-headed households in the Philippines, the archaic notions of patriarchal submissiveness are now being eroded, with alternative models of womanhood for single women. For example, female-headed households increased from 16.6% in 2008 to 21.2% in 2009 (Philippine Commission on Women, 2014).

## Conclusion

Catholic discourses about women remain the same as centuries ago, unchanged by modernity and the principles of equality laid out in law and in practice in the Philippines. The Catholic Church retains its prominent presence in the social fabric, and is very much a part in the rituals of life – from baptism to marriage and death. The symbolism of its moral power, particularly in the lives of women, however, has been contested by lived experiences quite different from what is prescribed. While ideals of womanhood are constantly raised to churchgoers, the particulars of lived realities present tangible bases of disconnect between discourse and practice, much like the official Catholic stance of Mary not as god, but contested by a strong popular Marian devotion as Mary being god-like that is central to many Filipinos, especially women.

In island Philippines, mainly in the Eastern Visayas region, the daily rudiments of life provide the backdrop to ascertain religious discourse and practice towards gender equality. The teachings of ideal mothers, wives and daughters resonate in rituals of church marriage and teachings. But the ethnographic details of life nowadays in the rural and urban centres reflect practices that demonstrate subtle subversions away from the once-prying colonial hold of elite women on social proprieties of being. Ostensibly, the times have changed where the facts of inclusion into the public domains of the economy, politics, education and health have meant Filipino women enjoying more gender-equal status in the 21st century than their counterparts in Asia, as indicated by the Global Gender Gap Index of the World Economic Forum (2015).

The practices towards gender equality or independent, autonomous and empowering choices made by Ludy and Nelia relative to their husbands, marriage and reproductive health speak of subversion of the ideals pronounced by the Catholic clergy. Observably, women like Ludy and Nelia in the Philippines may continue to hear Catholic mass on Sundays, but theirs are not the blind following of the faithful. Their actions are rooted in the realities of life, and not viewed as sacred transgressions. When women begin to rationally and practically delimit the influence of religion, of who they can be outside the discursive normative ideals of Catholic womanhood, and chart their own independent paths suited to their own situated lives, this allows for a truism beyond scriptural dogma.

## References

Aguiling-Pangalangan, E. (2010) 'Catholic fundamentalism and its impact on women's political participation in the Philippines', in C. Derichs and A. Fleschenberg (eds) *Religious fundamentalisms and their gendered impacts in Asia*, Berlin: Friedrich-Ebert Stiftung, pp 88–106.

Andaya, B.W. (2007) 'Studying women and gender in Southeast Asia', *International Journal of Asian Studies*, 4(1), pp 113–36.

Asian Development Bank (2013) *Gender equality in the labor market in the Philippines*, Manila, available at: http://digitalcommons.ilr.cornell.edu/cgi/viewcontent.cgi?article=1350&context=intl.

BC Philippines Lawyers (2009) 'Grounds for annulment of marriage in the Philippines', 1 March, available at http://www.bcphilippineslawyers.com/grounds-for-annulment-of-marriage-in-the-philippines/447/.

Blanc-Szanton, C. (1989) 'Collision of cultures: Historical reformation of gender in lowland Visayas, Philippines', in J.M. Atkinson and S. Errington (eds) *Power and difference: Gender in island Southeast Asia*, Stanford: Stanford University Press, pp 345–83.

Bonifacio, G. (2014) *Pinay on the prairies: Filipino women and transnational identities*, Vancouver: University of British Columbia Press.

Brewer, C. (2001) *Holy confrontation: Religion, gender and sexuality in the Philippines, 1521–1685*, Manila: Institute of Women's Studies.

Brewer, C. (2004) *Shamanism, Catholicism, and gender relations in colonial Philippines, 1521–1685*, Burlington: Ashgate.

Buch, E.D. and Staller, K.M. (2007) 'The feminist practice of ethnography', in S.N. Hesse-Biber and P.L. Leavy (eds) *Feminist research practice*, London: Sage, pp 187–221.

Carlson, M. (2016) 'Can the church be a virtuous hearer of women?', *Journal of Feminist Studies in Religion*, 32(1), pp 21–81.

Catholic Bishops Conference of the Philippines (1990) 'Guiding principles of the Catholic Bishops' Conference of the Philippines on population control', Media Office, CBCP, 10 July, available at: http://cbcponline.net/v2/?p=317.

Claussen, H.L. (2001) *Unconventional sisterhood: Feminist Catholic nuns in the Philippines*, Ann Arbor: University of Michigan Press.

De la Rosa, R. (2016) 'Do Catholics worship Mary?', *Manila Bulletin*, 18 September, available at: https://www.pressreader.com/philippines/manila-bulletin/20160918/281655369540604.

Delgado-Infante, M.L. and Ofreneo, M.A.P. (2014) 'Maintaining a "good girl" position: Young Filipina women constructing sexual agency in first sex within Catholicism', *Feminism & Psychology*, 24(3), pp 390–407.

Emery, R.E. (2013) *Cultural sociology of divorce: An encyclopedia*, Los Angeles: Sage.

Eviota, E.U. (1994) *Sex and gender in Philippine society: A discussion of issues on the relations between women and men*, Manila: National Commission on the Role of Filipino Women.

Feliciano, M.S. (1994) 'Law, gender, and the family in the Philippines', *Law and Society Review*, 28(3), pp 547–60.

Fernandez, R.J.T. (2016) 'Central Visayas has country's most number of pregnant teens', *Sun Star Cebu*, 9 August, available at: http://www.sunstar.com.ph/cebu/local-news/2016/08/10/central-visayas-has-countrys-most-number-pregnant-teens-490449.

Guillermo, A.R. (2012) *Historical dictionary of the Philippines* (3rd ed), Lanham: The Scarecrow Press.

Halili, M.C.N. (2004) *Philippine history*, Manila: Rex Bookstore.

Hesse-Biber, S.N. and Leavy, P.L. (2007) *Feminist research practice: A primer*, Thousand Oaks: Sage.

Lanzona, V.A. (2009) *Amazons of the Huk rebellion: Gender, sex, and revolution in the Philippines*, Madison: The University of Wisconsin Press.

Lanzoni, L. (2012) *The virtues of Mary*, New Bedford: Academy of the Immaculate.

Lauser, A. (2008) 'Philippine women on the move: Marriage across borders', *International Migration*, 46(4), pp 85–110.

Lema, K. (2012) 'Philippines defies church to push family planning', *FirstPost*, 3 October, available at: http://www.firstpost.com/world/corrected-philippines-defies-church-to-push-family-planning-477241.html.

Leyte Samar Daily News (2014) 'Cases of teen pregnancy in Eastern Visayas declines, said Popcom official', 6 October, available at: http://www.leytesamardailynews.com/cases-of-teen-pregnancy-in-eastern-visayas-declines-said-popcom-official/.

McHoul, A. and Grace, W. (2015) *A Foucault primer: Discourse, power and the subject*, New York: Routledge.

Miller, J. (2017) 'Religion in the Philippines', Center for Global Education, Asia Society, available at: http://asiasociety.org/education/religion-philippines.

Mills, S. (1997) *Discourse*, New York: Routledge.

Naples, N.A. (2003) *Feminism and method: Ethnography, discourse analysis, and activist research*, New York: Routledge.

Naples, N.A. (2004) 'The outsider phenomenon', in S.N. Hesse-Biber and M.L. Yaiser (eds) *Feminist perspectives on social research*, New York: Oxford University Press, pp 373–81.

National Statistical Coordination Board (n.d.) 'Eastern Visayas', Republic of the Philippines, available at: http://www.nap.psa.gov.ph/ru8/
Profiles/Regional_Provincial_City_Profiles.htm. Natividad, M.D.F. (2012) 'Reproductive politics, religion and state governance in the Philippines', unpublished PhD thesis, Graduate School of Arts and Science, Columbia University.

Parreñas, R.S. (2001) 'Mothering from a distance', *Feminist Studies*, 27(2), pp 361–90.

Peletz, M.G. (2006). 'Transgenderism and gender pluralism in Southeast Asia since early modern times', *Current Anthropology*, 47(2), pp 309–40.

Philippine Education for All 2015 Review Report, UNESDOC Database, UNESCO, available at: http://unesdoc.unesco.org/images/0023/002303/230331e.pdf.

Philippine Statistical Authority (2010) 'Philippine population went up by 12 million persons (Results from the 2007 census of population)', available at https://psa.gov.ph/content/philippine-population-went-12-million-persons-results-2007-census-population.

Philippine Statistics Authority (2015) *Philippines in figures 2015*, Republic of the Philippines, available at: https://www.psa.gov.ph/sites/default/files/2015%20PIF%20Final_%20as%20of%20022916.pdf.

Philippines Statistics Authority (2016) *Philippines in figures 2016*, Republic of the Philippines, available at: http://web0.psa.gov.ph/sites/default/files/PIF%202016.pdf.

Philippines Statistics Authority (2016a) 2015 Survey on Overseas Filipinos, available at: https://psa.gov.ph/content/2015-survey-overseas-filipinos-0.

Quimbo, S. (2014) 'Looking through the Leventhal lens: Is gender equity in the Philippines a puzzle?', in D. Foeken, T. Dietz, L. de Haan and L. Johnson (eds) *Development and equity: An interdisciplinary exploration by ten scholars from Africa, Asia, and Latin America*, Leiden: Brill, pp 156–66.

Republic of the Philippines (2009) Republic Act No. 9710, *Official Gazette*, available at: http://www.officialgazette.gov.ph/2009/08/14/republic-act-no-9710/

Robles, C. (2017) 'Philippine Supreme Court circulars', *Chan Robles Virtual Law Library*, available at: http://www.chanrobles.com/amno021111sc.html#.WI_Np9IrLIU.

Roces, M. (2008) 'The Filipino Catholic nun as transnational feminist', *Women's History Review*, 17(1), pp 57–78.

Sabangan, A.R. (2008) 'Number of Filipinos filing for annulment, legal separation cases up', *GMA News Online*, 1 April, available at: http://www.gmanetwork.com/news/story/87220/news/specialreports/number-of-filipinos-filing-for-annulment-legal-separation-cases-up.

Sobritchea, C.I. (2005) 'Representations of gender inequality and women's issues in Philippine feminist discourses', *Asian Journal of Women's Studies*, 11(2), pp 67–88.

Strother, J. (2013) 'Gender equality stats "don't tell full story"', *Deutsche Welle*, 9 November, available at: http://www.dw.com/en/gender-equality-stats-dont-tell-the-full-story/a-17082195.

University Center for Women's Studies, University of the Philippines (2001) *Women's role in Philippine history* (2nd ed), Quezon City: University of the Philippines Press.

Van der Hor, C. (2014) 'Teenage pregnancy among today's Filipino youth', *Philippine Daily Inquirer*, 15 May, available at: http://opinion.inquirer.net/74517/teenage-pregnancy-among-todays-filipino-youth.

Villegas, B.M. (2001) *The Philippine advantage*, Manila: University of Asia and the Pacific.

Vincent, S. (2012) 'Filipino church vows continued opposition to "reproductive health" bill', *National Catholic Register*, 20 December, available at: http://www.ncregister.com/daily-news/filipino-church-vows-continued-opposition-to-reproductive-health-bill.

Williams, L. and Guest, M.P. (2005) 'Attitudes toward marriage among the urban middle-class in Vietnam, Thailand, and the Philippines', *Journal of Comparative Family Studies*, 36(2), pp 163–86.

World Economic Forum (2015) *The Global gender gap report*, Geneva, available at: http://www3.weforum.org/docs/GGGR2015/cover.pdf.

# THREE

# A slow march forward: the impact of religious change on gender ideology in the contemporary United States

*Joshua D. Tuttle and Shannon N. Davis*

## Introduction

Gender ideology refers to societal beliefs that justify inequalities and differences across genders. Sociologists have studied shifts in gender ideology in the US since the late 20th century (Brooks and Bolzendahl, 2004; Cotter, Hermsen and Vanneman, 2011). The US provides a particularly interesting context for study because it is characterized by a relatively robust women's movement that has made historic gains in gender equality and women's empowerment. However, the march toward gender equality in the US has been rough and uneven. Progress was made in the 1970s and 1980s as women became more prominent in sectors of the economy that were previously dominated by men. At the same time, many Americans became more accepting of working mothers and economically empowered, independent women. However, American attitudes regarding gender equality trended downward in the 1990s, and grew slowly upward in subsequent years. Why did attitudes regarding gender equality trend downward, and then grow slowly upward, despite years of steady progress toward gender equality?

Some sociological research has addressed this question, connecting the observed trends in gender ideology to changing conditions in the US labour market and shifting perceptions of motherhood among women. However, these connections overlook other important cultural changes that have occurred in the US since the late 20th century, changes which may better explain the observed trends in gender ideology. Here we refer to the substantial decline of Mainline Protestantism and the tremendous growth of the religiously unaffiliated population. Mainline Protestantism began to decline in the late 20th century, while the religiously unaffiliated population began to grow at a quick pace in the mid-1990s. In this chapter, we ask how these cultural changes are related to the trends in gender ideology since the late 1970s, with a specific focus on the reversal in the trend toward gender egalitarianism in the mid-1990s, and the slow growth of gender egalitarianism throughout the 2000s. We begin our investigation with a deeper discussion of gender ideology and religious change in the US since the late 20th century. Subsequently, we apply a constrained age-period-cohort model to several decades of data from the General Social Survey (GSS) to evaluate the effect that religious change has had on gender ideology in the US. Our analysis suggests that the decline of Mainline Protestantism has attenuated progress toward gender egalitarianism, while the growth of the religiously unaffiliated population may have played a less straightforward role in progress toward gender egalitarianism in the US.

## Contemporary trends in gender ideology

Research on gender ideology in the US claimed that the national population became much more egalitarian during the 1970s, 1980s, and early 1990s (Brewster and Padavic, 2000; Brooks and Bolzendahl, 2004; Peltola, Milkie and Presser, 2004). US citizens became increasingly open to the idea of working mothers, and much more accepting – and desiring – of women occupying positions of authority. However, in the mid-1990s, the trend toward gender egalitarianism slowed, and then reversed. It was not until the year 2000 that the trend toward gender egalitarianism resumed, but at a slower pace than that which characterized the 1970s and 1980s (Cotter, Hermsen and Vanneman, 2011). Indeed, the general trend toward gender egalitarianism suggests that restrictive attitudes regarding women in non-domestic roles have given way to more liberal attitudes. But why did this trend reverse during the later years of the 1990s, and why did the trend resume at a slower pace in the years after the new millennium?

Several studies have addressed these questions in some detail. Cotter, Hermsen and Vanneman (2011) analysed data from the GSS to test the effects of demographic and social structural change on gender ideology in the US from 1977 to 2008. They found that the rapid progress toward gender egalitarianism in the 1970s and the 1980s was best explained by cohort replacement. That is, younger, liberal and better-educated individuals replaced older, more conservative and less-educated individuals. Those young, liberal and well-educated individuals were generally more accepting of egalitarian principles than those who preceded them.

The mid–1990s reversal of the trend toward gender egalitarianism is more difficult to explain. Cotter, Hermsen and Vanneman (2011) found that the effect of cohort replacement slowed after 1952. Thus, the similarity of post-1952 cohorts was greater than those born before 1952. This slow-down explained some of the mid-1990s turn around, but not all of it. Instead, it was found that a period effect in the 1990s better explained the mid-1990s turn around. With respect to this finding, Cotter, Hermsen and Vanneman (2011) theorized that a new cultural narrative had crystallized in the early 1990s, which framed gender equality as the right to choose between a career or raising a family. And while this narrative presented a false dichotomy, it effectively framed the decision to forego a career as a feminist decision. Thus, women who chose to be full-time mothers during the 1990s were able to use this cultural narrative to maintain their feminist identity while opting for more traditional family arrangements (Stone, 2007).

An ideology of 'intensive mothering' also manifested in the early 1990s, which emphasized the importance of choosing motherhood over a career. Hays (1996) defines this ideology as a gendered model of mothering in which mothers must maintain a career while simultaneously devoting tremendous amounts of time and resources to the rearing of children. The emergence of this ideology, coupled with increasing demands in middle-class and professional work environments in the 1990s (Cotter, Hermsen and Vanneman, 2010; Jacobs and Gerson, 2004), made it very difficult for women to feel successful at home and at work, and may have caused many individuals to question or even abandon liberal, feminist values.

The rise of a new cultural narrative regarding motherhood, and the manifestation of 'intensive mothering' may well explain the decline of gender egalitarianism in the mid-1990s. However, these developments do not explain the renewed, albeit slow movement toward gender egalitarianism in the years after the new millennium. Indeed, after the year 2000, it appears that the US population started to move back toward a more equitable understanding of gender in relation to politics, work and parenting. But what facilitated this renewed movement toward gender egalitarianism, and why has this movement occurred at a slower rate in comparison to the 1970s and 1980s? We argue that an analysis of recent changes in the religious landscape of the US may provide some answers to these questions. These changes refer to the decline of Mainline Protestantism, and the incredible growth of the religiously unaffiliated population.

## Contemporary religious change

Over the past several decades, Mainline Protestants[1] have declined as a proportion of the US population, while Evangelical Protestants[2] have maintained as a proportion of the national population (see Figure 3.1). In 1977, Mainline Protestants accounted for approximately 29% of the total US population, while Evangelical Protestants accounted for about a quarter of the population. At the dawn of the new millennium, Mainline Protestants accounted for about 17% of the population, and Evangelicals about 26%. By 2014, Mainline Protestants only accounted for approximately 13% of the population, while Evangelical Protestants accounted for about a quarter of the population. Across these years the remaining prominent religious affiliations, such as Black Protestants[3] and Roman Catholics, hovered around 9 and 24%, respectively.

The growth of the religiously unaffiliated population began in the mid-1990s and quickened in subsequent years (see Figure 3.1). In 1993, the religiously unaffiliated population accounted for about 9% of the population. In 2000, this figure increased to about 14% and continued to grow, to approximately 21% in 2014. At 21%, the religiously unaffiliated were the third-largest religious group in the US.

What effects have these shifts in religious affiliation had on gender ideologies in the US? Research on attitudes regarding gender ideology and religion argues that Evangelical Protestantism fosters traditional attitudes regarding gender and gender roles (Bolzendahl and Myers, 2004; Brooks and Bolzendahl, 2005; Cotter, Hermsen and Vanneman, 2011). Among Evangelicals, religious practices such as covenant marriage and a literal interpretation of Biblical scripture sanctify traditional gender roles, especially between husbands and wives (Baker, Sanchez, Nock and Wright, 2009).

Early work by Greeley (1989) suggested that the members of Mainline Protestant denominations were more accepting of women politicians than other, more conservative Protestant denominations. Further research has also found that Mainline Protestants have been more accepting of women clergy and lay leaders than Evangelical Protestants and Roman Catholics (Fobes, 2001; Nesbitt, 1997). Indeed, women's participation in leadership among Mainline Protestant denominations is now a norm, but women still struggle with a glass ceiling that limits the extent of their participation (Adams, 2007). Thus, Mainline Protestants appear to be accepting of women who hold religious and economic positions of authority, but only to a certain point.

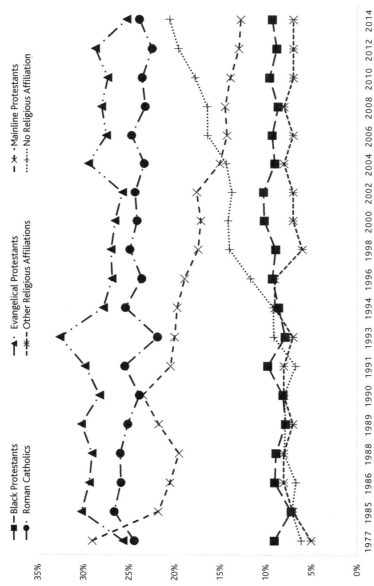

Figure 3.1. Trends in religious affiliation among US population, General social survey, 1977–2014

Source: Based on authors' analysis of GSS data.

With respect to Roman Catholics, research has indicated that they are characterized by a similar level of gender egalitarianism when compared to Mainline Protestants (Brooks and Bolzendahl, 2005; Cotter, Hermsen and Vanneman, 2011). However, Roman Catholics are more likely to value motherhood over professionalism in comparison to other Christian denominations in the US (Bartkowski and Shah, 2014). This finding suggests that Roman Catholics may be more traditional in their attitudes regarding gender roles when compared to Mainline Protestants.

In comparison to their religious counterparts, less is known about the gender ideologies that characterize the religiously unaffiliated in the US. Bolzendahl and Myers (2004) noted that the religiously unaffiliated became increasingly conservative between 1974 and 1998, and thus less receptive to gender egalitarianism. However, Cotter, Hermsen and Vanneman (2011) argued that the religiously unaffiliated were relatively supportive of gender egalitarianism across the years 1977–2008. Moreover, Hout and Fischer (2002; 2014) and Schwadel (2010) found that the religiously unaffiliated tend to be younger and more liberal than those who claim a religious affiliation. If this is true, it may be that the religiously unaffiliated are more supportive of gender egalitarianism when compared to those who belong to one or another denomination or sect.

It is also important to note that some religiously unaffiliated individuals are characterized by religious beliefs and behaviours. Thus, these individuals may consider themselves to be unaffiliated because they are 'unchurched', not irreligious (Lim, MacGregor and Putnam, 2010). Some of them may also have liminal attachments to religious organizations, but feel that they are not full members of those organizations. As such, they may worship, read religious scripture, and attend religious services. It is possible that these behaviours and beliefs foster traditional gender ideologies among some of the religiously unaffiliated.

With respect to gender egalitarianism and religious change, we posit several hypotheses. First, we hypothesize that Mainline Protestants will likely be characterized by a greater degree of gender egalitarianism than other religious affiliations in the US. If this is the case, the massive decline of Mainline Protestantism probably contributed to the reversal of gender egalitarianism in the mid-1990s, and its subsequent slow growth during the 2000s. Second, we hypothesize that the religiously unaffiliated will be characterized by a greater degree of gender egalitarianism than Evangelical Protestants and Roman Catholics, but a lesser degree of gender egalitarianism in comparison to Mainline

Protestants. If this hypothesis bears out, the substantial growth of the religiously unaffiliated contributed to the continued, albeit slow, growth of gender egalitarianism during the 2000s.

## Methods

### Data

We used data from the National Opinion Research Center's GSS (Smith, Marsden, and Hout, 2014) to analyse changes in gender attitudes in the US between 1977 and 2014. The GSS is a nationally representative survey of the entire US population, and has been administered biennially since 1972. The GSS contains eight items regarding gender role attitudes, but these questions were not included in every survey between 1977 and 2014. In fact, only four survey items about gender role attitudes were included in a consistent fashion during this time period. Prior research has already discussed the problems that this survey design has caused for time-series research on gender ideology (Cotter, Hermsen and Vanneman, 2011). Despite these problems, the GSS is still one of the best sources of data on gender ideology in the US because the data are representative of the entire US population, and the variables that measure gender ideology are standardized across a period of roughly 37 years. This data structure allows researchers to observe trends in gender ideology across recent US history, and it also allows researchers to relate demographic and economic change to trends in gender ideology as they unfold over time.

### Variables

#### Dependent variable

We borrowed our dependent variable from the work of Cotter, Hermsen and Vanneman (2011). They created a scale that measured changes in gender ideology using four different GSS survey items about gender role attitudes. Respondents were asked if they agreed or disagreed with the following four statements: 'Most men are better suited emotionally for politics than are most women'; 'A working mother can establish just as warm and secure a relationship with her children as a mother who does not work'; 'A preschool child is likely to suffer if his or her mother works'; and 'It is much better for everyone involved if the man is the achiever outside the home and the woman takes care of the home and family'. We recreated this scale by computing z-scores for each variable. We then combined each variable into a single scale by computing average scores across each variable. Higher scores on this scale corresponded to egalitarian gender ideology (accepting of working mothers, accepting of women in politics), while lower scores corresponded to traditional gender ideology (not accepting of working mothers, not accepting of women in politics).

### Independent variable

We measured religious affiliations using the 'RELTRAD,' or 'religious tradition' classification scheme that was developed by Steensland et al (2000). This classification scheme was later updated and improved by Chaves (2011). In its current state, RELTRAD sorts GSS respondents into the following religious affiliations: Black Protestant, Evangelical Protestant, Mainline Protestant, Roman Catholic, Jewish, other religious affiliations, and no religious affiliation. Respondents are categorized into one or another Protestant category according to the theological orientation and history of their self-reported Protestant affiliation. Respondents who self-identified as Roman Catholic or Jewish were classified as such. Respondents who self-identified as Buddhist, Mormon, Jehovah's Witness, Muslim, Hindu, or Unitarian were categorized as 'other religious affiliations'. Finally, respondents who reported 'no religious affiliation' were categorized as such. We decided to combine Jewish respondents with other religious affiliations because there were relatively few Jewish respondents in the GSS data. Evangelical Protestants were excluded from the analysis as a reference category.

### Period and cohort controls

We included several independent variables to control for the effect of periods and cohort replacement on gender ideology in the US. Survey years were included as a continuous variable to account for period effects. Survey years correspond to the year each respondent participated in the GSS. In keeping with the work of Cotter, Hermsen and Vanneman (2011), we also included two survey year splines: one spline in which the year 1994 served as the knot on the spline, and another in which the year 2000 served as the knot on the spline. This allowed us to control for the period effects that were observed by Cotter, Hermsen and Vanneman (2011).

Birth years were included in the model to account for the effect of generational change and cohort replacement on gender ideology.

A generation refers to a collection of individuals who were born during a relatively long, discrete historical period, while a cohort refers to individuals who were born within discrete time periods within a generation (Gilleard, 2004; Kertzer, 1983). Pew Research Center (2010a) has identified five generations in the US: the Greatest Generation (born before 1928), the Silent Generation (1928–45), the Baby Boomer Generation (1946–64), Generation X (1965–80), and the Millennial Generation (1981–97). Research suggests that a substantial portion of the religiously unaffiliated were born in 1981 or later years, which makes them members of the Millennial Generation (Hout and Fischer, 2002; 2014; Pew Research Center, 2010b). Thus, it was necessary to differentiate between Millennials and the religiously unaffiliated within our model. We differentiated between these groups by including a birth year spline in the model. The birth year 1981 served as the knot on the spline. By including this spline, we were able to clearly observe how the rise of Millennial birth cohorts affected gender ideology in the US, relative to birth cohorts from prior generations.

### Additional controls

We controlled for the effect of political identities and political ideologies with several dichotomous variables and one scale variable. In terms of political identities, we included self-described moderates and conservatives in the analysis, while excluding self-described liberals as a reference category. Political ideology was included as a scale, which was constructed by taking the average of the standardized scores of 18 different survey items. This scale has been used in prior work on gender ideology (Brooks and Bolzendahl, 2004; Cotter, Hermsen and Vanneman, 2011). The survey items used to construct this scale pertained to attitudes regarding freedom of speech, censorship, academic freedoms, sexual education, sexual freedoms, and same-sex rights. Higher scores on this scale corresponded to support for greater freedoms and sex education. Lower scores corresponded to the opposite.

Several socio-economic variables were included to control for variations in employment, education, and income across years of data. Employment was measured in two ways: whether or not a respondent was working full- or part-time, and whether or not a respondent was self-employed. We also included a measure of female spouses who work. We accomplished this by including males who were married to a female who works. All other women and men were excluded as a reference category. This allowed us to control for the rise of the dual-earner households in the late 1970s, the 1980s and the 1990s. Education was measured in years of completed education. Income was measured at the household level, and adjusted to control for inflation. Descriptive statistics suggested that the household income distribution was skewed across years of data, so the natural log of household income was computed to pull in the tails of the distribution.

Finally, we included several variables that measured respondents' gender and race, marital status, the number of children reared, and frequency of religious service attendance. Females were included in the model while males were excluded as a reference category. Blacks and those who self-reported as 'other races' were included in the model while Whites were excluded as a reference category. Frequency of religious service attendance was measured in the following manner: 0 'Never', 1 'Less than once a year', 2 'Once a year', 3 'Several times a year', 4 'Once a month', 5 'Two to three times a month', 6 'Every week', 7 'More than once a week'. Descriptive statistics for the dependent variable and each independent variable are listed in Appendix A.

### Analysis and results

We constructed a constrained age-period-cohort (APC) linear regression model to analyse changes in gender ideology in the US across survey years 1977–2014. An APC linear regression model is similar to a standard linear regression in the sense that both assume a quantifiable, linear relationship exists between a continuous dependent variable and a set of continuous or discrete independent variables. However, unlike a typical linear model, an APC model accounts for time-dependent effects, such as age effects, cohort effects and period effects (O'Brien, 2014). Age effects refer to changes that individuals experience as they get older. Cohort effects refer to the effects that shared life experiences have on the thought and behaviour of many individuals. Period effects refer to variations in thought and behaviour that are associated with the period in which those thoughts and behaviours were observed. Age, cohorts and periods tend to share strong correlations, which makes it difficult to control for all three with one statistical model. Thus, we chose to control for only period and cohort effects in order to account for how cohort replacement affects gender ideology across time. This strategy allowed us to better observe the effect of religious affiliation on gender ideology while holding other economic, social and demographic factors constant.

Average scores on the gender ideology scale across years and religious affiliations are presented in Figure 3.2. As noted in prior research, the US population has become increasingly egalitarian over time, apart from the reversal during the mid-1990s. The religiously unaffiliated have been characterized by a higher average score on the gender ideology scale relative to all other religious affiliations. Black Protestants and Mainline Protestants were also characterized by high average scores in comparison to Roman Catholics, Evangelical Protestants and 'Other Religious Affiliations'. Overall, Evangelical Protestants were characterized by the lowest average scores on the gender ideology scale, far below the national average across all years.

The results of the APC linear regression model are listed in Appendix B. The model predicted approximately 32% of the variation in gender ideology across survey years. All religious affiliations scored higher on the gender ideology scale relative to Evangelical Protestants. However, the effect of belonging to 'other religious affiliations' and the effect of being religiously unaffiliated were not statistically significant. These results suggest that Black Protestants, Mainline Protestants and Catholics are rather open to progressive ideas regarding gender, while those belonging to other affiliations, and the religiously unaffiliated, may be less so. These findings support our hypothesis regarding Mainline Protestants and undermine our hypothesis regarding the religiously unaffiliated. The dramatic decline of Mainline Protestantism has probably attenuated the growth of gender egalitarianism among the US population. However, our analysis was unable to determine whether the rise of a relatively large religiously unaffiliated population has had a significant effect on gender ideology in the US.

Frequency of religious attendance shared a negative association with gender ideology. That is, for each one–unit increase in religious service attendance, scores on the gender ideology scale dropped by about .036 units. This is a rather small effect, but significant nonetheless. We also included an interaction term between the religiously unaffiliated and religious attendance in order to test for the effect of liminal religiosity among the religiously unaffiliated (Unaffiliated*Religious Attendance). The coefficient associated with this interaction term was negligible in size and was not statistically significant.

A small, positive association was found between survey years and gender ideology. Each one–unit increase in survey years was associated with an increase of .024 units on the gender ideology scale. The 1994 survey year spline was negatively associated with gender ideology. Each unit increase on the spline was associated with .049 decrement on the gender ideology scale. Conversely, the 2000 survey year spline was

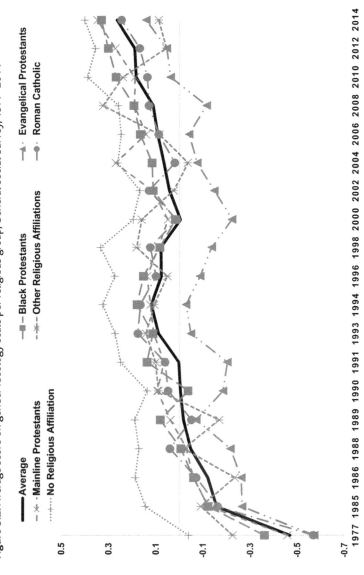

Figure 3.2. Average score on gender ideology scale per religious group, General Social Survey, 1977–2014

Source: Based on authors' analysis of GSS data.

positively associated with the gender ideology scale. Each one-unit increase on this spline was associated with an increase of .036 on the scale. These results confirm the findings of prior research and support the theory that a new cultural frame developed in the mid-1990s that pressured women to choose between a professional career and motherhood (Cotter, Hermsen and Vanneman, 2011).

Birth years were positively associated with the dependent variable. Each one-unit increase in birth years was associated with an increase of .005 on the gender ideology scale. Surprisingly, a small, negative associated was observed between the birth year spline and gender ideology. Each one-year increase on the spline was associated with a decrement of .022 units on the gender ideology scale. These findings suggest that Millennial birth cohorts are less egalitarian than birth cohorts from prior generations. We also tested the effect of being a Millennial and being religiously unaffiliated on the variation in gender ideology. This was accomplished by the inclusion of an interaction term (Birth Year Spline*Unaffiliated). The coefficient associated with this interaction term was very small and negative, and it was not statistically significant.

## Conclusion

This chapter has documented the effect that religious change has had on gender ideology in the US since the late 1970s. Our analysis demonstrated that all religious affiliations scored higher on the gender ideology scale relative to Evangelical Protestants, and Mainline Protestants were characterized by the greatest score on the gender ideology scale. However, the Mainline Protestant population has drastically declined since the late 20th century. The decline of Mainline Protestantism has been met by the growth of a rather large religiously unaffiliated population, but it is unclear whether this population is open to gender egalitarianism.

Our analysis also found that Millennials are characterized by slightly less egalitarian gender ideologies when compared to older individuals. This finding was surprising because research has found that Millennials are less socially conservative than other generations, and are more accepting of working mothers than other generations (Pew Research Center, 2010; Donnelly, Twenge, Clark, Shaikh, Beiler-May and Carter, 2016). However, some research suggests that support for gender egalitarianism has declined among young people in the US since the mid-1990s (Cotter and Pepin, 2017; Fate-Dixon, 2017).

**Appendix A.** Weighted descriptive statistics for all variables included in regression of gender ideology scale

| Continuous variables | | |
|---|---|---|
| | Mean | SD |
| Gender Ideology Scale | −0.021 | 0.744 |
| Civil Liberties Scale | 0.534 | 0.620 |
| Religious Attendance | 3.770 | 2.721 |
| Survey Year | 1993.930 | 11.426 |
| Year Spline (1994) | 5.231 | 7.296 |
| Year Spline (2000) | 2.884 | 4.944 |
| Birth Year | 1950.898 | 19.182 |
| Birth Year Spline (1981) | 0.326 | 1.618 |
| Number of Children | 1.880 | 1.740 |
| Years of Education | 13.14 | 2.986 |
| (LN) Household Income | 10.117 | 0.970 |
| Dichotomous Variables | | |
| | Per cent | |
| Black Protestant | 08.23 | |
| Mainline Protestant | 19.34 | |
| Roman Catholic | 25.43 | |
| Other Religious Affiliation | 06.58 | |
| No Religious Affiliation | 11.39 | |
| Black | 11.51 | |
| Other Races | 05.34 | |
| Female | 52.59 | |
| Married | 60.38 | |
| Working | 65.86 | |
| Self-employed | 10.79 | |
| Working Female Spouse | 16.31 | |
| Politically Moderate | 36.31 | |
| Politically Conservative | 33.24 | |

$N = 10,082$
*Based on authors' analysis of GSS data.*

Additional qualitative research also suggests that Millennials in the US are characterized by contradictory gender ideologies (Risman, 2017). Some Millennials reject the traditional gender binary and choose to rebel against gendered expectations to social roles, while other Millennials believe that there are immutable differences between men and women, and that it is best to conform to institutional rules and organizational policies that relate to such differences. These findings, in relation to our own, suggest that gender ideology among Millennials is a complex matter that varies among age cohorts within the Millennial generation. That is, relatively younger Millennials may be less egalitarian than relatively older Millennials.

The continuing trend toward gender egalitarianism among the US population is important to emphasize, and this trend is likely to continue in the coming years. The social factors associated with this trend are rather unclear. Our findings, which are consistent with Cotter, Hermsen and Vanneman (2011), suggest that a period effect was responsible for the renewed growth of gender egalitarianism in the year 2000. Future research should investigate this effect to better understand the historical context of the New Millennium, and why the momentum of the US gender revolution was renewed.

The decline of Mainline Protestantism and the rise of a relatively traditional Millennial generation casts some doubt on the future of gender egalitarianism in the US. As their numbers dwindle, Mainline Protestants will exert less influence on the social and cultural values that Americans hold regarding gender. Millennials will exert more influence on these values as they age into positions of authority. If Millennials – particularly younger Millennials – remain relatively traditional, the trend toward gender egalitarianism in the US could give way to gender traditionalism. Of course, the religiously unaffiliated population will inevitably play a role in this future. However, as of now, their disposition to gender egalitarianism is ambiguous.

**Appendix B.** Linear regression of gender ideology scale, 1977–2014

|  | Unstandardized Ordinary Least Squares Regression Coefficient | Standard Error of the Estimate |
|---|---|---|
| Evangelical Protestants | REF | — |
| Black Protestant | 0.097* | 0.038 |
| Mainline Protestant | 0.088*** | 0.019 |
| Roman Catholic | 0.068*** | 0.017 |
| Other Affiliations | 0.019 | 0.027 |
| Unaffiliated | 0.028 | 0.028 |
| Religious Attendance | −0.024*** | 0.003 |
| Unaffiliated*Religious Attendance | 0.013 | 0.013 |
| White | REF | — |
| Black | 0.103*** | 0.032 |
| Other Races | −0.130*** | 0.028 |
| Male | REF | — |
| Female | 0.327*** | 0.014 |
| Not Married | REF | — |
| Married | −0.075*** | 0.015 |
| Number of Children | −0.016*** | 0.005 |
| Years of Education | 0.020*** | 0.003 |
| Not Working | REF | — |
| Working | 0.086*** | 0.015 |
| Employee | REF | — |
| Self-Employed | −0.061** | 0.020 |
| Working Female Spouse | 0.193*** | 0.021 |
| (LN) Household Income | 0.014 | 0.007 |
| Politically Liberal | REF | — |
| Politically Moderate | −0.036* | 0.015 |
| Politically Conservative | −0.209*** | 0.016 |
| Civil Liberties Scale | 0.299*** | 0.012 |
| Year | 0.024*** | 0.001 |
| Year Spline (Knot = 1994) | −0.049*** | 0.005 |
| Year Spline (Knot = 2000) | 0.036*** | 0.006 |
| Birth Year | 0.005*** | 0.000 |
| Birth Year Spline (Knot = 1981) | −0.016*** | 0.005 |
| Birth Year Spline*Unaffiliated | 0.001 | 0.009 |
| Constant | −57.134*** | 2.882 |
| R-Square | 0.315 | — |

N = 10,082; * = p<.05; ** = p<.010; *** = p<.001
Based on authors' analysis of GSS data.

## Notes

[1] Mainline Protestants are individuals who belong to historically prominent and relatively liberal Protestant denominations in the United States. These denominations include the United Methodist Church, the Evangelical Lutheran Church, the Presbyterian Church, the Episcopal Church, American Baptist Churches, the United Church of Christ, the Disciples of Christ and several other smaller organizations.

[2] Evangelical Protestants are individuals who belong to conservative and fundamentalist Protestant denominations and sects. These denominations and sects include but are not limited to the American Baptist Association, the Assemblies of God, the Salvation Army, Southern Baptist Convention, the Pentecostal Holiness Church and many other smaller organizations.

[3] Black Protestants include African Americans who belong to historically Black Protestant denominations and sects in the US, such as the African American Episcopal Church, the African American Episcopal Church, the African Methodist Church and the Church of God in Christ, to name a few.

## References

Adams, J. (2007) 'Stained glass makes the ceiling visible: organizational opposition to women in Congregational leadership', *Gender & Society*, 21, pp 80–105.

Baker, E.H., Sanchez, L.A., Nock, S.L. and Wright, J.D. (2009) 'Covenant marriage and the sanctification of gendered marital roles', *Journal of Family Issues*, 30(2), pp 147–78.

Bartkowski, J.P. and Shah, S. (2014) 'Religion and gender inequality: from attitudes to practices', in Keister, L. and Sherkat, D.E. eds. *Religion and Inequality in America: Research and Theory on Religion's Role in Stratification*. Cambridge: Cambridge University Press.

Bolzendahl C. and Myers, D. (2004) 'Feminist attitudes and support for gender equality: opinion change in women and men, 1974–1998', *Social Forces*, 83(2), pp 759–90.

Brewster, K.L. and Padavic, I. (2000) 'Change in gender-ideology, 1977–1996: the contributions of intracohort change and population turnover', *Journal of Marriage and Family*, 62, pp 477–87.

Brooks, C. and Bolzendahl, C. (2004) 'The transformation of US gender role attitudes: cohort replacement, social-structural change, and ideological learning', *Social Science Research* 33, pp 106–33.

Chaves, M. (2011) *American Religion: Contemporary Trends*. Princeton: Princeton University Press.

Cotter, D., Hermsen, J.M. and Vanneman, R. (2011) 'The end of the gender revolution? Gender role attitudes from 1977 to 2008', *American Journal of Sociology*, 117(1), pp 259–89.

Cotter, D. and Pepin, J. (2017) *Trending Towards Traditionalism? Changes in Youth's Gender Ideology*, Council on Contemporary Families. Austin: The University of Texas at Austin, available at: https://contemporaryfamilies.org/2-pepin-cotter-traditionalism/.

Donnelly, K., Twenge, J., Clark, M., Shaikh, Samia., Beiler-May, A. and Carter, N. (2016) 'Attitudes toward women's work and family roles in the United States, 1976–2013', *Psychology of Women Quarterly*, 40(1), pp 45–54.

Fate-Dixon, N. (2017) *Are Some Millennials Rethinking the Gender Revolution? Long-Range Trends in the Views of Non-Traditional Roles of Women*, Council on Contemporary Families. Austin: The University of Texas at Austin, available at: https://contemporaryfamilies.org/2-pepin-cotter-traditionalism/.

Fobes, C. (2001) 'Searching for a priest ... or a man? Using gender as a cultural resource in an Episcopal campus chapel', *Journal for the Scientific Study of Religion*, 40, pp 87–98.

Gilleard, C. (2004) 'Concept: cohorts and generations in the study of social change', *Social Theory & Health*, 2(1), pp 106–19.

Greeley, A.M. (1989) *Religious Change in America*, Cambridge: Harvard University Press.

Hays, S. (1996) *The Cultural Contradictions of Motherhood*, New Haven: Yale University Press.

Hout, M. and Fischer, C.S. (2002) 'Why More Americans Have No Religious Preference: Politics and Generations', *American Sociological Review*, 67(2), pp 165–90.

Hout, M. and Fischer, C.S. (2014) *Explaining Why More Americans Have No Religious Preference: Political Backlash and Generational Succession, 1987–2012*, NYU Population Center, available at: http://populationcenter.as.nyu.edu/page/workingpapers.

Jacobs, J. and Gerson, K. (2004) *The Time Divide: Work, Family, and Gender Inequality*, Cambridge: Harvard University Press.

Kertzer, D. (1983) 'Generation as a sociological problem', *Annual Review of Sociology*, 9, pp 125–49.

Lim, C., MacGregor, C. and Putnam, R. (2010) 'Secular and liminal: discovering heterogeneity among religious nones', *Journal for the Scientific Study of Religion*, 48(4), pp 569–618.

Nesbitt, P. (1997) *Feminization of the Clergy in America: Occupational and Organizational Perspectives*, New York: Oxford University Press.

O'Brien, R. (2014) *Age-Period-Cohort Models: Approaches and Analyses with Aggregate Data*, New York: Chapman and Hall.

Pauly, D. (1995) 'Anecdotes and the shifting baseline syndrome of fisheries', *Trends in Ecology and Evolution*, 10(10), pp 430.

Peltola, P., Milkie, M.A. and Presser, S. (2004) 'The "Feminist" Mystique: feminist identity in three generations of women', *Gender and Society*, 18, pp 115–39.

Pew Research Center (2010a) *Millennials: A Portrait of Generation Next*, available at: http://assets.pewresearch.org/wp-content/uploads/sites/3/2010/10/millennials-confident-connected-open-to-change.pdf.

Pew Research Center (2010b) *Religion Among the Millennials: Introduction and Overview*, available at: http://www.pewforum.org/2010/02/17/religion-among-the-millennials/.

Risman, B.J. (2017) '2016 Southern Sociological Society Presidential Address: Are Millennials cracking the gender structure?', *Social Currents*, 4(3), pp 208–27.

Schwadel, P. (2010) 'Period and cohort effects on religious nonaffiliation and religious disaffiliation: a research note', *Journal for the Scientific Study of Religion*, 49(2), pp 311–19.

Smith, T., Marsden, O., Hout, M. and Kim, J. (2014) *General Social Survey*, Chicago: National Opinion Research Center.

Steensland, B. et al. (2000) 'The Measure of American Religion: Toward Improving the State of the Art', *Social Forces*, 79(1), pp 291–318.

Stone, P. (2007) *Opting Out? Why Women Really Quit Careers and Head Home*, Berkeley: University of California Press.

FOUR

# Divine shadows: Indian Devadasis between religious beliefs and sexual exploitation

*Manu Sharma*

## Introduction

The term Devadasi is a Sanskrit word, which literally translates to 'female slave of God'. Devadasi practice arises out of a crossroads of religion, poverty, gender stereotypes and social norms. This chapter aims to understand the origin and growth of the Devadasi system and highlight the present status of Devadasis in Indian society. It also envisages the exploitation of women in the name of religious tradition. In contemporary times, for various socio-historical reasons, the Devadasi tradition appears to have lost its status and is equated synonymously with prostitution and slavery in India. Devadasi practice is today a challenge to both the government and non-governmental organizations (NGOs).

Devadasi means a woman who performs the service for some deity in a temple: unmarried temple servants who had been dedicated to temple deities as young girls through rites resembling Hindu marriage ceremonies (Parker, 1998). To be a Devadasi is one of the services rendered by women in Hindu society; a woman readily marries a deity and serves him in the temple. Devadasis were an essential part of Indian temples. They performed regular functions at temples such as cleaning of temples, lighting lamps, dressing the deities and so on. They sang devotional songs and danced in devotion to the deities. They taught music and dance to girls. They kept alive and developed a tradition of classical music and dance. They lived in quasi-matrilineal communities, had non-conjugal sexual relationships with upper-caste men, and were literate when most South Indian women were not. Beyond these historical facts is a vast area of myths and false propaganda. Devadasis were meant to please the eyes of the Lord alone but their dancing unintentionally became a source of entertainment and attraction for the folk who happened to witness their swirl in worship. Essentially and originally during the period between the

10th and 11th centuries CE, when the system reached its pinnacle, a tumultuous erosion of its virtuous position took place, making the position of Devadasis vulnerable and docile. Presently, Devadasis are no longer considered historical temple dancers, and many of them belong to the low-caste *Dalit* (oppressed caste) section of society.

A report commissioned by the National Commission for Women (NCW) (Bharathi Harishankar and Priyamvadha, 2016) reveals that thousands of *Dalit* women continue to be forced into the Devadasi system in several states of India. Estimates suggest that approximately 250,000 girls and women in India are still dedicated to their local temple deities. More than half of the Devadasies become prostitutes (Zaidi, 2012). Most Devadasi communities exist in south India. (Shingal, 2015). In Andhra Pradesh, Devadasi practice is prevalent in Karimnagar, Warangal, Nizamabad, Mahaboobnagar, Kurnool, Hyderabad, Anantapur, Medak, Adilabad, Chittoor, Rangareddy, Nellore, Nalgonda and Srikakulam. In Karnataka, the practice has been found to exist in Raichur, Bijapur, Belgaum, Dharwad, Bellari and Gulbarga. In Maharashtra, the Devadasi practice exists in Pune, Sholapur, Kolhapur, Sangli, Mumbai, Latur, Usmanabad, Satara, Sindhudurg and Nanded.

Starting with these premises, this chapter questions the importance of the religious factor in explaining the logic of the Devadasis' institution. But the element of caste and socio-economic background – the two fundamental aspects – should be taken into account. These factors, strictly interwoven, contribute to keeping this practice alive. The Devadasi's consecration is deeply embedded both in the rural social structure and in religious beliefs and represents a form of dominance and social control of upper castes over lower ones.

The chapter begins with an overview of the Devadasi system in the past and in the present. In the following sections, temple rituals and cult practices are discussed. The chapter then focuses on the social reform movements aimed at abolishing the Devadasi system, on contemporary legislative activities and on the present situation of Devadasis. The chapter concludes with a critical discussion of the institution of the Devadasi, particularly with respect to the social attitude towards this phenomenon and some suggestions for the betterment of their status. To understand the history and culture of Devadasis, this chapter is based on data collected from national archives, published research articles, books and other materials. To discuss the present situation, interviews with Devadasis published in books, newspapers, periodicals and so on are taken into account.

## Historical background

A definite commencement point of time remains unknown as to when the Devadasi tradition began. A complete absence of the Devadasi tradition has been noticed in the works of Jatakas (the previous life stories of Lord Buddha), Kautilya or Vatsayana. The new opinion of many scholars is the view that the Devadasi practice has no sanction of the scriptures. These scholars treat Devadasi practice as 'Sacred or religious prostitution' and plead that Hindu religious scriptures do not have any mention of sacred prostitution. But various 'Smritis' (ancient Indian law books) have recognized prostitution and there are instances of prostitutes being taxed. Altekar opines that 'the custom of the association of dancing girl with temples is unknown to Jataka literature. It is not mentioned by Greek writers; the Arthashastra which describes in detail the life of Ganikas is silent about it' (Altekar, 1956, p. 185).

The custom of dedication of girls to 'Yellamma' and to the temples of the Goddess is traced back to the 3rd century AD during the period of the Puranas. Devadasis at that time worked in temples as entertainers. Dancing girls find a mention in Kalidas's 'Meghadoot', who was a classical Sanskrit writer of the Gupta Empire in ancient India. It is said that dancing girls were present at the time of worship in the Mahakal Temple of Ujjain. Devadasis and the other categories of dancing girls find a mention in the works of Hiuen-Tsang, a Chinese pilgrim traveller of the 7th century AD who visited India during the rule of Harshavardhana (the king of the Vardhan Dynasty); Kalhana, a historian who wrote *Rajatarangini*, a historical chronicle of Kashmir (the north-western Indian subcontinent) in the 12th century; Abul Fazal, the vizier and court historian of the Mughal Emperor Akbar in the 16th century; Domingo Paes and Fernao Nunz, the Portuguese travellers of the 16th century; and Abbé Dunois, a French Catholic Missionary of 19th century and many more.

Inscriptions dating back to 1004 AD on the Raja Rajeshwar temple at Tanjore in South India maintain that there were 400 Devadasis in the temples, who were second in importance only to the temple priests who performed the religious rituals. Parallel to this, there is a record of the Someshwer shrine at Gujarat, which maintained 500 Devadasis. They used to live in the streets surrounding the temples and received maintenance in return for service in the temple (Tarachand, 1992).

The affluent status of Devadasis has been found in Pallava and Chola dynasties in the southern parts of India between the 6th and 13th centuries AD. This phase shows that they were accorded with great respect and dignity in society, being the custodians of culture and the arts such as music and dance. There is no hint of ostracism. They were bestowed with grand gifts of land, property and jewellry by wealthy and royal patrons and were quite affluent.

As we will shortly see, the esteemed status of the Devadasis began to wane under Islamic and British rule (Shingal, 2015). By 1818, the Devadasis themselves had been reduced to the level of prostitutes for sustaining their finances. Especially during British rule (1858–1947), there had been a sea change in the economic system of the society, which led the Devadasis to lose the privileges that they had traditionally enjoyed. British rule in India put an end to the local royalty and temple treasuries. Most of the temples at that time ran with royal funding from local kings. All these faced decline with the rise of British power and one of the groups to be financially and socially pursued and victimized were the Devadasis. Gone was the respect they enjoyed as members of a class next only to the priests. Devadasis remained entertainers but their mode of entertainment changed drastically, being performed by their bodies. They evolved into practising courtesans, skilled in the art of love-making. The system spread across the Belgaum, Gulbarga and Bellary districts in Karnataka and the Satara, Kolhapur, Solapur and Osmanabad districts of Maharashtra.

Thus what began as being the slave of God culminated in prostitution. Presently, the Devadasi tradition has become a system of open prostitution in all Indian states except in few pocket areas where it still flourishes under the guise of dedication to Yellamma.

## Temple rituals and cult practices

The Devadasi had to participate in almost all the daily rituals and ceremonies, from the rousing of the deity from sleep in early morning to the time when the God went to sleep (Jain, 2003, p. 120). In the morning, the deity had to be awakened, to be bathed, dressed up in elaborate robes; a morning meal was followed by an afternoon nap, offering lamps, incense and perfumery; and the evening meal was enveloped by intense and elaborate decoration with flowers and then night refreshment. The day culminated with a 'putting to sleep' ceremony (Marglin, 1985).

Dusk and dawn marked the performance of the Devadasis. The morning rituals were devoid of songs to complement the dance, which took place simultaneously along with the first major offering in the inner sanctum. Offerings were inclusive of cooked food and other food offerings, and the public were not allowed to view the deities as this took place behind closed doors. However, the dance performed by the Devadasis in the dance hall was a public event.

The status of the Devadasi accorded with whom she was given to in marriage, that is, the deity, the God of the temple, and thus she was considered 'Sadasuhagan'– at all times married, hence always blessed. Being married to a deity, her adherence to maintaining strict discipline was mandatory, she was the personal possession of the temple and her elevated position made it unacceptable for her to mingle with the rest of the people and, more precisely, to keep in touch with men.

A Devadasi was meant to be revered; while she danced in worship, speaking to her or looking at her has been mentioned as a ritual offence in the sectarian texts that lay out the etiquette on blame in other varieties of indiscretion such as spitting in the temple, turning one's back to the shrine, looking covetously at consecrated property, and so on. A Devadasi's death was marked with an elaborate rite where she was granted life honours; flowers, sandal paste, and a garland were to be sent from the God of the temple. Unlike in other funeral processions, where no stops are to be made, in the case of a Devadasi, her pyre was momentarily placed on the floor near the entrance of the temple where the offerings were made to her.

A Devadasi as 'Nitya Sumangali', a woman who enjoyed the protection of a living husband – here the deity, was provided with a necessary excuse or approval to enter secular society and thus improve her artistic skills among the connoisseurs and their families, who were obliged to respect her and treat her with much chivalry. Ceremonial events in the big homes of the locality, such as welcoming the bridegroom and guests, singing songs of festivity at marriages and puberty ceremonies, tying the red beads on a woman's marriage necklace and so on were performed by Devadasis, which ordinarily in homes were conducted by Sumangalis (Chakraborty, 2000).

## Status degradation and legislation

The glorious golden days of Devadasis ended with their exploitation by wealthy and powerful class of men as their conditions, beset with poverty, drove them to prostitution. As Shingal writes (2015, pp 110–11):

> The esteemed status of the *devadasis* began to wane under the Islamic and British rule. Following their successful invasion of North India, Islamic rulers began to destroy Hindu temples throughout the region .... With the

destruction of the temples, *devadasis* lost not only their patronage but also their status in society, leading to the beginnings of their exploitation. The result of the loss of patronage forced the *devadasis*, who previously danced at religious temple events, to dance at wedding feasts or other private entertainments. The system was further limited under British rule, which unlike the Islamic Empire reached the entirety of the subcontinent.

The Muslim invasion (between the 12th and 16th centuries) was the first gateway to their slaughter as the Hindu Empire went to subjugation and the Devadasis lost their royal patronage. By losing virginity earlier, they had to resort to prostitution to earn their living. The testimony of Al-Beruni (Sachau, 1910, p. 157), a traveller during the Muslim invasion, states that kings maintained this institution for the benefit of their revenues, as here the Brahmana or priest was detained to allow into their temples women who sang, danced and played. The kings, however, made them a source of attraction to their subjects so that they might meet the expenditure of their armies out of the revenues derived from there.

The arrival of Europeans and their perspective regarding the Temple Devadasis is marked with suspicions about the immorality of Indian religion. The French missionary Abbé Dubois, who had spent 30 years (1792–1823) in South India, in his classic *Hindu Manners, Customs and Ceremonies*, (Abbé Dubois, J.A., 1993, p. 585) condemned them in no uncertain terms: 'Once the Devadasi's temple duties are over, they open their cells of infamy and frequently convert the temple itself into a stew. A religion more shameful or indecent has never existed amongst a civilized people.'

Towards the end of the 19th century, Indian socio-religious practices were challenged, which also led to social movements against the Devadasi system. The social movements to deal with the Devadasi system can be classified as the Reformist movement and Revivalist Movement. Reformists urged the abolition of all ceremonies and practices by which young girls were dedicated as Devadasis of Hindu shrines (Srinivasan, 1985). To create public opinion, seminars and conferences were organized in Madras to attack the Devadasi system in 1882. In 1892, an appeal was made to the Viceroy and Governor-General of India and to the Governor of Madras against the Devadasi system, known as an anti-nautch movement (a corruption of the Hindi term *nach*) (Srinivasan, 1985; Shankar, 2004, p. 39). In the appeal made by Hindu social reforms associations, it was claimed that there existed in the Indian community a class of women community commonly known as nautch-girls who were invariably prostitutes. The anti-nautch supporters, largely educated professionals and Hindus, began their attack on the Devadasis' dance in 1892 (Shankar, 2004, p. 39). Marches and protests were held in the houses of the elite, who refused to heed the call for boycotting the dance at private celebrations, which led to the complete suppression of 'Sadir' and its secular performance long before the final legislation was enacted in 1947.

During the same period there emerged a movement urging the 'revival' of Sadir or traditional dance of Devadasis. The revivalists feared that the emergence of the anti-nautch movement would lead to a ban on classical dance, which was performed only by Devadasis. In 1882, the Theosophical Society of India had set up its headquarters in Adyar, Madras with the set goal of working towards the restoration of India's ancient glory, her art, science and philosophy. The revivalists tried to present Devadasis as the model of the ancient temple dancer, as pure sacred and chaste women, and emphasized the absence of immorality. The revivalists wanted to preserve the traditional form of Sadir dance by purifying it. In 1930, Dr Muthulakshmi Reddy launched a vocal anti-dance campaign, demanding the abolition of the Devadasi system. She brought a Bill in the Madras Council, prohibiting the performance of the dedicatory ceremony in any Hindu Temple and enabling the dedicated woman to contract a legal marriage (*The Fort St. George Gazette*, Madras, Part IV, 28 January 1930, p. 191). According to Jordan (2003), Dr Reddy's campaign prompted scores of pleas and protests written by Devadasis. She recounts one such plea from a Devadasis association: 'Our institution is similar to the mutts presided by sanyasis for the propagation of religion. We can be compared to female sanyasis who are attached to respective temples. We marry none but God and become devotees of God' (Jordan, 2003, p. 47) Hence, even among the protests, Dr Reddy's campaign prevailed, and initial punitive legislation in 1927 was followed by an outright ban in 1948 with the Madras Devadasis Act 1947:

> Dancing by a woman, with or without kumbhaharathy (pot-shaped temple arti lamp), in the precincts of a temple or other religious institution, or in any procession of a Hindu deity, idol or object of worship installed in any such temple or institution or at any festival or ceremony held in respect of such a deity, idol or object of worship, is hereby declared unlawful ... Any person who performs permits

or abets (temple dancing) is punishable with imprisonment for six months. (Marglin, 1985, p. 306)

The Bombay Devadasis Protection Act 1934 prohibits the marriage of girls with idols. This act sets out to protect Devadasis and to prevent the dedication of women to Hindu deities, idols, objects of worship, temples and religious institutions in the state of Bombay. Section III is about the illegality of the dedication of a woman as a Devadasi. The performance of any ceremony or act intended to dedicate or having the effect of dedicating a woman as a Devadasi is declared unlawful. According to the Tamil Nadu Devadasis (Prevention of Dedication) Act 1947, also known as Act No. XXXI of 1947, all forms of the Devadasi system were abolished in the Madras Presidency and Devadasi girls were also permitted to marry in the Southern province. 'The Prohibition of Dedication Act 1982 of Karnataka considered dedication as a Devadasi to be unlawful (*Karnataka Gazette*, Part IV-2A, No. 75, 3 February 1982, p. 5). The Andhra Pradesh Devadasis (Prohibition of Dedication) Act 1988 prohibited the dedication of women as Devadasis in the State of Andhra Pradesh, whereas Maharashtra Devadasi (Abolition of Dedication) Act 2006 completely prohibited such practices. In 1992, the Karnataka State Government passed the 'Prohibition of Dedication' Act, which criminalized the activities of a Devadasi, but not those of her patrons. This Act was also amended in 2010 to rehabilitate the existing Devadasis. However, following Bharathi Harishankar and Priyamvadha (2016), stakeholders and Devadasis are not aware of the existing legislation.

## Present social status of Devadasis: challenges and recommendations

Today, the Devadasi tradition appears to have lost its status and is equated synonymously with prostitution and slavery. At present, the practice of dedicating girls to temples continues. Although mass dedications have stopped, women are still devoting themselves to the practice in small 'Devi' temples. As we have seen, approximately 250,000 girls and women in India are still dedicated to their local temple deities (Zaidi, 2012; Shingal, 2015; also The Hindu, 2006). The majority of active Devadasis are in Karnataka, Andhra Pradesh and Maharashtra. Following the Report of the National Human Rights Commission (National Human Rights Commission [NHRC], 2009), the Devadasi system prevails in Karnataka and Andhra Pradesh, where 80,000 Devadasis still exist. In northern Karnataka, the Devadasi system remains a culturally and economically valued form of sex work, and approximately 1,000–10,000 young girls are inducted into the system annually. Over the years, the Devadasi system has resulted in trafficking and commercial sexual exploitation of women, with almost 64% of these women forced into prostitution to survive (Chakraborty, 2000). Parents, mostly of *Dalit* communities, still force their girls to become Devadasis: economic hardship pushes poor families to consecrate their daughters. The majority of Devadasis comes from poor landless families: many *Dalit* women are dedicated to the Goddess at a very young age by parents hoping to receive divine help to cure a disease or as an offering for the fulfilment of a wish (Torri, 2009). Young girls initiated into the Devadasi system are potentially at high risk of becoming victims of health and psychological stress factors (Bharathi Harishankar and Priyamvadha, 2016): the girls are forced to perform dances and are subjected to cruel beating. The health risks are multiplied by poor nutritional and health support from their families and the community. The livelihood problems faced by Devadasis increase when they become mothers: the legitimacy and upbringing of children remain a major problem for Devadasis. Devadasi mothers make huge efforts to send their children to school despite all the financial difficulties: most Devadasis have little or no education with very limited work opportunities. These difficulties increase when they reach old age – which happens prematurely, usually in their 40s – and they become too infirm for heavy work on a daily basis, for example on construction sites. The traditional institution of Devadasi endows masculine privileges to the dedicated girls. A Devadasi is entitled to inherit her parents' property and perform their funeral rites. Her children belong to the lineage of their mother and not to the lineage of their biological father. If she has a son, he inherits her property and perpetuates her father's family. If she has a daughter then the daughter is again initiated into the same system. This has an interesting but evil twist. In some regions based on superstition, it is customary that a *jogati* must dedicate her own daughter, otherwise, her funeral rites would not be held and the corpse would be eaten by dogs and other beasts. Though an economic aspect is also involved, her daughter would take her responsibility when she becomes old. No matter what social respect the *jogatis* enjoy, their daughters do not have a match if they want to marry. No one comes forward to marry a *jogati's* daughter. So there is no other way left for the innocent girl but to be dedicated and this helps her mother as a means of livelihood when she becomes old. This continues the tradition from generation to generation.

Thus, the Devadasi system has become nothing more than commercial sex work in the name of religion. The real question is not whether to change the custom or not but how and who should change it, differentiating the good and bad part from making Devadasi women vulnerable today. There are various projects and schemes introduced by the government and NGOs to help Devadasis improve their status. However, there is misuse and abuse of the funds allocated for the Devadasis over the years. There are also problems related to pending funds for the various schemes, scepticism of senior officials, and lack of serious concerns at the administrative level being responsible for the failed execution of policies. The biggest challenge is how to integrate Devadasi girls into local communities: community participation is essential as the Devadasi system is deeply embedded in the local culture; simultaneously, efforts are needed to build confidence and self-esteem among Devadasi-initiated girls.

As written (Torri, 2009), the struggle against the Devadasi system is arduous and needs the active role of several partners such as government, NGOs, health workers, social workers and social movements. The custom can be eradicated through a multidimensional perspective able to offer different kinds of social and economic support such as: vocational training and skills to enhance women's economic status; rehabilitation through self-employment; bank loans and income-generating activities; economic and social development programmes for 'ex-Devadasis'' rehabilitation. In addition to this, there is need for access to primary healthcare services, health education and counselling services; scholarships and hostels for Devadasis, particularly girls; assistance to Devadasi culture-challenged girls and awareness campaigns targeting young girls; financial assistance and incentives for a man to marry a Devadasi. Sensitizing the family members of the Devadasis will also help in reducing the number of dedications. However, it seems particularly difficult to change community attitudes and practices towards the Devadasi system in order to build a Devadasi-free community: for the very poor, the Devadasi system can still be seen as providing a way out of poverty while gaining access to the blessings of the Gods (Dalrymple, 2008). Moreover, the stigma attached to the Devadasis' identity is very difficult to remove through rehabilitation programmes. Village communities are often not ready to accept ex-Devadasi families. For this reason, in a number of villages the Devadasis, through the support of local NGOs, organize themselves to form cooperatives (Bharathi Harishankar and Priyamvadha, 2016). There are also some attempts made by stakeholders to reintegrate Devadasis into their communities, for example through Self Help Groups (SHG) of women. The NGOs initiate networking exercises with local SHGs, collaborating with community-based organizations and enhancing the participation of families and key community members in an attempt to merge Devadasis into community life (Bharathi Harishankar and Priyamvadha, 2016).

Many NGOs are working to support Devadasis. One example is Mahila Abhivruddi Mattu Samrakshana Samsthe (MASS), based in the Belagavi district of the Southern Indian state of Karnataka, which mainly works with *Dalit* women, with a focus on ex-Devadasi women and their children. 'BIRDS' (Belgaum Integrated Rural Development Society) also works for women who are sex workers. Bangalore-based MYRADA (Mysore Resettlement and Development Agency) works to bring social justice and equality to Devadasis in the Belgaum district. Humanitarian Aid Relief Trust (HART) strives to promote gender equality, with numerous projects worldwide focusing on women's issues. One such scheme is 'Operation Mercy India', which partners with HART to work with one of the most disempowered groups across India – the Devadasis. The work of HART's partners, Operation Mercy India (OMI) with the Devadasis is vital in providing these women with access to healthcare, education and security to support themselves and enabling them to give their children a better future. Their pioneering projects work to support the Devadasis and break the cycle of exploitation. OMI provides Devadasis and their children with education, counselling support and medical care.

Among the institutional efforts aimed at eradicating the Devadasi system we may mention the Devadasi Rehabilitation Project (DRP), set up by Karnataka State Women's Development Corporation in 1991. DRP was aimed at helping those who have been exploited by the Devadasi system. Women were trained in income-generating skills: they were provided counselling, awareness, and protection in safe houses. Karnataka State Women's Development Corporation, with the assistance of the social welfare department, provided subsidy and loans from banks to help them become self-sustaining. The Karnataka government has planned financial assistance to those who marry Devadasis, and Devadasis are also given priority in getting employment. Under the 'Scheme of financial assistance for remarriage of destitute widows and marriage of Devadasis' (Women and Child Development Department, Karnataka State), financial assistance is given for the remarriage of destitute widows and also for the couple where the bride is a Devadasi. The age limit of Devadasi women should be between 18 and 35 years and they must be resident in Karnataka for more than two years.

## Conclusion

The system of the Devadasi institution no doubt originated from the religion itself but the shape it took with the passage of time was a complete distortion of its goal. Initially, it was done with the idea of dedicating dancing girls to the temples who would dance in front of the deity as a typical religious ritual and who were supposed to be a kind of devotee who would give up their material life for the sake of worship. However, the religious-socio-political-cultural-economic factors of different times, in particular during colonialism, worked on it brutally and changed the total purpose and intention of the institution. We all know that it is prevention which is better than cure. The distortion of the system, with whichever selfish motives, made it so ugly and unhealthy for society that this had to be addressed vigorously, not only to improve on the situation, but also to put an end to the entire system. Today, the current status of the Devadasis requires urgent attention as society and religion do not require the system anymore so not only should ample measures taken to improve the condition of these women and their children, but also a strict invigilation of the proper execution of the facilities and measures taken is to be done efficiently. Starting from the very introduction of the system we have seen how the historical background played an important role in the development of the institution followed by the temple rituals and practices of the cult gradually formulating the shape of the institution rather in a derogatory sense. The different sections of this chapter have shown how the system of Devadasi witnessed its degradation of status, gradually reaching the present-day social status with its own unique challenges. Therefore, we must come up with appropriate recommendations in order to prohibit the exploitative practice and to ensure that no illegal activities of subjecting women to forced prostitution take place. Multidimensional intervention programmes involving multiple actors are urgently needed: above all, a stronger commitment of the Indian government to women's economic empowerment through educational support, vocational training for them and their children, effective poverty eradication schemes, health support and, most importantly, the deconstruction of gender and religious stereotypes.

### References
Abbé Dubois, J.A. (1993) *Hindu Manners, Customs and Ceremonies*, Rupa & Co. Calcutta (original edition, 1906), Oxford: Clarendon Press.
Altekar, A.S. (1956) *The Position of Women in Hindu Civilization*, Benaras: Motilal Banarasidas.

Bharathi Harishankar, V. and Priyamvadha, M. (2016) *Exploitation of Women as Devadasis and Its Associated Evils*, Report submitted to the National Commission for Women, New Delhi, available at: http://ncw.nic.in/pdfReports/Exploitation_of_Women_as_Devadasis_and_its_Associated_Evils_Report.pdf.

Chakraborty, K. (2000) *Women as Devadasis: Origin and Growth of the Devadasi Profession*, New Delhi: Deep & Deep Publications.

Dalrymple, W. (2008) 'Serving the Goddess: The dangerous life of a sacred sex worker', *The New Yorker*, 4 August, available at: http://www.newyorker.com/magazine/2008/08/04/serving-the-goddess.

Jain, S. (2003) 'The Devadasi System', in *Encyclopaedia of Indian Women through the Ages: The Middle Ages*, vol 2, New Delhi: Kalpaz Publications, pp 119-135.

Jordan, K. (2003) *From Sacred Servant to Profane Prostitute: A History of the Changing Legal Status of the Devadasis in India 1857–1947*, New Delhi: Manohar.

Marglin, F.A. (1985) *Wives of the God-King: The Rituals of the Devadasis of Puri*, New Delhi: Oxford University Press.

National Human Rights Commission (2009) *Annual Report 2008–2009*, New Delhi, India, available at: http://nhrc.nic.in/Documents/AR/Final%20Annual%20Report-2008-2009%20in%20English.pdf.

Parker, M.K. (1998) '"A Corporation of Superior Prostitutes": Anglo-Indian legal conceptions of temple dancing girls, 1800–1914', *Modern Asian Studies*, 32(3), pp 559–633.

Sachau, E.C. (trans.) (1910) *Alberuni's India*, London: Kegan Paul, Trench, Trubner & Co.

Shankar, J. (2004) *Devadasi Cult: A Sociological Analysis*, 2nd revised edition, New Delhi: Ashish Publishing House.

Shingal, A. (2015) 'The Devadasi system: temple prostitution in India', *UCLA Women's Law Journal*, 22(1), pp 107–23.

Srinivasan, A. (1985) 'Reform and revival: The Devadasi and her dance', *Economic and Political Weekly*, XX(44), pp 1869–76.

Tarachand, K. (1992) *Devadasi Custom: Rural Social Structure and Flesh Markets*, New Delhi: Reliance Publishing House, pp 19–23.

Torri, M.C. (2009) 'Abuse of lower castes in South India: The institution of Devadasi', *Journal of International Women's Studies*, 11(2), pp 31–48, available at: http://vc.bridgew.edu/jiws/vol11/iss2/3.

*The Hindu* (2006) '"Project Combat" launched to eradicate Devadasi system', available at: http://www.hindu.com/2006/01/30/stories/2006013020130300.htm.

Zaidi, Z. (2012) *Devadasi System in Indian Temples*, M.A.S.E.S-Movement Against Sexual Exploitation and Sexism, 7 April, available at: https://masessaynotosexism.wordpress.com/2012/04/07/devadasi-system-in-indian-temples-zoya-zaidi/.

# Part 2
## Identities, women's movements and religion

FIVE

# Formation of 'religious' identity among British Muslim women

*Masoumeh Velayati*

One of the manifestations of Islam in the 'west' is its assertive female adherents, publicly visible by observing religious symbols in the so-called 'secular' domain. This chapter will contribute to the current debates on women and religion as well as cross-cultural perspectives and interreligious dialogues. It also corresponds with the aim of the book in exploring the association between social changes, religiosity and women's self-definition in the contemporary world. Despite a temptation to exclude religion from the public space, a process of 'de-privatization' of religion is evident among Muslim women.[1]

In the UK, Muslim women, as a faith group, are generally disadvantaged, despite policies to reduce the diversity gap in the labour market based on gender and religious affiliations (Bunglawala, 2008; Heath and Martin, 2012; Velayati, 2015, MCB, 2015). To examine the extent to which limitations in social mobility are due to their religious commitments or religious expectations of womanhood in 'Islam', I include 'religion' as an investigative tool in my research. Gendering religion as a social practice is central to all religions, including Islam (King, 2005), which has practical implications traditionally understood, observed and performed in any society.

Applying feminist theory and questioning Muslim women's place as a marginalized group at the centre of social inquiry, this chapter aims to explore the ways in which Muslim women negotiate religious and cultural norms and values to promote their interests in everyday lives. It will reflect on the meaning of 'Islam' and the formation of 'religious' identity among this specific social group. Within the large forces of globalization and increased intercultural relations, accounts of personal or collective religious affiliation by Muslim women need to be explored and understood.

The format of this chapter is to first present the methodological aspect of the research. The following sections will focus on 'religion as a source of identity' and its importance for the majority of my informants, particularly in terms of discovering selfhood and modes of expression. This will lead me to explore my informants' desire to understand Islam, which among some is decoded into conformity with orthodoxy and traditional discourses of Islam, and among others into finding liberal and moral wisdoms of Islam.

## Methodology

This chapter is built on empirical data drawing from personal narratives collected from 64 questionnaires[2] and 53 semi-structured interviews with Muslim women from different ethnic and cultural backgrounds in the UK between 2012 and 2013. The demographic makeup of the interviewees is demonstrated in Tables 5.1, 5.2 and 5.3.

The chapter will also reflect on my observations through attending meetings and events organized by Muslim women. Being a member of various national, regional and local organizations[3] run by Muslim women, I also receive news of their activities and often collective responses to national and international concerns.

The questionnaire titled 'Muslim women and work in the UK' aimed to explore how women's experiences of work in the UK labour market fit with their Islamic identity and how religio–cultural norms and values

Table 5.1. Age group of interviewees during the interview process (*n*= 53)

| Age group | Under 20 | 21–30 | 31–40 | 41–50 | 51–69 | Total |
|---|---|---|---|---|---|---|
| N. | 1 | 15 | 14 | 19 | 4 | 53 |
| % | 2 | 28 | 26 | 36 | 8 | 100 |

Notes: Almost one third of the demographic cohort of the interviews is Millennials falling between early 1980s and 2000. My youngest informant was a 19-year-old university student and the oldest one was 69 years old.

Table 5.2. Migration pattern among the interviewees (*n*= 53)

| Migration background | N | % |
|---|---|---|
| First-generation migrants* | 21 | 40 |
| Second- and third-generation migrants** | 28 | 53 |
| Non-migrants (Native British) | 4 | 8 |

* First-generation migrants refer to those who migrated as adults for various reasons, such as education, family reunion, and so on.

** Second-generation migrants came to the UK either in childhood, with no role on migration decisions, or were born to migrant families in the UK; and third-generation migrants are those whose grandparents were the first migrants in the UK, mainly as labour migrants to the port towns or industrial cities.

were negotiated in relation to work, mainly outside the home and in the formal setting. The questionnaire included 47 questions, grouped in three sections: personal details (13 questions); migration history (13 questions); and economic activities (21 questions).

**Table 5.3.** Ethnic background of interviewees (*n*= 53)

| Ethnic Background | N | % |
|---|---|---|
| White converts (4 British and 1 Italian) | 5 | 9 |
| Middle Eastern (non-Arabs) | 4 | 8 |
| Middle Eastern (Arabs) | 6 | 11 |
| African (including North Africa) | 5 | 9 |
| Mixed parents (British mother) | 1 | 2 |
| Indian origin | 6 | 11 |
| Pakistani origin | 25 | 47 |
| Bangladeshi origin | 1 | 2 |

Note: Overall, 60% of the interviewees were originally from the Indian subcontinent, the majority being Pakistani; 21% were from Middle Eastern countries including Arabs and non-Arabs (Turkish and Iranians); and 18% were equally divided between white converts and African origins.

In the third section, 14 of these questions mainly focused on religious and cultural beliefs and practices and their potential impact on women's engagement in the labour market. They included questions on women's preference in terms of working in Muslim only and/or women-only work places; the attitude of their male family members towards their paid work; their own attitude towards work, and whether they believed women's work outside the home was against religion and if that makes them less Muslim; whether they would consider a job in another city or give up their jobs after marriage; and if they consider women's work as empowering. Questions also addressed what prevents many Muslim women from working outside the home; how they dress in public; how they maintain Islamic values and behaviours; the types of problems Muslim women face in British society; and what their suggestion was to empower them.

The interview process covered similar questions, but also focused on the women's individual circumstances. The interviews were conducted individually or in groups of no more than three women, with some being conducted over the phone. I aimed to examine the diversity among Muslim women, who are seen as a homogeneous group. I sought to talk to women from diverse socio-economic and ethnic backgrounds with different religious or non-religious affiliations and educational attainments. However, women who participated in the research tended to hold a more prominent role in society, with most having tertiary education and being from middle-class backgrounds.[4] Informants were initially sought through social networks and voluntary organizations, and later mostly through snowballing and being introduced by those who were interested in the research. The in-depth interviews gave cross-generational accounts on different aspects of women's own lives and that of other female friends and relatives.

## 'Religion' as a source of identity

Religion is the realm of the sacred that provokes strong feelings of piety and admiration (Parekh, 2006). It gives a sense of power to its adherents in terms of meaning and significance of their lives, activities and relations with others. Religious identity seemed to be vital for the majority of my informants, despite diversity. In response to my question of how they identify themselves, most, even those who did not wear hijab, mentioned a hyphenated identity of British or Scottish Muslim. First-generation migrants – with no British citizenship – identified themselves with a hyphenated identity of their country of origin. One of the informants responded: "… number one is my religion, and I am Palestinian. Of course, I am also a female." Some responded in terms of a single identity as Muslim. One woman stated:

> 'I think, I am just Muslim … a Muslim woman, that's it. Everything else doesn't mean anything to me. I was born in Malawi, moved here when I was 6 months old. I know nothing about Malawi. My forefathers are from India, but I've never been to India. The only thing I know is how to be a Muslim in Britain.'

Many of my young educated informants, who were often second- or third-generation immigrants, resonated discursively the uncertainty about their identity. One of them who was confused with her identity responded in this way:

> 'Sometimes I feel like I really don't know who I am! Sometimes the only thing I know about myself is my belief. I also describe myself as a woman and a mother. I also have a western upbringing – I think that is very dominant and has a big impact on how I see things, or how I deal with them in my life. I also think that I am not entirely like a Turkish person but also not a German, definitely. Maybe

I have multiple identities, and at some point maybe an unsettled identity. I don't know!'

Uncertainties about identity sometimes lead to the formation of a religious identity. This involves dealing with both traditional invisibility within the Muslim community and marginalization and discrimination in the wider British society. One woman stated: "In Muslim countries, religion is part of education, but here, you learn it from your parents along with the cultural elements that they have been taught. Lots of things are not understood, especially in places like India or Pakistan, where they emphasise how to read the Quran, but not understanding what the Quran is saying."

Most of the informants developed a desire to know more about their religion to make a sense of the world around them. One of the women put it this way: "at some stage in your life you start asking questions ... you do come into religion, then it's a very confusing path for a lot of people, of what can I do and what can't I." The above quotations demonstrate how religious belief or interests in religious identity affect women's well-being, decision making and psychological functioning, in terms of the level of devotion to faith, which at times leads to self-restriction and voluntary withdrawal. One informant put her thoughts in this way:

'When you get a bit mature and actually look back at the history, you realise that yes you can still contribute to society and be an active Muslim woman. At the same time, there are a lot of things that can get confusing; like when it comes to segregation in the work force, things are not as clear, like what can a Muslim woman do and what shouldn't she be doing. Sometimes I think it's just easier to draw the line, and think "well, I am not sure if I can do that, so I better not".'

For many of my informants, seeking religious identity manifested in the form of social practices. The most visible manifestation of belief and moral intentions among Muslim women has been to consciously display their faith in the public sphere, by wearing Islamic dress and very occasionally the face cover, niqab.[5] This is despite the disproportionate discrimination,[6] and negative attitude towards veiled women in the 'west' and the widespread assumption that women are the passive victims of patriarchal Islam, which imposes a dress code on them. One informant, who was very active in teaching Islamic studies to women, reflected on some women's experiences:

'In Liverpool there are many Muslim women who are very qualified, lawyers and accountants etc, who are not married, don't have children, and can't get jobs. Discrimination definitely happens. Your image just doesn't fit in with the company and that's it. I know women, who move out of the city and go to bigger cities like London, Manchester, and Birmingham – it's very common. There, they are more open to hiring people from different cultures, but when you live in other cities it's very closed. It's almost like an institutionalised racism, nobody talks about it.'

When I pointed another informant to the diversity and equal opportunity legislation through which the UK government encourages promotion of minorities' engagement in the public sector, she responded:

'I think it depends on the sector. I have seen 1st generation immigrant doctors who for years struggle to find jobs. I can't comment on government policies because despite its rhetoric, if the institutions have certain policies and internal structures which discriminate against blacks or Muslims, it's very hard to pin down what is happening. My Sudanese friend with a PhD in agricultural economics, eventually left England to the UAE to find work, leaving her son and husband behind. It is very hard to get through. The competition is extremely high. I think the preference is for white home graduates. Very few Arabs manage to get jobs.'

This issue was raised many times by the informants when they were talking about their own or their close friends' experiences. Having Muslim names or appearance, in terms of wearing Islamic dress, were perceived as possible explanations. A convert woman who was married[7] to a Muslim man stated that "whenever I apply with my own name, I get an interview, but when I apply with my married name, I don't."

However, it can be said that, compared to other European countries, veiling in the UK is an accepted or at least a tolerated subject. Unlike some other European/western countries, in the UK there is no prescribed regulation or legislation to outlaw veiling practices in public places (Hadj-Abdu and Woodhead, 2012). Most debates are often around the face covering and security issues.

## Desire to (re)discover one's religion

Due to the centrality of religion in social life[8] and culture, and religious belief systems regarding women's role and family commitments,[9] Muslim women show more and more interest in the study of Islam, religious texts and even the Arabic language in attempts to understand their religion better. I encountered four groups of women in this endeavour.

Group one, who are a minority, are scholars of Islamic studies, who obtain their disciplinary training in Islamic studies in western universities in accordance with the model of established Christian theology. They focus on Islamic theology and engage with core sources of Islam in their research on Islam, Quranic exegesis and intellectual thoughts, some with particular interest in women and gender. One of the informants, a university lecturer, reflected on her interest in Islamic studies in this manner:

> 'I did my PhD on classical Islam; I was interested in the literature theory, a critical approach which is much more modern than *Sharia*. I am interested in the social processes; my thesis is really on the semantics of that. I am interested in hermeneutic theories and theological approaches to women.'

Although in terms of her employment, she thought she received positive discrimination, she felt drawbacks in terms of how her colleagues perceived her. Whenever she expressed an interest in other subjects, she felt she was being slotted into the category of being only able to do gender and Islam. She explained: "it has not been easy; it took me time to work with my colleagues and engage with them in dialogue and discourse."

The second group are British-born and -raised individuals, mostly from ethnic minority backgrounds, who became interested in learning Islam, mostly in terms of theology and religious knowledge. Some of them obtain their training in Islamic education from religious institutions, mostly based in the Islamic world, such as Jordan, Syria, Saudi Arabia, Yemen and Al-Azhar University in Egypt.[10] The graduates of these institutions are called *alima* or *ustadha*,[11] who gain authorization from their mentors to teach other Muslims, mainly women and girls, the Quran and *Hadith* (narrations of the Prophet) and to offer services and counselling in creeds and other religious matters and questions. One of my informants studied for three years in Syria and about six years in Yemen, in the historical town of Tarim.[12] When I interviewed her, it had been five years since she and her husband had returned to the UK and they were teaching the Muslim community through their registered charity.[13] I did not interview any woman who had studied in Saudi Arabia to observe differences in attitudes, behaviours, belief system and tendencies between women trained in different religious institutions in the Arab Sunni world. However, all those who studied in countries other than Saudi Arabia were grateful that they did not study there.

The third group are also British born and bred, who go to either after-school supplementary mosque classes, or to day-time Islamic faith schools. Some are also sent to boarding schools called *Darul Ulooms*[14] or Islamic Academy, which mostly cover secondary education onwards, and they also study the national curriculum. These schools are mainly operated under the broad framework of the Islamic ethos, providing an Islamic environment to promote pupils' moral and spiritual development through teaching various Islamic principles and sciences in a confessional setup.[15] Students of some of these schools have a tendency to lead a more segregated life from wider British society.

The fourth group are mostly Muslims with a limited knowledge of Islam, who at one point in their lives want to learn about their religion. They either attend Islamic classes run by trained tutors in traditional overseas religious institutions or study on their own. One of the informants in this group mentioned:

> 'When I went for pilgrimage, I realised there is a lot to Islam that I need to learn. I took up the learning. We are brought up with culture mixed into religion, so then trying to differentiate them is a battle in itself. Our parents were not educated to the level of understanding religion the way we can now. I think a lot of times people are quite illiterate to what religion is saying.'

The interlocking of religion with culture was mentioned by many of the informants. However, religion cannot be culture-free (Parekh, 2006). Rather, the degree and level of the cultural contamination determines gender expectations, as "… the divine will cannot acquire a determinate human meaning without cultural mediation" (Parekh, 2006: 147). With globalization and the establishment of Muslim communities from many cultural and ethnic backgrounds in the UK, a cross-cultural fertilization takes place. In December 2012, with the recommendation of one of the *alima/ustadha* informants, I joined a three-day 'Sister's Winter Retreat', as part of a spiritual gathering. About 70 other women from diverse ethnic backgrounds and of diverse walks of life attended the programme in an attractive resort. Childcare facilities with qualified child-carers were also provided. Most of the women were from England, and had embarked on Islamic studies and attended some Islamic classes. Two qualified female preachers,[16] trained at different levels in Islamic institutions in Damascus and Trim, led the programme.

As I have observed thoroughly, desire in religious knowledge among Muslim women can broadly be translated into 'passive acceptance of faith' and 'positive commitment to faith'. While the former relates to the conformity with orthodox and traditional discourses of Islam, the latter involves discovering liberal and authentic voices of Islam. I will expand on these in the following two sections.

## Devoted acceptance of faith

Orthodoxy among religious women is highlighted in two main areas of gender relations and rituals and practices. Most of the women in this category often stressed the centrality of proper behaviour and correct conduct of religious rituals and practices. Their strong beliefs often prevented them from serious engagement in theological debates. The morality aspect of religion or 'Islamic forms of sociability' (Mahmood, 2005) becomes more important than theological aspects of religion, particularly in terms of gender equality.

Islamic forms of sociability are demonstrated in many forms. Veiling and restrained forms of dress as the most important external expression are a clear form of pious identity. Veiling was regarded as a religious obligation, a sign of deeper piety and devotion to the will of God. Women who wear the niqab often assert that they feel closer to God. They often ignore the cultural dimension of dressing, choosing the conservative forms of sartorial traditions in terms of colour, length and shape, as the most religiously proper attire.[17] Only one of my informants wore niqab. She did not have a deep knowledge of Islam, but her affiliation to the faith was reflected through her strong feelings about her understanding of rights and wrongs. Her strong beliefs on the one hand, and everyday realities of life on the other, led to some struggles and challenges. She worked in the voluntary sector and had very friendly relations with her colleagues, who were moderately dressed. Her husband was educated in Islamic studies and often reminded her that some of her practices were not Islamic requirements. She put her feelings this way:

> 'Some things for me don't feel right whether it is music or things that I think are totally forbidden. ... There are a lot of things that go on in our life that I am quite stern with. Whether you practise it or not, this is what the command is. My brother and I have debates about music and stuff in Islam. We understand religion totally differently, though we both come from the same family.'

Among very conformist religious women, stress on the hereafter and fear of God is very strong, which leads to self-restraint and the rejection of materialistic enjoyments of life. They often impose these restrictions on their family members, including their children. The same lady stated:

> 'My daughter likes music, but I don't. ... sometimes she sings in the shower and I knock the door and say: "remember you are going to go to your grave, these are not good things for you", and she'll say: "oh yeah mum, okay" ... She is practising her faith, but she just has to balance it herself. You know I'll just remind them of the hereafter, and of certain things that I don't like them doing. She sometimes hears music through ear phones at school ... she knows the lyrics to everything. I say to her it's a fight with her own self. I don't put the fear of me in her, no, but the fear of God.'

One of the informants emphasized the importance of daily prayers by stating that

> '... praying was not a part of our everyday life when I was growing up. It was there, but it wasn't really enforced in the home. The way my children are being brought up by me, praying is a part of life because it's important. When I started practising Islam, it took me a while, a good year or so to embed five daily prayers in my life, whereas both my children do it naturally. I thank Allah for that.'

Devotion to the family is also considered another important religious manifestation. Overall, family is very central to the Muslim psyche. However, for religiously oriented women, femininity and womanhood is centred on motherhood and being a good wife, leading to domestic dependency, self-sacrifice, self-denial and dedication to family as their natural and religious duty. They normally do not oppose women's work and quite often they refer to the Prophet's wife, Khadija, as an example of a very successful businesswoman who devoted her wealth to Islam. However, for them, the type of work outside the home is very important and according to one of the informants: "… first and foremost, obligations of a Muslim woman are her husband and her family, but if she has skills and qualifications, she should make sure that everything is fine within her first obligation before she goes out into society." In the retreat (mentioned above), more conservative gender and behavioural expectations of Muslim women were promoted, such as avoiding makeup or deciphering suitable jobs for Muslim girls. One of the teachers, for instance, told the group "we don't need doctors but social workers." She herself was an engineering graduate who devoted her life to family and Islamic education.

Another very devout woman who was also trained and worked as pharmacist, stated:

'I think as a Muslim woman, work is not everything for us. We are juggling family and work and voluntary work. I think life satisfaction and living a purposeful and worthwhile life are really what we are looking for. I am not looking to my work to get empowerment, but to make a difference in people's lives and to contribute to society.'

In terms of gender relations, they believe in the Islamic model of a 'virtuous family' in terms of traditional gender roles; such as men being the breadwinners and the main decision makers − though they believe that they should consult with their wives − and that to uphold the welfare of the family, women should not do anything that makes their husbands unhappy. One of the women said: "I believe in team work − working for the betterment of the family and making their unit strong, rather than the wife being subservient to a tyrannical husband who tells her what to do, which is the case in some cultures." In response to my question about domestic violence and how *Al-Meezan*, the organization that promotes the understanding of the Islamic faith for women and children, deals with this issue, one of the very active women, who enjoys a very harmonious married life, stated:

'We actually get criticised from the community for empowering women to know their rights in Islam. There are some men in the community that prefer women not to know (laughs). We are causing trouble in the home with our teachings, but we don't do it to rebel. We give the teaching that both husband and wife have to work together to make things work. But ultimately if there is an issue which creates disorder or difficulty in the home, then one party has to compromise ... And a lot of the time it is woman; it should be men as well. But because we are addressing women we say to them: "if you compromise today, then you will humble him tomorrow". We say: "live with your family, make your family work, if it means that you have to sacrifice then be the one to sacrifice, because spiritually you will be rewarded by God even though your right is not being fulfilled. You be the one to create the peace in the home".'

In the case of domestic violence, the organization's position is to provide mostly comfort and support to women rather than actively engaging with the community to tackle and reduce the wrong and harmful behaviours or advocate women to free themselves from an abusive life:

'Women will come and talk to us. Sometimes they just need to talk. The problems are so deep that they are not asking for a solution, they know how to deal with it. Generally women who are abused know what triggered him, how that situation came about and that they are not actually victims of a blind brutality. They come back and say: "I shouldn't have said this, I shouldn't have triggered it, because he is like this, he is capable of this and I was the one who pushed the wrong buttons to have faced this." All they really want from us is a shoulder to cry on, a bit of support and encouragement to be patient. If they ask for help then, we would advise them that they need to protect themselves. Patience should not be to the point of someone's body getting damaged, but we don't advocate this. Islamically, a woman is not a lamb for a slaughter, you know!'

These interviews and my observations highlight the importance of ritual practices such as prayers, the sartorial practices of veiling, devotion to the family, denial of materialist aspects of life and voluntary withdrawal from some social life such as work, for the realization of a virtuous life. Therefore, any public gaze or experience of discrimination for these devout Muslim women becomes more tolerable.

## Positive commitment to faith

There is also a growing commitment and compassion among the young educated and religiously oriented informants to enter the public sphere and be involved in social and cultural activities and to help the community as a religious obligation. They raise challenging questions about religion and culture, contest male-oriented definitions and interpretations of womanhood and discover liberal and authentic voices of Islam in regard to women's issues, aiming to distinguish 'religion' from culture and cultural expectations of womanhood. This is even reflected in the diversity of dressing practices and of their conscious choices about wearing or not wearing the veil, while at the same time remaining committed to appropriate clothing codes.[18] Woodhead calls it "the affirmation of partial domestic femininity and simultaneously embracing more independent, entitled self-hood" (2016, 155). They search alternatives that are attractive and can reflect their desire for being both 'religious' and 'modern'. This is very evident among millennial informants and those in their thirties, and occasionally older women in their forties.

Due to the importance of religion in cultures as a point of belonging and reference as well as religious conviction vis-à-vis women's role and family commitments, Muslim women often experience a series of paradoxes, such as incompatible interpretations of 'Islam' and cultural gender expectations. In recent decades, the equal opportunity polices in the UK have expanded minority groups' access to educational and employment opportunities, which have positively affected many Muslim women's aspirations. Unlike very religious women, for whom the ritual/sartorial practices and deliberate withdrawal from materialistic aspects of life are regarded as righteous, younger women are striving for a more active participation in and usefulness to society. They demonstrate new images of Muslim women engaged in civic and political life and overcome paradoxes they see between religion and their interests.

Unlike orthodox women who agree on limited kinds of professions outside the home on the condition that they do not compromise their main duty of motherhood/wife-hood, these women expose themselves to a variety of professions and activities. Over many decades, young women's contribution to British society, including public participation, interventions in civil society, the voluntary sector and advocacy positions on issues affecting social justice and promoting ethnic minorities' rights, including Muslim women, is clearly evident.

Hadj-Abdou and Woodhead (2012, 195–97) attribute these to the importance of citizenship as an important factor for empowering minorities in terms of claiming rights and freedom of expression, compared to other European countries. The citizenship recognition is also significant for resource mobilization. Apart from *Al-Meezan*, other organizations mentioned above have access to government funding to secure financial resources and continue their missions and activities at different levels. Within this "institutional structure" (Hadj-Abdou and Woodhead, 2012) and a multicultural context that promotes individual rights and the freedom of religion and its practices, is that Muslims, including women, as religious minorities in the UK, most of whom hold full British citizenship, identify themselves as 'British Muslims'. One of the women in her forties stated: "These young women are managing to become international citizens. We in the 80s and 90s were coming out of closed societies. We had limited exposure compared to this generation. They are simultaneously connected, talking to everyone all over. It's a different generation." They see any sort of engagement beneficial for social cohesion and their own integration into the wider British society. One of the informants stated:

> 'People don't just look at the appearance; they see that you are helping them and that you have something to give. Muslim women should contribute to the society; it doesn't have to be paid employment. It could be being an active parent in your child's school. We just need to let the society see beyond our veil, people are very open and happy with that. Sometimes as a Muslim woman if you are a good communicator you can talk your way through anything really, and really reach the hearts of people, I think that's a key thing.'

It seems a collective conscience has been developed among some young women in terms of prioritizing their family and children over their own profession, particularly if the family can afford one income. More and more women referred to the role of men culturally and religiously as providers for the family, which takes away the burden from women. One of the informants stated: "working in the house shouldn't be underestimated, it's also like work." Some married women with young children demonstrated an interest in voluntary work and getting training so that they would be able to go back to work when their children grew up. A young mother with two children stated:

'I studied engineering but when my children came along, I felt that the greatest contribution I could give to society was to raise my children, and give them the love, care and attention they need. There was no pressure from my husband. He is an engineer himself and we actually met at university. I see this is really growing, not just amongst Muslim women, but amongst educated women in society that they now feel that they want to take more time to invest in their children.'

Another young woman put it this way:

'Friends of mine who are doctors, especially those who were in quite high positions, sometimes question themselves, because they had no quality time with their children and all of a sudden the child is 15/16 and seeing their parents like foreigners. A friend of mine is a Consultant and says her children are adults and it's like she doesn't know them.'

When I asked the reason for the poor involvement of Muslim women in society, one of the women responded: "Well, I don't believe that they are not there. I just believe that they are in a different capacity."

Overall, younger Muslim women have benefited from the expanded opportunities, including political opportunities, as more women are now entering political life as politicians, activists, public servants, and members of local councils and political parties.[19] At the general election in June 2017, for instance, two Muslim women contested the same constituency,[20] one as the Labour Party candidate and the other as an independent candidate.

In terms of gender relations, younger active Muslim women promote more egalitarian relationships within the family. A woman in her late twenties was bitter about cultural expectations of women within Muslim communities. She reflected her feeling:

'I hate differentiation between men and women. I hear it all the time: "Muslim girl can't do that (referring to relationships out of wedlock); what kind of Muslim girl she is?" I would say: "all these boys are doing it". They would say: "that is different". But no, it is not the case in the religion; it's the same sin; it has the same punishment, if we don't repent. I hate this idea of girls bringing more shame.'

Many young mothers also spoke about their desire to raise their children more equally. Some were very critical of negative cultural expectations and norms, which privilege boys and disadvantage girls from childhood. They also discussed such matters with their partners. As the daughter of an Arab migrant father and a British mother, who had married her Pakistani-origin classmate, one of the informants reflected on her dialogue with her husband on how to avoid double standards within their own family by raising their children equally:

'I say to my husband we have to raise our son and daughter the same. I am not having one rule for him and one rule for her. That's one thing I think from the way I've been brought up – that a man is fine if he gets loads of women, but a woman is called a "slut".'

These women engage intellectually in reading the Quran, not just in Arabic, but also the translation, to find out and discuss the meaning. One of the women stated:

'... obviously everything is open to interpretation. My husband and I were reading the Quran during Ramadan and we read something on how men and women were equal in the eyes of Allah. He was like: "oh I didn't know that, I really thought men were a little bit higher than women"! Thank God my husband is very easy going; but a man that thinking he's superior to his wife could be very dangerous to the dynamics of family and relationships.'

For younger self-directed women, while femininity is also about cherishing family values, they are more attentive to a compassionate and egalitarian involvement in the family, moving away from 'selfless to expressive selfhood' (Sointu and Woodhead, 2008). For most of the women I spoke to, self-assertion is reflected more in terms of awareness of rights, dignity, equality and entitlements as important tools for self-development and self-fulfilment, rather than full economic independence or achievements.

## Conclusion

This study of Muslim women from various ethno-cultural backgrounds indicates dynamic and reciprocal relations between religion and gender among women in Muslim communities in the UK. Although there is a greater tendency to explore religious expectations about gender roles and women's religious commitments, Muslim women offer complex and often contradictory negotiations of religion. The multicultural context of British society, which allows freedom of religion and religious expression, as well as contemporary political events in the international arena, has instigated numerous debates about religion, particularly Islam, and its positive or negative function in contemporary western/European society. Since within the wider cultural and political scene, Muslim women are seen as one of the manifestations of Islam in the 'west', they inevitably become interested in searching their identity as well as the principles of 'Islam' on gender. As a result, multifaceted and sometimes contradictory outcomes become evident among the women. Some initiate conformity with traditional notions of femininity, female modesty and Islamic gender roles and expectations as part of their religious duties, in exchange for a greater eternal reward, while others, also tapping into the Islamic framework, challenge some notions that create gender inequalities in Muslim families and communities.

While a minority of women engage in a theological endeavour to gain a fresh and culture-free reading of Islam, particularly the Quran, to challenge patriarchal interpretations of Islam with regard to women, others engage at the civil activity level. They often take the spirit of the religion as an enabling means for personal empowerment and social good in a rapidly changing world. The work of Muslim Women Network UK (MWNUK) to a great extent deals with issues and injustices against women in the name of religion.

Socio-political changes have allowed younger generations of Muslim women to reconstruct their life and selfhood by finding new opportunities, while maintaining their 'Muslim' identity. They see these as an empowering opportunity for discovering their potential and gaining confidence. For some Muslim women, the search for a distinct social identity means exercising their 'religious' manifestations in a way that reflects both modern and Muslim simultaneously. Further study should focus on religious activities and negotiations of religion and gender within that context, among traditional and reformist religious women.

## Notes

1  Further demographic characteristics of the informants and their ethnic backgrounds will be covered in the methodology section.

2  The questionnaires were collected via online survey and printed copies. The ages of the participants were between 19 and 57 (only three women in their fifties). Responses to the online surveys were mainly from younger women, mostly in their twenties and thirties. The informants were from different parts of the UK, mainly Glasgow, Dundee, Edinburgh, Aberdeen, London, Birmingham, Blackburn and Luton. One of the shortcomings of the survey was lack of engagement with the explanatory questions by the informants.

3  Apart from the national organization, the rest are Scottish based due to the residency of the author of this paper in Scotland. These organizations predominately include: (1) Muslim Women' Network UK: Connecting Voices for Change – http://www. mwnuk.co.uk/ – a national organization, located in Birmingham; (2) Amina, The Muslim Women's Resource Centre, widely known as Amina – http://www. mwrc.org.uk/ – a regional organization in Scotland, with its headquarter based in Glasgow and two additional offices in Dundee and Edinburgh; (3) Al-Meezan: Balancing Life with Islamic Learning – https://www.almeezan.co.uk – a charitable organization working in Glasgow with a primary focus on the Islamic educational and social needs of Muslim women and children; and (4) Dundee International Women's Centre: Engagement, Education, self-Empowerment (DIWC) – http:// diwc.co.uk/ – a local organization based in Dundee.

These four organizations are committed to promoting the rights of Muslim women and girls as well as women from black and ethnic minority backgrounds who face challenges and discrimination from within Muslim communities and the wider society. They address matters that adversely affect women through various activities that could be broadly divided into: cultural, social, political, economic and religious activities. They mostly provide helpline and counselling services; recreation activities; awareness-raising events; advocacy and campaigns; training and workshops to improve capabilities and employability skills; as well as confronting Islamophobia by addressing stereotypes and misconceptions around Islam and Muslim women. They also provide resources such as books, booklets, reports and videos.

4  Many women from Muslim backgrounds whose lives were influenced by diverse sources other than religion refused to take part in the research as they might have considered it to be irrelevant to them. Some Muslim women, mostly the less educated and less qualified, also refused to take part in the study.

5  Niqab wearers are donned in full, long, black-coloured attire, hiding their faces and exposing only their eyes.

6  For accounts of Muslim women's experience of discrimination in the labour market, see Velayati (2015).

7  It should be noted that not all conversion to Islam is due to marriage. There are women who convert to Islam and then meet Muslim men. There are also women who are married to practising Muslim men, while keeping their own religion, though this is not very common.

8  This is mainly in terms of point of reference or belonging, not necessarily in terms of the depth of knowledge or practice (Maréchal, 2003).

9  See Velayati (2016) on family responsibilities among Muslims.

[10] Although all these countries are Sunni Arab and have mainly confessional approaches to religion and religious teachings, there are great differences in their denomination and dominant creeds and Islamic doctrines. In Saudi Arabia, Wahhabism has become the dominant creed. It is an ultra-conservative form of Sunni Islam insisting on literal interpretation of the Quran with *jihadi* trends, which has had global influence due to missionary trends in Wahhabism (DeLong-Bas, 2011: 1369–70).

[11] *Alima* and *Ustadha* are both Arabic terms. *Alima* means a learned and qualified female scholar, and *Ustadha* means a female master, mainly teaching Islamic knowledge at a rudimentary level.

[12] Tarim, located in South Yemen, is widely known for being a centre for Islamic learning and religious educational seminaries for both foreign and domestic students.

[13] One of the main activities of their charity is to provide sacred literacy for adults in two locations of Liverpool and on the university campus of Huddersfield. The organization also has other cultural and sports activities and attracts many young professional Muslim men and women, born and raised in the UK and interested in learning about their religion.

[14] *Darul Uloom* institutions are Islamic seminaries, mostly influenced by the Indian Deobandi model, which was originally set up in the late 19th century to train religious scholars. Currently, in the UK, there are six religious schools for girls and nine for boys, some boarding and others day schools.

[15] For further information on the history and development of Islamic education in secular societies, see, among others: Jackson, Miedema, Weisse and Willaime (eds) (2007) and Berglund, Shanneik and Bocking (eds) (2016).

[16] One of them was a highly respected Syrian in her fifties and the other a young woman in her early thirties with a very diverse multicultural background: born to Indian parents, raised in Saudi Arabia, studied at boarding school in the UK, graduated in engineering and married to a convert man. The senior preacher led the prayers and provided commentary on a classic Islamic text which is used in religious institutions as a guidebook for a life in accordance with religious tenets and canons. The text, titled *The Book of Assistance*, has also been translated into English. The younger one provided explanation for some selected narrations from and about the Prophet. Her knowledge of English/western culture and her good communication skills and rhetoric and ability to relate to younger women made her sessions enjoyable, which could also be considered as a means for social cohesion. The group also gathered together to praise the Prophet of Islam by singing and playing *daf* (drum), a musical instrument used mainly in classical and religious music. The activity, which is called *nasheed* (chanting), as a vocal and musical art, is part of spiritual expressions and Sufi rituals.

[17] For more information on veiling and its various meanings and forms, refer to Amer's *What is Veiling?* (Amer, 2014).

[18] I have encountered some women who removed hijab and/or niqhab after a while, due to either external or internal factors such as harassment or not feeling comfortable. Some women also consciously demonstrate a freedom to choose when, where, how and in what form to practise veiling, while others elevate it to a more fashionable but still modest style of dressing. All these reflect different conceptions of female modesty, act of morality and sartorial practices. For fashion aspects of dressing practice, see Lewis (2015).

[19]  For further information on Muslim women's political and civic participation, see Joly and Wadia (2017).
[20]  The non-veiled Muslim woman was re-elected with an increased majority of 65% in Bradford West, traditionally a male-dominated Muslim community (BBC News, 2017: Bradford West).

## References

Amer, S. (2014) *What is Veiling?*, Edinburgh: Edinburgh University Press.

BBC News (2017) *Election 2017: Bradford West*, available at: http://www.bbc.co.uk/news/politics/constituencies/E14000589.

Berglund, J. Shanneik, Y, and Bocking, B. (eds) (2016) *Religious Education in a Global-Local World. Boundaries of Religious Freedom: Regulating Religion in Diverse Societies*, vol 4, Cham: Springer (e-Book).

Bunglawala, Z. (2008) *Valuing Family, Valuing Work: British Muslim Women and the Labour Market*, London: The Yong Foundation; London Development Agency.

DeLong-Bas, N.J. (2011) 'Wahhabis', in M. Juergensmeyer and W. Clark Roof (eds) *Encyclopedia of Global Religion*, Los Angeles, London, New Delhi Singapore, and Washington DC: Sage Publications, vol 2, pp 1369–70.

Hadj-Abdou, L. and Woodhead, L. (2012) 'Muslim women's participation in the veil Controversy: Austria and the UK compared', in S. Rosenberger and B. Sauer (eds) *Politics, Religion and Gender: Framing and Regulating the Veil*, London, New York: Routledge, Routledge Studies in Religion and Politics, pp 186–204.

Heath, A. and Martin J. (2012) 'Can religious affiliation explain "ethnic" inequalities in the labour market?', *Ethnic and Racial Studies*, 36(6), pp 1005–27.

Jackson, R. Miedema, S., Weisse, W. and Willaime, J.P. (eds) (2007) *Religion and Education in Europe: Developments, Contexts and Debates. Religious Diversity and Education in Europe*, vol 3, Münster: Waxmann.

Joly, D. and Wadia, Kh. (2017) *Muslim Women and Power: Political and Civic Engagement in Western European Societies*, London and New York: Palgrave Macmillan.

King, U. (2005) 'General introduction: gender-critical turns in the study of religion', in U. King and T. Beattle (eds) *Gender, Religion and Diversity Cross-Cultural Perspective*, London, New York: Continuum, pp 1–10.

Lewis, R. (2015) *Muslim Fashion: Contemporary Style Cultures*, Durham, NC: Duke University Press.

Mahmood, S. (2005) *Politics of Piety: the Islamic Revival and the Feminist Subject*, Princeton and Oxford: Princeton University Press.

Maréchal, B. (2003) 'The question of belonging', in B. Maréchal, S. Allievi, F. Dassetto and J. Nielson (eds) *Muslims in the Enlarged Europe: Religion and Society*, vol 2, Muslim Minorities, London, Boston: Brill, pp 5–18.

MCB (The Muslim Council of Britain) (2015) 'British Muslims in numbers: a demographic, socio-economic and health profile of Muslims in Britain drawing on the 2011 Census. Available at: http://www.mcb.org.uk/muslimstatistics/.

Parekh, B. (2006) *Rethinking Multiculturalism: Cultural Diversity and Political Theory*, 2nd edition, New York: Palgrave Macmillan.

Sointu, E. and Woodhead, L. (2008) 'Spirituality, gender, and expressive selfhood', *Journal of the Scientific Study of Religion*, 47(2), pp 259–76.

Velayati, M. (2015) 'Muslim Women and Work in Scotland', in S. Jackson (ed) *Routledge International Handbook of Race, Class and Gender*, London and New York: Routledge, pp 84–100.

Velayati, M. (2016) 'Gender and Muslim families', in C.L. Shehan (ed), *The Wiley Blackwell Encyclopedia of Family Studies*, vol 2, pp 933–37.

Woodhead, L. (2016) '"Because I'm Worth It": Religion and women's changing lives in the West', in K. Anue, S. Sharma and G. Vincett (eds) *Women and Religion in the West: Challenging Secularisation*, 2nd edition, London and New York: Routledge, pp 147–64.

# SIX

# Christian women's movements in secularizing and diversifying contexts: a case study from Belgium

*Nella van den Brandt**

This chapter explores the relationship between social change, religion and women by focusing on the specific experiences of secularization of a Christian women's movement in Belgium. It does so by thematizing how secularization experiences in a European context need to be understood in relation to discourses regarding Islam/Muslims.

Since the 1960s, Western European countries have witnessed two important factors of social change, namely secularization and ethnic-religious diversification, taking place unevenly across contexts, regions and communities. In Belgium, secularization is understood in terms of sociological statistics pointing to decreased levels of churchgoing as well as unprecedented low levels of trust in the Catholic authorities, especially since the 2010 paedophilia scandals in the Catholic Church (Billiet, Abts and Swijngedouw, 2013). Sociologists and historians have connected secularization and individualization to major shifts in the relationship between religion and politics, and in majority-held norms and values since the 1980s regarding work and family life, sexuality and ethical issues. In 2000, Belgian sociologists at Dutch-speaking universities captured what they perceived to be a shifting collective consciousness throughout Belgium with the phrase 'lost certainty' (*verloren zekerheid*) (Dobbelaere et al, 2000).

Ethnic–religious diversification is understood as the increased presence and visibility of various minoritized communities in Belgium due to globalization and migration since the 1960s. While (postcolonial) migrants, asylum seekers and refugees have represented a

* I would like to thank the editors for supporting and including this chapter in this volume, and for their feedback. Thanks also go to Anne-Marie Korte and Marco Derks, who provided insightful thoughts and critical remarks on earlier versions of the chapter, and to Eyad Abuali for helping out with language editing. I take full responsibility for the final version, including potential omissions and mistakes.

wide variety of ethnic and religious backgrounds, the term diversity is often associated with the presence of Muslims. While only comprising 6% of the Belgian population, many citizens grossly overestimate the number of Muslims (Temmerman, 2014). Muslims' increasing visibility and integration in all sectors of public life, and their claims to equal rights and opportunities as well as the right to profess the Islamic faith outside the home or the mosque, are contested in various ways, such as through political and media debates (Zemni, 2011), everyday life interaction and sensibilities (Fadil, 2009) and local policy making that demonstrates difficulties or refusal to accommodate Muslims' specific needs or practices (Kanmaz and Zemni, 2005; Coene and Longman, 2008).

In this setting, Christian feminists and Christian women's movements face numerous challenges. Due to secularization, individualization, ethnic-religious diversification, and inequalities on the basis of gender, ethnicity, 'race', class and sexuality, they feel the need to rethink their contemporary relevance and priorities. In Flanders, the Dutch-speaking northern part of Belgium, Christian feminist theologians recently began posing questions about feminist theology and religious studies for contemporary times (Maes, 2012). They also started rethinking the relationships between women belonging to different religious and ethnic groups in order to build more inclusive feminist thinking and practices suitable for a postcolonial context (Decoene and Lambelin, 2010).

In Flanders, Christian women's movements belonging to Catholic civil society used to draw on a large following, and historically contributed to the political, religious and social emancipation of Catholic women (van Molle, 2004). In recent years, these movements have faced declining membership and have felt a need to 'reinvent' themselves according to what they consider women's current needs. This chapter explores, against this background of social change, how Femma, a large Christian women's organization uniting 65,000 members, has reinvented its identity and self-presentation in order to maintain religious, social and cultural relevance. This exploration is theorized as a specific secularization experience that is related to discourses surrounding Islam/Muslims.[1]

The following section reviews literature on secularization and women, and argues for further diversifying our understandings of secularization by considering not only particular social groups, but also the experience and position of religious social movements. The second part of the chapter examines Femma. Besides its empirical contribution, the chapter furthers the development of critical perspectives on secularization by bringing together different fields of discussion and priorities.

## Theoretical approach: diversifying secularization

Various sociologists of religion have emphasized that the classic secularization thesis cannot account for diverse contexts. Instead, secularization takes place in different ways according to national and regional settings, and the religious and political traditions involved. Theories of secularization have therefore become multiplied in recent decades (for example Casanova, 1994; Martin, 2005; Davie, 2002; Berger, 1999). Feminist and gender critical scholars have argued for the importance of a contextualizing approach starting from gender and sexuality. Sociological and anthropological approaches in this field can be understood as having launched a 'diversifying secularization' paradigm. In the Western European context, recent impulses in favour of this paradigm emerged mainly from UK-based scholarship. In this section, I aim at connecting these insights in order to rethink the specificity of Christian women's movements.

British sociologists of religion have pointed at women as influencing processes of secularization. In the introduction to *Women and Religion in the West: Challenging Secularization*, editors Kristin Aune, Sonya Sharma and Giselle Vincett argue that a 'one-size-fits-all' explanation for secularization simply does not exist. The argument for looking at secularization processes through multiple angles and experiences is made through various perspectives. First, the editors mention the significance of the rise of the feminist movement in the 1960s and many second-wave feminists' rejection of traditional religions and religiosity as irredeemably patriarchal. Feminist critique historically contributed to secularization processes by concurring in the loss of Churches' authority in defining women's proper role.

Second, the editors and authors argue that attention should be paid to the specific experiences and positions of women, or particular groups of women, in order to understand current patterns of religiosity and change in Western contexts. Societal change such as women's increased emancipation and participation in the public sphere, increasing diversity of family life and women's sexual lives make women fit less well with Christian ideals of heterosexual marriage and traditional gender roles (Aune, 2008; Sharma, 2008). According to Penny Long Marler (2008), constructions of femininity and female religiosity explain why some women remain connected to Churches, while other women have started experimenting with spirituality outside of the Church.

Spanish sociologist Jose Casanova (2009) and Belgian historian Patrick Pature (2004) emphasize the role of women and sexuality in secularization processes in Catholic-majority contexts. Similar to Aune, Sharma and Vincett, Pasture (2004) mentions the impact of feminist counter-narratives and developments in popular culture and society. Traditional women's roles were undermined, which included work outside of the home becoming ideal for women's self-expression, and the abandonment of piety as part of proper female identity. Importantly, the discrimination women suffer in most Christian denominations – in particular the denial of the right to be ordained – are increasingly perceived to be morally unjust. For Catholics, the expectations raised by the Second Vatican Council (1962–65) and the spirit of time could not be met (Pasture, 2004, p 86). Pasture (2004) points to sexuality as another challenge the Catholic Church faces, an argument that is further developed by British sociologist Linda Woodhead. Her essay 'Sex and Secularization' (2007) explores the importance and controversy of sex in contemporary Christian Churches. Woodhead argues that Christian Churches' heightened concern (US and UK Protestant and Catholic Churches) with sexual regulation in general, and female sexuality in particular, may be a significant factor contributing to their recent decline. Since the 1960s, mainstream culture has increasingly emphasized subjective life and individual emancipation, which has involved, Woodhead claims, a widespread rejection of attempts by external authorities to impose order on sexual life. In this context, the Churches' stance on sexuality has alienated large numbers of Christians, who have started to find individual desires more trustworthy than the imperatives of external obligation and authority. As Woodhead puts it, 'In the West at least, "sexualization" may be an important factor in secularization' (2007, p 230).

The above diversifying secularization approaches have emerged mainly in the social sciences and investigate processes (and disruptions) of secularization. They aim, in short, at specifying and nuancing secularization theories through investigating women and sexuality. Secularization, individualization and religious/spiritual proliferation are the paradigms through which cultural phenomena and the experience of specific groups in society are assessed and understood. However, the above literature does not give many tools for understanding the specific role of Christian women's *movements*. I suggest that social movements be considered as actors in a particular dynamic of representing/constructing collective priorities and needs. When Christian women's organizations articulate, for example, notions of women's religiosity, this needs to be understood as emerging from and therefore *representing* the collective experience of their members. However, these notions simultaneously need to be perceived as *constructed*, as they might not include the experiences of all members, and there might be other reasons for articulating certain notions besides representation.

This chapter aims to contribute to the above diversifying secularization paradigm by exploring the particular experience of Femma. It moreover links to dynamics of ethnic-religious diversification by addressing the ways in which images of Islam and Muslims influence Femma's secularization experience. Sociologist Sarah Bracke (2013) discusses the secularization of the Netherlands by addressing the position of Islam and Muslim communities. She demonstrates how the secularization of the Dutch majority population and institutions is linked to the 'Muslim question' – that is, concerns and anxieties about the 'Muslim other'. While Bracke's argument revisits the dominant Dutch narrative of a history of institutional secularization ('depillarization'), this chapter nuances existing narratives in Belgium about secularization and socio-cultural Christianity by looking at a Christian women's movement. In a similar vein, however, I draw attention to the constitutive role of Muslims in ongoing processes of secularization and socio-cultural Christianity.

On the basis of the empirical analysis I present in the next section, I demonstrate that Femma's secularization experience is influenced by discourses regarding Islam and Muslim women. I therefore argue that, theoretically, there is a need for furthering insights into social movements and civil society actors in secularization processes, and into the ways in which secularization experiences might be tied to discourses surrounding religious, gender, sexual and ethnic differences.

## Case study: introduction

The Christian Working Class Women's Organization (*Kristelijke Arbeiders Vrouwen* – KAV), was officially established in the early 1930s, as part of the Christian working class movement (Willems, 2011).[2] The Christian working class movement used to have enormous popular support in Flanders (more than in French-speaking Wallonia) in terms of membership and active commitment as it could more evidently draw, unlike the socialist workers' movement, from a predominantly Catholic working class (Witte, Craybeckx and Meynen, 2006). KAV contributed to Flemish working class women's emancipation at two levels: as women, and as members of the lower social classes (Osaer, 1991, p 317).[3]

KAV had a following of 153,000 members around 1960, which increased to 300,000 members in 1980 (KAV, 1980). The Flemish community included 5.6 million people in 1980, and KAV was its largest women's organization (van Molle, 2004, p 372). KAV established throughout Flanders hundreds of local women's groups under the auspices of priests. These groups encouraged cooperation among women, and educated women in household matters, child rearing and Catholicism. At the same time, KAV collaborated with other women's organizations and movements to further women's political, reproductive, juridical and educational rights. KAV has defined itself since the 1950s as a social-cultural organization that combines a political agenda on behalf of women with working class women's education and personal development (Willems, 2011, pp 70–1).[4]

The current steady decline of KAV's membership numbers is part of a larger context in which the traditional pillars and its organizations are decreasing in importance for individual identity and daily life. Since the 1960s, the Catholic pillar has been confronted with growing Church disaffiliation, which has forced the pillar's leadership to adapt its collective consciousness. This has led to the Catholic credo, values and norms being replaced by 'so-called typical values of the Gospel integrated in what is called a Socio-Cultural Christianity' (Dobbelaere, 2010). I understand Femma as situated in this context, and simultaneously a specific actor in shaping 'socio-cultural Christianity', starting from what it considers to be women's needs in terms of emancipation, community and *zingeving*[5] (see Moerman, 2013). With at least 65,000 members today, KAV should still be regarded a mass organization, however many of its local groups are aging. In 2012, KAV changed its name to 'Femma'.[6] Femma's policy makers and staff currently focus on attracting young women to the organization and establishing new local groups. The recent decision for the name change is part of the organization's aim to reach out to young women (Femma, 2012, pp 7–37).[7]

What message does this recent name change convey about a Christian women's movement's identity and position in a changing context? This question emerges from literature review, media reports, and interviews conducted in 2013–14. All interviews addressed the name change and the subsequent internal discussions about women's *zingeving*. In this case study, I focus on the discussion and analyse what it reveals about Femma's understanding of itself and its potential as a women's movement; about the young women it reaches out to; and about those women whom it has difficulty imagining as potentially being part of the regeneration it aspires to.

The material for analysis consists of policy documents and media statements produced by Femma policy makers, and eight interviews: three with current and former policy makers; three with policy makers at provincial main offices (Brussels, Hassel and Antwerp), and two with key volunteers (organizing local groups in Antwerp and Brugge). All interviewees are involved in devising and/or implementing Femma policies that aim at supporting women's emancipation, community building and *zingeving*.

## Discussing the name change

Femma's policy makers describe the change to 'Femma' as a 'successful rebranding' but emphasize that the organization's primary goals remain the same.[8] The name change became a topic of discussion both outside and inside the women's organization. The new name was announced in various mainstream media (for example De Morgen, 2012; De Standaard, 2012), and voices emerging from Catholic media criticized the loss of an explicit reference to Christianity (Pollefeyt, 2012). Femma's policy makers therefore decided to provide an elaborate explanation in the July 2012 issue of Femma's magazine. Countering some of the responses the new name evoked, Femma director Eva Brumagne humorously writes in the editorial introduction: 'Femma is not a cream to treat hemorrhoids, and I am not – I give my word of honour – a mercenary to steer our organisation towards Frenchification. And we have nothing against headscarves, but we are not going to wear them ourselves' (2012, p 3).[9]

I first start by outlining two main foci of the arguments in favour of the name change: generational shift and the disconnection from an explicit Christian identity. After that, I analyse the internal discussion and the strategies in dealing with the objections. This will explain the seemingly out-of-context reference to the Islamic headscarf by Eva Brumagne cited above.

## *The generational shift argument*

The main argument embraced by the interviewees in favour of the name change is connected to the idea of a generational shift; of differences between generations of women. The argument is formulated as such: the name KAV sounds old-fashioned and is not attractive for young women. This clashes with the crucial task of attracting young women as potential members. The assumption is that young women especially do not identify with the category 'workers' and identify as Catholic even less. What complicates the issue is that the 'K' of the acronym KAV stands for *kristelijk* (Christian), which is an old Dutch notation nowadays replaced by *christelijk*. This means that the Dutch-speaking outsider to the movement, young and old, will interpret the 'K' in 'KAV' automatically as standing for *katholiek* (Catholic) instead of *kristelijk*.

Fran, a volunteer organizing groups and activities in Antwerp, for example, speaks about the old-fashioned connotations of the name KAV:

> 'I am going to put that honestly: for many women who want to come to us, this is a threshold. Like: I do not want to be associated with KAV, because I do not want to have anything to do with the Catholic pillar. And a couple of years ago we received some people [to our activities], who said ah, there are young women too! Well, today I am a little older, but they did say: ah, there are young women at KAV. Because KAV has somewhat an image problem. That it attracts predominantly elderly women. They are working hard to attract also young women.'

The generation argument holds that especially young women today find it hard to identify with Christian identity, and even more with the Catholic pillar. It assumes that they are generally non-religious or 'religious differently' in the sense of embracing individually constructed religiosities drawing on various sources of inspiration and on the basis of a disconnection from Catholicism, which, as an institutionalized form of Christianity, does not support women's contemporary lifestyles. And so, the argument goes, in order to attract young women as members and regenerate the movement – and save it from extinction – the women's organization urgently needs to adopt a new name without any reference to religious inspiration or a specific worldview.

### *No need for an explicit Christian identity*

While my interviewees were generally positive about the new name Femma, they also claimed that the name change provoked both positive and negative responses among Femma members. They spoke of some Femma members' resentment regarding the loss of an explicit identification with Christianity as the women's organization's historical source of inspiration and religious belonging. As Antwerp staff member Margo states:

'After our name-change, I was at a meeting at the Groenplaats [well-known square] in Antwerp where all kinds of organisations and associations presented themselves. I received many responses. Responses from our members who were very irritated and angry because we changed that name. Because they actually felt that: "there is so much value in our name, so what have you done?"'

Not limited to Femma's own members, other organizations that are part of Catholic civil society expressed their disappointment regarding the new name in terms of the loss of an explicit connection to Christian roots and faith. The explanation of one of Femma's national policy makers, Liza, about the choice for the new name can be considered a reworking of socio-cultural Christian identity (Dobbelaere, 2010) from the perspective of a women's organization:

'Yes, [the identification with] Christianity is not part of it anymore. I think that is important. I think it is true that we open our doors widely by removing the Christian aspect. But in our mission and vision we refer to those values, such as solidarity and justice. Some say: those are not Christian values, they are humanist values. Yes, that is true in fact. Yes. Actually, any individual with a Christian framework for constructing meaning is very much welcome here. We do not throw away our Christian roots. They have an important role in the viewpoints we take up, and our choice for specific target groups. So, the ideas and thoughts of Cardijn [priest who organised the early Catholic working class youth movement] certainly have a place. But those who do not have that framework, they should be as much welcome. So that is a clear choice.'

Socio-cultural Christianity needs to be understood as the particular form in which Catholic civil society in Flanders secularizes. Arguably, Femma's furthering of socio-cultural Christianity is inspired by the need for the women's organization to further disconnect from Church hierarchies on behalf of young women's contemporary lifestyles and dis-identifications.

As narrated above, this furthering of socio-cultural Christianity is not without contestation. The internal discussion about the loss of an explicit Christian identity emerges from differences in worldview and religiosity existing within the Catholic pillar of Flanders. The stories of Margo and Liza reveal that not all members of the women's organization are in favour of the (re)construction of social-cultural Christian identity, or at least not in favour of one that is secularized to the extent that explicit references to Christianity disappear altogether.

## Secularization contested: the fear of Islam/Muslims

This section analyses the various discourses regarding generational change and Christian identity by paying attention to the ways in which they are tied to different degrees of distancing from Islam and Muslim women. Reaching out to young women was not contested, but as pointed out, some Femma members did resist the loss of an explicit link with Christianity. While differences in worldview and religiosity were deemed important in internal conversations, the need to hold on to an explicit Christian identity articulated by some members at times went hand in hand with a fear of Islam. In this understanding, the name change closes off any explicit link with Christianity in order to deliberately open up to Islam. These members' words convey an anxiety about the presence of Muslim women.

My interviewees' strategy to respond to this assumption of 'opening up to Muslim women' was to deny the existence of any such intention underlying the name change. They also point to the irrationality of this concern, emphasizing that following the name change, the influx of a large group of Muslim women as new Femma members never took place. While it is productive to point at this statistical reality in order to counter irrational claims, on the other hand, it does not counter the fear itself. Some interviewees, however, emphasize that although the name change was not primarily meant to attract Muslim women, Muslim women are as welcome as all other women to become new Femma members.

Esra, a Femma staff member in Hasselt, reflects on what she dubs 'Islamophobia' among Femma members. Various strategies of dealing with negative responses regarding the name change are reflected in Esra's narrative:

> 'Now, one year and few months later, it is not that much alive anymore as back then. But I was surprised that it wasn't that much about the disappearance of the "K", of the Christian roots and identity. It had to do with that too, but immediately, when I asked questions and continued asking further questions, then I encountered Islamophobia. Yes. At a certain moment I asked: well, the "K" disappeared,

but how important is that really for you? Whose daughters are still going to church? And then they often said: actually, not only our daughters, but we ourselves do not go often anymore. And in that case, I continue to pose questions. And then [the response is as such]: in fact, yes, Europe is Islamising. One put it literally: you put the doors wide open for Islam. And I thought: no! Now they understand better. This year in May, we brought together local groups in each region of the province. And … someone posed the question: how many women of other ethnic origins became new members since the name-change? And I made clear once again: look ladies, we have the name-change, a long process took place before that, and it also happened to do justice to reality. Also regarding those women [Muslim women], but that wasn't our primary target group. We primarily started from the idea that *zingeving* today takes place in another way. And the "K" and the "A" do not attract young women, they don't recognise themselves in that. And one year later, they [local Femma groups] start to understand that. … [I] don't know whether it is jealousy, but … church attendance is decreasing, and … more and more mosques are being built. And also in the streets, you see women with headscarves. So, there is a counter movement. And I think that that is considered a bit painful … Yes, maybe it is competition. But a threat also, literally a threat.'

Esra's story demonstrates the use of various strategies simultaneously: referring to the importance of reaching out to young women ("daughters"); connecting the 'secular' name to a reality of secularization ("to do justice to reality"); refusing the assumption that the new name was meant to attract Muslim women ("not our primary target group"); and at the same time emphasizing that Muslim women are welcome, too ("[It was] also regarding those women"). As such, Esra builds a critical (and exceptionally reflexive and complex) narrative that aims at countering Islamophobia. Anthropologist Nadia Fadil (2011) similarly speaks of the sense of threat as an important aspect of Islamophobia among the white majority population in Flanders. Esra's story above demonstrates that this idea of threat is directly linked to the sense of an incoming flood. In a period of change for KAV/Femma, in which the women's movement feels itself forced to rethink and reform in the face of declining membership and social importance, the feeling of crisis and insecurity becomes the ground on which the potential arrival of Muslims appears as a threat for some of its members.

The above analysis provides an explanation for Femma's director Eva Brumagne's comment in Femma's magazine of July 2012 that '*we* have nothing against *headscarves*, but we are not going to wear them ourselves' (Femma, 2012, p 3, my emphasis). 'We' refers here to Femma's policy makers, staff and volunteers. Initially, it seems strange that Brumagne feels compelled, as a non-Muslim woman, to underline that she is not going to wear a headscarf. The analysis suggests, however, that it is a response to the existing resistance regarding the new name based on the women's organization's presumed embrace of Muslim women. According to Carland (2011), Islamophobia in Western contexts often includes a fear of loss of freedom, and Muslims are assumed to import restrictive and oppressive behavioural codes and morals, especially related to sartorial practices. This reading explains why Brumagne feels the need to assert her autonomy (and implicitly that of the women's organization at large) vis-à-vis Islamic dress.

Here, a multifaceted collective self-image constitutes a related image of the 'other', in this case Islam/Muslim women, by which negative perceptions become 'free-floating signifiers' that have recently moved, in the European context, from Judaism to Islam. Building on what Freud called 'the narcissism of minor differences', cultural historian Sander Gilman argues that in creating categories (in this case the name Femma) that elide differences and stress similarities, one believes that one is bridging differences. But in fact, in secular/izing contexts, (minor) differences are being heightened instead of bridged (2015, p xiv). The differences being heightened here are, in various ways, the generational one, and (socio-cultural) Christianity versus Islam/Muslims.

## Conclusion

This chapter started from the assumption that Christian women's organizations and movements have particular experiences in broader contexts of secularization and ethnic-religious diversification. Its analysis focused on a large Christian women's organization in Flanders, Femma, and its current self-positioning through a recent name change and the discussions tied to it. Femma's self-representation is theorized as part of, and contributing to, secularization in general, and the emergence of socio-cultural Christianity in particular. The analysis examined the arguments in favour of the name change and what they reveal about the understandings of Femma's policy makers and staff regarding Femma's future relevance. It demonstrated that an important axis of identification is youth. As Femma hopes to attract more young women to the organization, its new name is primarily meant to be attractive to 'young women'. A second important axis of dis/identification is Christianity. Young women are presumably not attracted to Catholicism and do not care about an explicit reference to Christian identity, which leads to the embracing of a 'secular' name. The analysis showed that the arguments in favour of the new name are forced to deal with the objections/resistance of some Femma members. An important objection presented by the interviewees was framed as the need to defend oneself against Islam/Muslim women. While the interviewees themselves were in favour of the new name and did not explicitly exclude Muslim women from membership, their discursive strategies to counter the Islamophobic resistance often do not criticize the fear of Islam/Muslim women directly.

Examining the internal controversy about the new name in terms of secularization being contested reveals that despite the differences, the discourses share, to varying degrees, a disconnection from Islam/Muslim women. This leads me to conclude that a women's organization the size of Femma experiences difficulties in bridging differences, not only regarding worldview or religiosity, but also with respect to the perception of Islam as a minoritized religion, and women belonging to Islamic communities.

The process of becoming (more) secular needs to be seen as part and parcel of local histories of secularization, but also as influenced by discourses regarding Islam/Muslims. In this process, constructions of gender, religion and ethnicity are central. Femma's name change reveals what is at stake for this Christian women's organization in current times. In its aspiration to become a large socio-cultural organization 'fit' for contemporary times, it embraces 'other women' at best reluctantly.

## Notes

[1]  This book chapter emerges from my 2010–14 doctoral research on women's movements and feminist activism in Flanders and their connections to religious traditions and secularisation/secularity. The study of Femma was its fifth comparative case study, and was developed through in-depth interviews and an analysis of Femma's policy papers and media statements. See for a further methodological explanation, pp 122–23 of this chapter.

[2]  The emergence of Belgium as a state and society is historically based on three politically, religiously and socially institutionalised 'pillars': the Catholic, the socialist and the liberal. The pillars were supervised by political parties (and in the case of the Catholic pillar, the Catholic hierarchy), and its members were supported by the pillar's unions, health care, civil society organisations, and schools (Witte,

Craybeckx and Meynen, 2006). The Christian working class movement has always been embedded in the Catholic pillar.

3   Up until today, two autonomous Christian working class women's organisations exist in Belgium, divided by language and region: KAV in Flanders, and LOFC-Vie Feminine in Wallonia.

4   The main functions of social-cultural organisations, as outlined by the Flemish government, are community building, social participation, education and cultural activities.

5   *Zingeving* is a Dutch umbrella term that refers to religiosity and spirituality, as well as broader patterns of meaning making.

6   In the Dutch language 'femma' is not an existing term. However, in Belgium, where French, Dutch and German are the three officially recognised national languages, 'femma' easily reminds one of the French 'femme' (woman). In combination with a new logo and new magazine design, which use playful letter types and bright pink as their main colour, 'femma' leads to associations with women and femininity.

7   Other contemporary Flemish women's organisations historically embedded in the 'Catholic pillar' are: Vrouw & Maatschappij, KVLV, Markant and Vrouw en Geloof. An example of 'gender mainstreaming' of Catholic civil society organisations is the ACV-Gender team of the Christian working class movement (ACV). Not just Femma, but all these Christian women's organisations and groups feel the need to rethink their political, social and religious relevance and future audience.

8   Femma's Progress Report 2013 (*Femma vzw Voortgangsrapport 2012–2013*) describes the process of name change (Femma, 2013, pp 5–6), and concludes that '[l]ess than a year after our name-change, we dare to speak of a highly successful rebranding' (p 6).

9   All citations are my translations from Dutch to English.

## References

Aune, K. (2008) 'Evangelical Christianity and women's changing lives', *European Journal of Women's Studies*, 15(3), pp 277–94.

Aune K., Sharma, S. and Vincett, G. (eds) (2008) *Women and religion in the West: Challenging secularization*, Aldershot/Burlington: Ashgate.

Berger, P. (1999) *The desecularization of the world: Essays on the resurgence of religion in world politics*, Washington: Ethics and Public Policy Center.

Billiet, J., Abts, K. and Swyngedouw, M. (2013) *Rapport: De evolutie van de kerkelijke betrokkenheid in Vlaanderen tussen de voorbije twee decennia en het verlies van vertrouwen in de kerk in het bijzonder tussen 2009 en 2011*, Leuven: Instituut voor Sociaal en Politiek Opinieonderzoek (IPSO) and Centrum voor Sociologisch Onderzoek (CeSo), Katholieke Universiteit Leuven.

Bracke, S. (2013) 'Transformations of the secular and the "Muslim question". Revisiting the historical coincidence of depillarisation and the institutionalisation of Islam in the Netherlands', *Journal of Muslims in Europe*, 2, pp 208–26.

Brumagne, E. (2012) 'Vooraf', *Femma Magazine*, June, 3.

Carland, S. (2011) 'Islamophobia, fear of loss of freedom, and the Muslim woman', *Islam and Christian-Muslim Relations*, 22(4), pp 469–73.

Casanova, J. (1994) *Public religions in the modern world*, Chicago/London: The University of Chicago Press.

Casanova, J. (2009) 'Religion, politics and gender equality: Public religions revisited', in J Casanova and A. Phillips, *A debate on the public role of religion and its social and gender implications*, Gender and Development, Program paper number 5: United Nations Research Institute for Social Development, pp 1–34.

Coene, G. and Longman, C. (2008) 'Gendering the diversification of diversity: The Belgian hijab (in) question', *Ethnicities*, 8(3), pp 302–21.

Davie, G. (2002) *Europe: The exceptional case*, London: Darton, Longman & Todd.

De Morgen (2012) 'KAV heet voortaan Femma', 12 May. Available at: https://www.demorgen.be/binnenland/kav-heet-voortaan-femma-b405a158/ (last accessed: 28 February 2018).

De Standaard (2012) 'Christelijke vrouwenvereniging KAV heet voortaan Femma', 12 May. Available at: http://www.standaard.be/cnt/dmf20120512_086

Decoene, A. and Lambelin, J. (2010) 'Feminisme a–Dieu? De transformatieve kracht van feministische theologieen in België', in Sophia (ed) *Genderstudies: Een genre Apart? Een stand van zaken. Colloquium 2009/Savoirs de genre: Quel genre de savoir? Etat des lieux des etudes de genre. Colloque 2009*, Sophia: Brussels, pp 369–91.

Dobbelaere, K. (2010) 'Religion and politics in Belgium: From an institutionalized manifest Catholic to a latent Christian pillar', *The Politics and Religion Journal*, 2, pp 283–96.

Dobbelaere, K., Elchardus, M., Kerkhofs, J., Voye, L. and Bawin-Legros, J. (2000) *Verloren zekerheid: De Belgen en hun waarden, overtuigingen en houdingen*, Tielt: Uitgeverij Lannoo/Koning Boudewijn Stichting.

Fadil, N. (2009) 'Managing affects and sensibilities: The case of not-handshaking and not-fasting', *Social Anthropology*, 17(4), pp 439–54.

Fadil, N. (2011) 'Islamofobie als laatste strohalm voor het Eurocentrisch denken', *Manazine*, 3, pp 4–13.

Femma (2012) 'Een naam krijgt een ziel als hij leeft', *Femma Magazine*, June, pp 44–6.

Femma (2013) *Voortgangsrapport 2012–2013*, Brussels: Femma.

Gilman, S. (2014) 'Introduction: The Abrahamic religions in an age of diaspora', in S. Gilman (ed) *Judaism, Christianity and Islam: Collaboration and conflict in the age of diaspora*, Hong Kong: Hong Kong University Press, pp ix–xix.

Kanmaz, M. and Zemni, S. (2005) 'Religious discrimination and public policies: "Muslim Burial Areas" in Ghent', *Migration Letters*, 2(3), pp 265–97.

KAV (1980), *Jubileumboek*, KAV.

Marler, P. (2008) 'Religious change in the West: Watch the women', in K. Aune, S. Sharma and G. Vincett (eds) *Women and religion in the West: Challenging secularization*, Aldershot/Burlington: Ashgate, pp 23–56.

Moerman, E. (2013) 'Z.O.Z.: Ubuntu onder vrouwen!', Voorstel Femma zingevingsbeleidsplan 2014–2015 (versie november 2013), unpublished draft policy papers.

Osaer, A. (1991) 'De Christelijke arbeidersvrouwenbeweging', in E. Gerard (ed) *De Christelijke arbeidersbeweging in België 1891–1991*, Leuven: Universitaire Pers Leuven, pp 316–410.

Pasture, P. (2004) 'Christendom and the legacy of the sixties: Between the secular city and the age of Aquarius', *Revue d'Histoire Ecclesiastique*, 99(1), pp 82–117.

Pollefeyt, D. (2012) 'Femma, Fama, Femka: Waarom het om meer dan een letter gaat', Tertio, 13: 641. Available at: http://www.kuleuven. be/metaforum/page.php?FILE=opiniestuk_pers&PID=149#384.

Sharma, S. (2008) 'When young women say "yes": Exploring the sexual selves of young Canadian women in Protestant churches', in K. Aune, S. Sharma and G. Vincett (eds) *Women and religion in the West: Challenging secularization*, Aldershot/Burlington: Ashgate, pp 71–82.

Temmerman, J. (2014) 'Weet u hoeveel moslims er in België wonen?', *De Standaard*, 29 October. Available at: http://www.standaard.be/ cnt/dmf20141029_01348354.

Van den Brandt, N. (2014) 'Religion, secularity and feminism in a West-European context: A qualitative study of organisations and activism in Flanders', PhD thesis, Ghent University.

Van Molle, L. (2004) 'De nieuwe vrouwenbeweging in Vlaanderen: Een andere lezing', BTNG/RBHC XXXIV(3), pp 357–97.

Willems, L. (2011) *Maria Baers (1883–1959): De constructie van een vrouwbeeld ten opzichte van een manbeeld. Genderdiscourse in de Belgische katholieke zuil*, Ghent University, MA thesis.

Witte, E., Craybeckx, J. and Meynen, A. (2005) *Politieke geschiedenis van België: Van 1830 tot heden*, Antwerp: Standaard Uitgeverij.

Woodhead, L. (2007) 'Sex and secularization' in G. Loughlin (ed) *Queer Theology: Rethinking the Western Body*, Malden/Oxford/Carlton: Blackwell Publishing, pp 230–44.

Zemni, S. (2011) 'The shaping of Islam and Islamophobia in Belgium', *Race & Class*, 53(1), pp 28–44.

# SEVEN

# Muslim women in contemporary Argentina

*Mari-Sol García Somoza and Mayra Soledad Valcarcel*

## Introduction[1]

Taking as our starting point the contributions of the debates and considerations around the 'voice of the subaltern', *discursive colonization* and *epistemic violence* (Spivak, 2009; Mohanty, 2008), some initial questions are inescapable: what happens when that Other that we work with and that interpellates us is not strictly a 'subaltern', or in other words, does not necessarily fit the classical description based on supposed racial and/or class parameters? Furthermore, what dilemmas do we face when the *otherness* or *alterity*[2] that confronts and affects us includes, in addition to the tensions inherent in diversity, others that are the result of similarities? Who is the 'subaltern', who are they for and in what context? And lastly, what happens to empathy and distance when the Other is *our neighbour*? (Ginsburg, 2004). Can we really avoid indefinite forms of discursive violence and narrative authority even if our stance in the social field is similar to the Other? How to train 'the eye' and 'the ear' to recognize instances of resistance and normativity in diffuse and unusual spaces?

Many of these questions have arisen out of our own experience of fieldwork with Muslim women in Buenos Aires. We started our work at different times but our paths crossed along the way. The goals and desires driving our two research projects are quite distinct; however, as Argentinean trainee researchers, we agree on the vital importance of a knowledge of the past and present of Muslim communities in the Global South.

Our main objective is to describe, understand and explain the process of identity building among women professing Islam in Argentina by analysing the ways they articulate and reconstruct their different loci of identity belongings (sex/gender, Arab, Argentinean and Muslim identities). This enables comparisons to be drawn between the religious

135

careers of women occupying different positions in the social field, and tries to understand and describe how Muslim women experience (embodiment) and externalize (performance) their religiosity and religious identity, while at the same time paying attention to the different types of female agency (Mahmood, 2005).

This chapter is the result of sharing thoughts on the experiences of fieldwork in the framework of our two doctoral research projects. Both pieces of research retrieve a sociological and anthropological approach, emphasizing participant observation as their main methodological strategy. We endeavour to overcome the objective–subjective dichotomy by opting for a relational dialectical perspective that allows us to link up structural, institutional and quotidian levels with subjects' experiences, discourses and meanings (Achilli, 2005, p 39). Underlying this perspective is an intersubjective, dynamic complex idea of the social world. This research seeks to contribute to the development of gender and social studies of Islam in contemporary Argentina. It adopts an interdisciplinary perspective that reclaims the contributions offered by sociology and anthropology, including critical approaches from and on post- and decolonial feminism. We take it that identity building takes place within the framework of a specific grammar of identity politics and of globalized and deterritorialized Islam.

The religious subject, states Bracke (2008, pp 61–62), inevitably highlights the issue of *agency*, and its secular, genderized and ethnicized Eurocentric definition. We would therefore ask whether 'subalternizing' – that is, associating or standardizing alterity to subalternity – is just another form of discursive colonization. One possible alternative to avoid the fetishization of otherness is indeed to emphasize agency, experience and subjectivity as dimensions for analysis. We take gender to be a relational category and an analytical tool that allows us to deconstruct and conceptualize what has been naturalized (Scott, 1988). Accordingly, we recognize the intersectional, translocational and transversal nature of gender (Anthias and Yuval-Davis, 1983; Crenshaw, 1989; Staunæs, 2003).

The methodology of this research has relied primarily on qualitative tools: in-depth (ethnographic) interviews[3] with Muslim women (natives and converts) of different generations from Argentina's Muslim community in Buenos Aires, as well as participant observation in different places of worship, celebration, political demonstrations, and spaces of conviviality and everyday community life. Among the interviews we each conducted was a corpus of some 50 testimonies. One of us prioritized interviews with women born into Muslim families, while the other included women converts. We also coincided over the age range of the interviewees: between 22 and 55 years of age. This allows us an insight into changes and continuities across different generations (across those born before and those born since the restoration of democracy, or across those belonging to second- or third-generation Muslims in Argentina and those recently embracing Islam).

This chapter opens with a section stating its objectives and a brief overview of works on Islam, gender and religion in Argentina, particularly those dealing with the local Muslim community. We go on to describe the different forms of identity building, emphasizing the existence of various paths and models of womanhood. We then develop our analysis of Muslim subjectivity and identity building from a gender-, religiosity- and corporality-focused perspective. We pay attention to how the Islamic way of life is lived and experienced, resignifying and managing the 'female role' as defined by religious normativity and (re)composed through different discourses in circulation (García Somoza, 2017). This opens up new issues and debates for future contributions, intersecting gender and social studies of Islam in Latin American contexts.

## Argentina's Muslim community

In contrast to the English-speaking and French academic fields, the study of Islam both in Argentina and Latin America has been slow to develop. The studies available and most visible are concentrated in the Brazilian academic field, where interest in the study of Islam has been growing since the 1980s. The results of such researches are primarily reflected in the production of master's and doctoral theses.

While the momentum to know about Islam and its particular attributes in Latin America has been gathering fairly steadily, this area of study is still confined to a minority in academia. Islam certainly represents a minority population in the region, but this does not mean it is of minor importance within the local social set-up and the memories or political participation of Muslims in civil society and government as some recent studies in countries such as Brazil, Argentina, Colombia or Mexico have attempted to show (Montenegro, 2015). Yet within this scientific production we find very little literature that intersects with gender studies and works on Islam in the region (Caña Cuevas, 2006; Ferreira, 2010, 2013; Voigt Espinola, 2013). This is even truer in Argentina, where, despite the socio-anthropological interest in Islam that has flourished for a little over a decade (for example Moreno, 2010; Montenegro, 2011), there has at the same time been no significant catalogue of works addressing religious processes from a gender perspective.

Argentina's Muslim community has its roots in Arab immigration, mainly from Syria and the Lebanon, and to a lesser extent Iraq and Palestine (most professing Christianity and Catholicism), who arrived in the country in the late nineteenth and early twentieth centuries (Akmir, 2009). This community has nevertheless recently gained in public visibility and the number of conversions to Islam among atheists or people from other religious traditions – not necessarily Arab in origin – has risen. Nowadays migrant groups from Senegal, Pakistan, India, Turkey and South Africa can also be found. In terms of demographic composition, the majority of the community's members are therefore second-, third- and fourth-generation descendants of those first waves of migration and belong to the so-called middle class sectors of Argentinean society. More than a century old, the diverse Muslim community in Argentina has been building its social identity and memory on a shared national identity (*argentinidad*), while containing cultural traditions of its own Arabization and de-Arabization processes (Montenegro, 2015), and redefining the religious beliefs in its diasporic condition (Roy, 2002; Sayyid, 2012).

This Muslim community is not interpellated by the debates and conflicts arising in countries with Islamic majorities or societies where Islam is the primary religious minority. However, personal and collective identities – *musulmanidades* – have been changing and reconstituting in light of shifts in the local society and the influence of global and transnational processes, resignifying a number of symbolic and iconographic resources (García Somoza and Valcarcel, 2016a). We wish to analyse processes of identity from a gender perspective that sheds light on women belonging to the local Muslim community. We try to grasp the changes in identity formation – strategies, tensions and politicizations – inside and outside their community of membership, as well as the challenges they face as women and members of a religious minority, building to an analysis of their praxes and discourses surrounding the negotiation and acceptance of socio-cultural and religious normativity.

## Ways of inhabiting the Muslim matrix

In the Islamic tradition *dīn* is a way of life and a system comprising action, ethics, politics, spirituality and corporeality. It establishes a Muslim matrix that allows different yet specific ways to build and live religious identities.

One significant finding was that the narratives of women from Arab Muslim families were grounded in their father's or grandfather's biographies. The 'pioneer' and his voyage of migration organized the family memory. On the other hand, the female figure – the mother or grandmother – featured on a secondary level as the male's companion. Their biographical descriptions tended to recapture the process of settlement, participation in the community and establishment of a family. At first sight everything seemed to point to males being the ones who were narrating the history of the community through the voice of women. What then is the place of these women? Where are they speaking from? If women appeared to make themselves invisible in memories that are *spoken* where might we find them? Where could we listen to them?

The female figure kept slipping in between the interstices from the margins to claim a central place in the account. From her own experiences and drawing on the biographies of her mothers and grandmothers, the 'maternal' figure imposed herself on the autobiographical account and then refracted into specific roles: militancy or political commitment, work/professional activity and religious observance (García Somoza, 2017). "Paradise lies under the mothers' feet," Flora[4] proudly told us in one conversation. This dictum was repeated in many guises throughout both our experiences of fieldwork (García Somoza, 2017; Valcarcel, 2016a, 2016b).

According to Chanfrault-Duchet (1983), what is being set in motion here is the exercise of detecting 'key patterns of narrative structure', namely the elements whereby a recognizable behavioural matrix that imposes a coherence on the speaker's life experience and translates into a coherence of the I is reproduced in the narrative. Each of these figures of identity is associated with a particular role. By 'role' we mean a position that defines individual places in a network of relationships; it can be described as both an individual and a collective construction.

Different institutions and actors from the Muslim community develop and deploy *visibility strategies* in order to (re)define their position within the public space. We therefore hold that the public could be read from three perspectives (García Somoza, 2017): (a) the *symbolic-nominative*, or the transmutable definition of people and/or community – like the *Ummah* – evoked in the local context by certain leaders of the Muslim community in Argentina; (b) the *material*, or what is common to all – be it a square or a space of transit – and is 'inhabited' and reincorporated into both institutional and individual daily practice; and (c) the *practical/ praxeological*, or what seeks to 'manifest itself' publicly, in the words of Hannah Arendt (1988 [1958]), what wishes to be seen, heard and known by all.

Anya was born in the city of Buenos Aires in the 1980s. She comes from an Alawi family with a long tradition in Argentina. Anya has a degree in Political Science and has taken post-graduate courses in Spain and the United States. But what is most interesting about Anya's biography is her political education, a bastion in the family history. Like her parents and relatives before her she belongs to the youth movement of the Federation of Arab Entities in the Americas (FEARAB).

Anya makes no secret of her political position as a Peronist, anti-imperialist and populist, with a strong accent on the empowerment of women. She does not usually wear a *hijab* on a daily basis, save for religious celebrations. While the *hijab* does flag up part of her *musulmanidad*, it is not something her militancy is built on (in contrast to Zahra's account below).

The model of woman that Anya constructs over her narrative is demarcated by elements that identify her as actively militant, both socially and politically. The following features stand out from her narrative structure: the fight for her ideals, the search for equality, the defence of women's rights and the rights of the disadvantaged. To Anya the militant woman is represented in the figures of Eva Perón, Zeinab and Fatima (the Prophet Muhammad's granddaughter and daughter, respectively):

> 'I think a great deal about Peronist feminism. The feminism of fighting women. I think of Fatima as a model too, more from a religious point of view maybe. It depends on the situation: if we're talking politics, Eva Perón; if we're talking religion, Fatima. And if we're talking religion, Zeinab too ... I believe in the image that women can go far and be great leaders, charismatic leaders, and can be good representatives of the female sex. [Eva Perón] .... She's been a real figure-head for lots of persecuted women. Personally, ... I actually find thinking about it really moving because for me she's like this model woman' [García Somoza, 29 December 2010].

In this account, Eva Perón embodies the local militant fighting woman par excellence, the protective mother of the 'shirtless' (*descamisados*). Here the woman appears as the 'mother of the nation' and a political comrade, someone who is visible and her own woman. In this model are distilled the values of struggle and conviction in search of social justice, emblematic of the Peronist dictatum but also combined in

Anya's narrative in line with the Islamic value of justice (*adl*). Justice in Islam is one of the attributes of perfection (*iḥsān*). At the religious level, Anya retrieves a political reading of Fatima and especially of the figure of Zeinab, highlighting their struggle against 'all forms of injustice and oppression'. These three characters in her account reflect the image of the militant woman in terms of both national party politics and Islamic tradition. Anya belongs to this line of women militants and fighters. The female model she constructs visibilizes women's agency within community institutions and the space of civil society.

Nabira is a young sociologist born in the city of Córdoba in the early 1980s. She is from a Sunni Muslim Arab family largely of Lebanese origin, with Syrian origins on her maternal grandmother's side. Her grandfather – the pioneer – was the first member of the family to come to Argentina and find a nostalgic reminder of his native Lebanon in the landscape of the Córdoba sierra. From what she told us, religion in her family environment is passed on through the maternal line, specifically through her maternal grandfather. Nabira's family is one of the 'traditional' families within the community, which centres around the Islamic Centre of the Republic of Argentina (CIRA). Her cousin, the daughter of the Consul of Jordan, belongs to the CIRA's Ladies Committee. The model woman constructed by Nabira in her account is also reflected in several women in CIRA's circle of leaders: a professional businesswoman with a strong character who emphasizes the outline of her body by wearing business suits. Like Anya, Nabira only wears the *hijab* for religious celebrations. To her, it is part of her *musulmanidad* but not the main element. She stresses that she does not feel less Muslim for not wearing it. Although the outstanding image here is one of an independent woman developing her professional career, Nabira's account at the same time expresses the importance of preserving the family space and the transmission of inherited religious values.

By way of contrast there is Sumaya, another young woman from a Muslim family linked to the CIRA community. Sumaya is a French teacher and translator, work she currently carries out within the domestic sphere. She is far more categorical about the position of women within the composition of the family:

> 'As a woman I put my family first. I'm not saying not to work or anything. ... Even less if I want to give my children a religious education, I have to educate by example. I can't do that if I'm completely absent. ... So there are things about nature [sexual difference] you have to respect ...

because I feel it's a priority to be the educator of the family. To me that's the priority' [García Somoza, 5 May 2008].

Finally, we share the stories of Siam and Jasmine. They are cousins and were born in the city of Buenos Aires in the early 1990s. Of Lebanese origin, their families belong to the traditional Shīa community located in the Floresta district. Both are actively engaged with their community institution. When we met Siam, she had only very recently decided to wear the *hijab* on a daily basis. Although she had had no major difficulties in her job working for the state, she did however report receiving negative comments on the street. Jasmine for her part does not wear the veil in public but expresses a desire to do so. She needs to find the courage to do this the way Siam has. For both women 'being a good Muslim' implies regular religious practice (fasting during Ramadan, the daily *salat*, the *zakat*, dietary restrictions and so on). Siam explained to us: "To us religion is the most important thing and having to try and follow that path without isolating yourself is hard. God willing, we lay far more claim to the insertion of Muslim women and all Muslims in society economically, politically and socially" [García Somoza, 6 October 2007].

Both Siam's and Jasmine's stories include the search for spiritual elevation in order to become good – devout, modest – Muslim women. This model is commonly represented through Fatima. On certain other occasions they mention Khadija, the Prophet's first wife, Zeinab and especially the Virgin Mary. Jasmine says:

'For us, our woman, our lady is the Prophet's daughter, who was called Fatima. … One goal in our lives is to become a thousandth of the person she was. Her patience, her love and respect towards her parents, towards her children, the caring attitude she had for everything, her kindness towards the rest of the world. … Her love of God' [García Somoza, 6 October 2007].

The qualities associated with religious observance and motherhood are aspects that shape the 'role' upheld by certain women. These aspects do not necessarily limit their presence in the public space but rather redefine their status and participation in the dialogic continuum comprised of public-private spheres. Each of the above profiles can be presented with varying degrees of emphasis depending on the course of each woman's life.

The Muslim matrix contained in the nature of *dīn* echoes through the narratives of women in the ways they construct their identity and redefine their position. Women may feel included within this Muslim matrix either through militancy and the pursuit of social justice, intellectual and professional labour linked to rationality as a privileged attribute within the Islamic tradition, the primacy of motherhood or strict religious observance.

So how do gender and religion relate and intersect? Or rather gender and *dīn*? Being relational in nature, gender is inevitably a regulator of generic identification. Bodies and consequently sexed *subjectivities* are pervaded by culture, putting the 'I' in relation, situation and position through transitive and contingent articulations (Richard, 2002, p 100). We may, therefore, rethink identities from a nomadic (Braidotti, 2004), intersectional and translocational (Anthias, 2006) perspective. Here we would question the juxtaposition of different identities. What tensions, strategies and representations come into play as a Muslim woman in Argentina? Below we share excerpts of the account of a young convert to Islam. Her life story no doubt reflects certain aspects of the matrix discussed above, but certain discontinuities with the stories of the women born into Arab Muslim families can also be discerned.

## "I'm still just as Argentinian as the next woman": beyond identity politics

Argentinean popular culture constitutes a complex heteroclite constellation that embraces anything from slogans like 'Not One Less'[5] to the most naturalized forms of micro-machismo, inequality and gender-based violence. Discourses from conservative Catholic – of great weight and influence in Argentinian society – and politically reactionary agents also converge in this mainstream. The internal Other (popular sectors, indigenous peoples, religious minorities) and the external Other (especially migrants from neighbouring countries) are perceived either as inferior or as a threat to Argentina.

What happens in this context to women from a religious minority (erroneously) associated with an ethnicity? The Muslim woman who wears the *hijab* on a daily basis is more likely to receive negative feedback in the public space, the result of either ignorance or *genderized Islamophobia* (Zine, 2006). Therefore the negotiation of identity acquires a different, clearly political complexion, though not always formulated as such: a *politics of identity* through the *voice*, the *body*, the *image* and its *symbolization*. Also, what happens when against all odds religious normativity, and its sexual and family morality are used to combat certain mainstream imaginaries and gender technologies, and to reverse what they conceive as certain female privileges that culturally would have been lost?

Zahra is a 25-year-old Argentinean woman who embraced Islam more than six years ago. She first came in contact with the religion through Arab culture by learning the *derbake* (a percussion instrument) and the Arabic language in the mosque she regularly attends. Zahra, who described herself as an agnostic from a relatively non-religious family, began to take an interest in the religion of friends she was sharing these spaces of socialization with. She felt Islam furnished her with answers to the different questions she had been asking herself for some time, with arguments, she told us, that met both the criteria of rationality and the fundamentals of the faith. She fell in love with a young Muslim (also a convert), whom she married and started a family with. She has three children and is trying to continue her university studies while freelancing on the side. She takes a strong and clearly defined religious line (as a Shīite Muslim) and political stance (defending governments like Cristina Fernández de Kirchner's, and repudiating US international policy and Zionism, while vindicating – albeit not from a feminist standpoint – certain claims by women's movements, such as respected/humanized childbirth and the fight against gender-based violence).

Zahra decided to start wearing the *hijab* every day shortly after 'converting'. She sees it as a way of remembering – and of making visible – that she is just a servant of Allāh (Valcarcel, 2016a). It acts as a technology of the 'I',[6] allowing her to define her being-in-the-world[7] and commitment to divinity as a symbol of female religiosity (Ferreira Barbosa, 2013). It is a way to publicly express her religious choices (inside and outside the community of membership), to confront the reification of the female body, and to show that women can and should be valued for their ethical qualities and intellectual capabilities. She said,

> 'The hijab isn't just a hankie on your head. It's a way of life and conduct. ... Inwardly it's a way of relating to others, of relating to God. Of knowing you're a servant of God and that he's provided these tools for you to be more peaceful in life .... I'm talking about not being dependent on the physical, about being more focused on the intellectual and the spiritual. ... And God is giving me this tool. ... And actually, when you put it into practice, it's absolutely the way God says it is. ... You start relating to other people and impose a different kind of respect' [Valcarcel, 29 May 2013].

On the question of interactions with other social actors and reactions to Islamic attire she differs with Siam and Jasmine. Zahra narrates,

> 'I've never experienced aggression of any kind at all. This is a very open country. In Spain or France it's very different. But here we're a mixed bag, we're all children of immigrants, nobody's a native of this country ... it also depends on how you present yourself to others. ... You have to break down the prejudices one by one, with your daily actions. I've come across people who are surprised at me drinking maté: but aren't you [Muslim]? Yes, but it's my religion; this is my culture, Argentinian culture. ... I haven't lost my culture because of my religion. Customs change, but I'm still just as Argentinian as the next woman' [Valcarcel, 29 May 2013]

Zahra's account reveals the complex processual nature of *identitarian assemblages* (Puar, 2013). On the one hand, Islamic ethics and attire appear as 'tools' that help to counteract what she regards as negative aspects of society (emphasis on physical attributes, lack of respect, disintegration of families, violence and so on). On the other hand, there is an emphasis on membership of a national community, and the unequivocal differentiation of culture from religion, even when the first approach to Islam has been through the cultural dimension. Narrative as discursive and performatic interpretation of her personal history is part of a particular normative socio-historical horizon (Ricœur, 2006; Butler, 2005): the experience that it is never transparent but always a constituent part of subjectivity has to be put into context. This involves recognizing its historicity (Scott, 1991).

It is no coincidence Zahra mentions France and Spain as contrasting examples, or pairs the Palestinian resistance with the governments of Latin America and the Islamic principle of social justice. The attack of 11 September 2001 redrew the geopolitical map of the world. The fight against terrorism, imperialism and Zionism should be given a local reading (García Somoza and Valcarcel, 2016b), and interpreted and approached through the Latin American colonial wound (Lugones, 2008).

We are also witnessing a transnational phenomenon in the politics of identity (Segato, 2007), and of the globalization and Westernization of Islam (Roy, 2002). The diacritics that were once camouflaged are today politically expressed (Sayad, 1989). They are becoming icons in motion (García Somoza and Valcarcel, 2016a), whose impact depends, to paraphrase Rancière (2010), on the regime of visibility and social tolerance. Making the choice of religious identity visible by adopting the *hijab* on a daily basis therefore acquires a different (personal, symbolic, political) meaning. It is countered by the idea that any non-Catholic religious symbol is foreign, in this case by appealing to the myth of a 'nation of immigrants' ('Argentinians are descended from the boats') and the 'melting pot', an imaginary that, paradoxically, has contributed to the hypercorrection of the 'real Other' and the homogenization of diversity through various institutions and discourses.

Another aspect revealed through Zahra's testimony is the issue of the subject's agency, specifically her *religious agency* (Bracke, 2008). Mahmood in her constantly cited work *Politics of Piety* (2005) suggests that agency is not reduced to the subversion of norms; on the contrary, it also includes the government of normativity in line with the possibilities offered by the context. She argues that pious subjects are also political subjects. Agency and experience are subject to a social temporality (Butler, 2005, p 19). Zahra explained in her interview that the wearing of the *hijab* and the ethics associated with it serve to preserve family harmony, as well as avoiding distractions and misunderstandings: a way of imposing respect and of constructing – what we might venture to term – a subtle femininity marked by such characteristics as decency, modesty, religious cultivation, acquisition of knowledge, and the role of wife and mother. All things that form part of the (female) Muslim matrix. To illustrate this further we share the testimony of Habi, a 50-year-old Argentinean medic who embraced Islam more than 15 years ago.

> 'To me the basic thing for a Muslim woman, if she has no family, is for her to try and start one, and it should be built on the foundations of Islam, and she has to respect her husband's right all the time, just the way her rights will be respected ... Islam is well adapted to the modern world ... It isn't an anachronism ... Islam doesn't look kindly – and I think it's right – on a woman in a man's place, on a woman wanting to occupy a man's space, what we strive for is to respect creation as Allāh made it, not to change it. You can't change a woman's energy, it isn't good for a woman's health, so if she goes out to work, she should choose a profession that's appropriate to female energy, a profession with a certain tranquillity, which she can do from home or somewhere with an atmosphere of peace and quiet' [Valcarcel, 19 September 2015].

In the same vein Nabira told us that women should not lose sight of the special nature of the female essence. "I believe it's important," she says, "for women to construct themselves on an image of difference, not of equality with men ... Let's occupy a space with the same opportunities, but based on a platform of difference. Difference has to mean equal opportunities" [García Somoza, 10 September 2007]. Discourses of this kind do not confront hegemonic sex/gender normativity directly. Indeed, many Muslim women who are strongly religious and respectful of norms defend the heterosexual family model and the complementarity of roles. Nevertheless, from the same perspective and as mouthpieces of the social function traditionally attributed to women, they legitimize and reposition their status, demanding respect and recognition, claiming a collaborative conjugal bond and rejecting gender-based violence.

The social subject, says Butler, vitally appropriates the norms governing its feasibility (2005, p 20). Argentinean Muslim women can choose – and here lies their capacity for agency – to espouse certain principles of the religious family and sexual morality, precepts that guarantee their membership of and position in the community, while not violating or contradicting socially obtained and recognized rights. These are women with a series of tools and resources available to them (symbolic, political, intellectual, cultural, economic) that enable them to articulate – with greater or lesser capacity for action and decision – a variety of normative discourses, as well as their multiple locus of identities. These are certainly different from the negotiating possibilities of many Muslim women in some countries with Islamic majorities or those occupying a position of marginality within the fabric of other Western societies.

There are no conflicts in Argentinean society like 'the veil issue': women may wear the *hijab* to school or university, or even on their national identity documents. Yet specific instances of genderized Islamophobia can and do occur (Zine, 2006). The fight against the stigmatization of Muslim women in particular (with the emphasis on intellectual capacity, ethical values, free choice or female leadership, as against the stereotype of the submissive oppressed woman) and against the 'thingification' of the female body in general. To this effect, women not only take part in panels about inter-religious dialogue, lectures and various cultural and religious events, but also employ the potential of the Internet (social media, websites) and social networks to disseminate what they label 'the unknown side' or 'the true face' of Islam in an attempt to demystify the representations prevailing in the Western mainstream.

An approach emphasizing the institutional and *the public space* can in turn be enriched by one that makes room for Muslim agency and corporeality – personal, social and political – as dimensions of analysis. Both approaches are useful in addressing, for example, the discretional adoption of Islamic dress in a society like Argentina's (García Somoza and Valcarcel, 2016a). Scott claims that 'identities don't pre-exist their strategic political invocations' (2009, p 285). They are, on the contrary, rooted in (gendered and racialized) bodies and (ethnic and religious) cultural traditions. In certain Western contexts, *Muslim identity* (in generic terms) and the *hijab* (as a symbolic condensation) are invoked as 'a rhetorical political strategy'. Taking up Scott's concept again, Muslim identity presents its own 'fantasy echoes'.[8] In other words, 'constructed in complex and diffracted relation to others' (2009, p 292).

The Islamic way of life (*dīn*) presents itself to us in the local context of Argentina as a choice: either to continue, preserve and disseminate the traditions of ancestors from other lands or to embrace a minority religion made invisible and/or stigmatized by Argentinean society. For converts, it involves gradual changes in their everyday lives (food, behaviour, dress, discursive apparatus and so on). Islam satisfies various personal needs for each of these subjectivities. But, at the same time, it offers a support or frame through which to reposition themselves as social and/or political actors: for example, to claim certain women's rights or tackle machismo by deploying a 'tolerable'[9] moral discourse while at the same time anchoring themselves in the status of mother, wife or believer; or to make possible the construction of a certain politico-religious trajectory or militancy when it comes to international causes (Syria, Lebanon, Palestine) given a local reading – that is to say, the development of a *political Islam* – and in some sectors of the local community there are even traces of a *nationalization of Islam* (García Somoza and Valcarcel, 2016a). On the contrary, this sometimes offers the opportunity to differentiate oneself (by a token of ethnicity or class) through the adoption of an *Arabized Islam* with a hint of exoticism and associated – through common sense – with luxury or purchasing power.

In a nutshell, the display of diacritics serves in many cases to anchor the membership of the (local and transnational) community and to establish affective, ethical and political bonds towards such common goals as the struggle against Islamophobia, solidarity with whatever national or international cause or public visibility. Through these fantasy echoes Islamic discourse and Muslim identity (re)compose a situated imagination (Stoetzler and Davis, 2002) and therefore the interpretation of the past (the exemplary memory of the Prophet and the women of his family), the present (the diagnosis of 'social ills') and the future (the yearning for better times). Hence the reconstruction of a politico-religious memory that emerges out of the juxtaposition of various historicities, discourses, identities and subjectivities, alongside the formation of other models of femininity or womanhood available in the fabric of post-feminist 'popular culture' (McRobbie, 2004).

## Concluding thoughts

By telling us fragments of her story, each Muslim woman interviewed is accounting for herself. She reflects on her personal and religious experience. She reprocesses and interprets it, constructing her singularity. She explains it using the various discursive regimes she has available, which at the same time interpellate and condition her. To put it succinctly, she is framed within the 'temporality of a set of norms that contest the singularity of my [her] history' (Butler, 2005, p 81). The selection, omission and valuation of certain aspects of her narratable life manifests the agency of every woman, the way she reconstructs and shapes her narrative identity (Ricœur, 2006). Language in Scott's words is the 'stage on which history is performed' (Scott, 1991, p 793). In this sense, the exhibition and operation of the norm also make possible the emergence of reflective being and *being-with-memory* (Butler, 2005, p 160).

The question about ethnographic authority, the role of researchers and operations of power returns again and again on recalling each interview. During each interview, an ethical relationship is established that has us as a counterpart, enabling mutual recognition and legibility. The asymmetry arising from the fact that the interviews are informed by the interests of our research projects is inescapable. Yet, when the Other agrees to participate and is willing to talk about aspects of her life, she is to an extent 'desubalternizing' herself. Her narrative constitutes identity formation. It may be sheer accident that Zahra was wearing the *hijab* despite our meeting taking place at her home in the presence of a female interviewer with no other participants and no visual recording equipment of any kind. Nevertheless, this detail prompted our question about the politics of the image (the government of physical appearance) and the politics of the voice (Dolar, 2006).

The voice is situated between the subject and the Other. The opening of being makes a reflection about oneself possible (Dolar, 2006, p 117). This perspective allows us to conceive of the testimony beyond the asymmetrical relation between scholar and 'subject of study'. It is not only a matter of trying to reduce distances through methodological strategies but of rethinking this instance as a moment when the other person's voice interpellates us, and attempts to be intelligible and audible (Dolar, 2006, p 122). Zahra, her beautiful young face defined by the Islamic headscarf, *giving her account of herself* at the anthropologist's request; on the other, the person listening to her and asking questions, trying (erroneously and absurdly) to find 'a revelation' or absolute correspondence and transparency between discourse and religious practice; Zahra's *hijab* lending form and body to her *voice*, making her visible as a political subject (Mahmood, 2005) with a form of agency that may not subvert normativity but nevertheless implies the politicization of identity and therefore the social relation that permeates our interview.

'The ideological interpellation can never quite silence this other voice, and the distance between the two voices opens the space of the political' (Dolar, 2006, p 123). This (de- and re-) constructive – albeit codified – aspect of sonority acquires a new dimension when we think about it in terms of its texture or symbolic fabric. It is of particular significance that the first pillar of religious practice is the aš-šahādah, or *shahada* (statement of faith): a ritual formula publicly recited in Arabic testifying that 'There is no god but God. Muhammad is the messenger of God.' Such testimony takes on even greater significance for those who embrace Islam. The voice, the message and the public (human and divine) form a network whereby the subject's spiritual choice is made visible: a watershed in the narrative identity.

The *matrical Islamic body* in its personal, social and political dimension[10] intervenes in and shapes the daily lives of each of the women, not just during community rituals and events. Appearance (the wearing of Islamic dress, the kind of behaviour) and voice (moderate tone, avoiding unseemly vocabulary, use of Arabic religious phrases and specific political terms) acquire a surprising relevance during daily presentations and in interviews. Speaking out against the stigmatization and 'thingification' of women is a way of positioning themselves as individuals. And, in community terms, the transformation of *historical alterity* into *political identity* may be a way of confronting the subalternization of difference.

Finally, we wish to emphasize that the gender perspective[11] allows an analysis of any social process or phenomenon, but also facilitates and promotes empathy with our female interlocutors. It, thus, gives us an insight into various facets of female agency – and hence of empowerment – as against the mainstream, the media or even hegemonic religious discourses. We came across Muslim women who by choice undermine the myths of submission and false consciousness. There are women who use Muslim ethics to redefine their status within the couple and the family, and others who make themselves visible in the public space through their membership of a given community (by tackling head-on the 'thingification' of the female body, the stigmatization of their religion and other praxes). They differently inhabit and connote the dialogical continuum that makes up the public–private space (Benhabib, 1993), which they do not see as divided given their understanding of the Islamic *dīn* as a way or system of life.

We believe that addressing Argentinean Muslim women's discourse and agency in the framework of the communal process of identity (re) construction would help to anchor these historical subjectivities in their specific cultural and spatio–temporal coordinates, allowing us to study the female modalities of government, resignification and politicization of their image and *voice* in greater depth in the future. They speak, narrate themselves, tell us … and so begin to rewrite their history.

## Notes

[1] We are grateful to Ian Barnett for the English translation of this manuscript. We would also like to acknowledge Alejandra Oberti PhD and Constanza Tabbush PhD for the bibliographical contributions in drafting the conclusions.

[2] This is an epistemological position. It is directly linked to the emergence of the anthropological question, which originates in cultural contact and forces us to reflect on it (Krotz, 1994, p 8). Krotz explains that alterity or otherness is not synonymous with differentiation. The anthropological question, perspective and practice are built on the dialectical game that tries to make familiar what we find strange ('exotic' in the discipline's jargon) and to make strange – that is, to dequotidianize or denature – what is familiar to us, thus creating a tension between the Us/Others and even dislocating our own subjectivity.

[3] As Guber (2001) points out, the ethnography interview is characterized by its threefold nature: the *approach*, which falls under a register of non-separation with ordinary communication; the *method*, which relies on a particular form of information gathering based on the exchange between the ethnologist and her interlocutors; and the *text*, which produces a particular form of interpretation of the information.

[4] A Muslim woman of around 50 years of age, housewife and the mother of two daughters. Interviewed by García Somoza in 2013. Pseudonyms are used to protect the identity of all interviewees.

[5] 'Ni una menos': a slogan popularized in Argentina after the mass demonstrations of 3 June 2015, 2016 and 2017. It arose as a collective rallying cry against male violence and femicide in Argentina, Brazil and Chile, and quickly spread to other countries in Latin America.

[6] We follow Foucault's definition (1990).

[7] We understand the concept of *being-in-the-world* as defined by Merleau-Ponty (1993) and taken up again by Csordas (1994) in his *embodiment* paradigm.

[8] In her analysis, Scott defines the echo as 'an imperfect return of sound' (2009, p 287). She sees identifications as imagined repetitions in which echo and fantasy

are interwoven. The echo, on the other hand, repeats and prolongs the sound, making possible the interpretive processes.

[9]  Less often confronted and rejected than feminist discourse due to the nature of its aims and rationale.

[10]  An analytical distinction made by Scheper-Hughes and Lock (1987) used in Valcarcel (2014) García Somoza and Valcarcel (2016a).

[11]  We draw on Monica Tarducci (PhD, University of Buenos Aires, member of the Feminist Anthropologists' Collective, IIEGE, FFyL-UBA). We acknowledge her contributions.

# References

Achilli, E. (2005) *Investigar en antropología social. Los desafíos de transmitir un oficio.* Rosario: Laborde.

Akmir, A. (2009) *Los árabes en América Latina. Historia de una inmigración.* Madrid: Siglo XXI – Biblioteca de Casa Árabe.

Anthias, F. (2006) 'Belonging in a Globalising and Unequal World', in N. Yuval-Davis, K. Kannabiran and U. Vieten (eds) *The Situated Politics of Belonging.* London: Sage, pp 17–31.

Anthias, F. and Yuval-Davis, N. (1983) 'Contextualizing Feminism: Gender, Ethnic and Class Divisions', *Feminist Review*, 15, pp 62–75.

Arendt, H. (1988) [1958]) *La condition de l'homme moderne*, Paris: Agora/Pocket.

Benhabib, S. (1993) 'Feminist Theory and Hannah Arendt's Concept of Public Space', *History of the Human Sciences*, 6(2), pp 97–114.

Bracke, S. (2008) 'Conjugating the Modern/Religious, Conceptualizing Female Religious Agency: Contours of a "Post-Secular" Conjuncture', *Theory, Culture & Society*, 25(6), pp 51–67.

Braidotti, R. (2004) *Feminismo, diferencia sexual y subjetividad nómade.* Barcelona: Gedisa.

Butler, J. (2005) 'Dar cuenta de sí mismo', in J. Butler, *Dar cuenta de sí mismo: Violencia ética y responsabilidad.* Buenos Aires: Amorrortu, pp 13–60.

Caña Cuevas, S. (2006) 'Islam y relaciones de género en San Cristóbal de las Casas, Chiapas', in *Centro de Investigaciones y Estudios Superiores en Antropología Social* (CIESAS). Mexico City.

Chanfrault-Duchet, M-F. (1983) 'L'énonciation et les ruses du sujet', *Revue des Sciences Humaines (Récits de vie, II)*, 192, pp 99–107.

Crenshaw, K.W. (1989) 'Demarginalizing the Intersection of Race and Sex: A Black Feminist Critique of Antidiscrimination Doctrine, Feminist Theory and Antiracist Politics', *The University of Chicago Legal Forum*, 140, pp 139–67.

Csordas, T.J. (ed) (1994) *Embodiment and Experience: The Existential Ground of Culture and Self.* Cambridge: Cambridge University Press.

Dolar, M. (2006) 'The Politics of the Voice', in M. Dolar, *A Voice and Nothing More*. Cambridge-London: The MIT Press, pp 104–25.

Ferreira Barbosa, F. (2010) 'Olhando para o feminino em circulação. Notas etnográficas sobre mulheres muçulmanas', *Fazendo Gênero*, 9: (online) http://www.fazendogenero.ufsc.br/9/site/anaiscomplementares.

Ferreira Barbosa, F. (2013) 'Diálogos sobre o uso do véu (hiyab): empoderamento, identidade e religiosidade', *Perspectivas: Revista de Ciências Sociais*, 43, pp 183–98.

Foucault, M. (1990) *Tecnologías del Yo y otros textos afines*. Barcelona: Paidós.

García Somoza, M.S. (2017) *Entre Fátima et Evita: Identités, espaces de participation et de sociabilités religieuses des femmes musulmanes en Argentine*, unpublished PhD thesis, Université Paris Descartes-Universidad de Buenos Aires.

García Somoza, M. and Valcarcel, M. (2016a) 'Íconos, sentidos e identidades en movimiento: estrategias, prácticas y discursos en una comunidad musulmana de la Ciudad de Buenos Aires', *Revista Estudios Sociales*, 56, pp 51–66.

García Somoza, M. and Valcarcel, M. (2016b) 'My Heart Beats Hussein: Identity, Politics and Religion in a Shi'a Community in Buenos Aires', paper presented at the Conference *Shia Minorities in the Contemporary World: Migration, Transnationalism and Multilocality*, 20 May, Chester University (UK).

Ginsburg, F. (2004) 'Cuando los nativos son nuestros vecinos', in M. Boivin and A. Rosato (eds) *Constructores de Otredad. Una introducción a la Antropología Social y Cultural*. Buenos Aires: Antropofagia, pp 186–93.

Guber, R. (2001) *La etnografía. Método, campo y reflexividad*. Bogotá: Grupo Editorial Norma.

Krotz, E. (1994) 'Alteridad y pregunta antropológica', *Alteridades*, 4(8), pp 5–11.

Lugones, M. (2008) 'Colonialidad y género: hacia un feminismo decolonial', in W. Mignolo (ed), *Género y descolonialidad*. Argentina: Ediciones del Signo, pp 13–54.

Mahmood, S. (2005) *Politics of Piety: The Islamic Revival and the Feminist Subject*. Princeton: Princeton University Press.

McRobbie, A. (2004) 'Post-Feminism and Popular Culture', *Feminist Media Studies*, 4(3), pp 255–64.

Merleau-Ponty, M. (1993) [1945] *Phénoménologie de la perception*. Paris: Gallimard.

Mohanty, Ch. (2008) [1984] 'Bajo los ojos de Occidente: Academia feminista y discursos coloniales', in L. Suárez Navaz and R.A. Hernández Castillo (eds) *Descolonizando el feminismo: Teorías y prácticas desde los márgenes.* Madrid: Cátedra, pp 112–61.

Montenegro, S. (2011) 'Actualidad de los estudios sobre el Islam. Reflexión a partir de temas y abordajes globales y locales', *Pensar: Epistemología, política y Ciencias Sociales*, 2, pp 115–29.

Montenegro, S (2015) 'Formas de adhesión al Islam en Argentina: conversión, tradición, elección, reasunción y tránsito intra-islámico', *Horizonte*, 13(38), pp 674–705.

Moreno E. (2010) *El proceso de conversión al islam en la construcción de la identidad religiosa en Buenos Aires: el campo islámico como un fenómeno multiforme.* Bachelor dissertation in Anthropology, Universidad de Buenos Aires.

Puar, J. (2013) 'I Would Rather Be a Cyborg than a Goddess: Intersectionality, Assemblage, and Affective Politics', *Meritum, Revista de Direito da Universidade FUMEC*, 8(2), pp 371–90.

Rancière, J. (2010) *El espectador emancipado.* Buenos Aires: Manantial.

Richard, N. (2002) 'Género', in Altamirano, C. (ed) *Términos críticos de la Sociología de la Cultura*, Buenos Aires: Paidós, pp 95-101.

Ricoeur, P. (2006) 'La vida: un relato en busca de narrador', in *Ágora, Papeles de Filosofía*, 25(2), pp 9-22.

Roy, O. (2002) 'Islamisme, fondamentalisme et néo-fondamentalisme: de quoi parle-t-on ?', *Politique Autrement*, 26. Available at: http://www.politique-autrement.org/Lettre-no-26-Islamisme-fondamentalisme-et-neo-fondamentalisme-de-quoi-parle-t-on.

Sayad, A. (1989) *La Double Absence*. Paris: Seuil.

Sayyid, S. (2012) 'La umma como diáspora', in G. Martín Muñoz and R. Grosfoguel (eds) *La islamofobia a debate: la genealogía del miedo al islam y la construcción de los discursos anti-islámicos.* Madrid: Casa Árabe, pp 191–218.

Scott, J.W. (1988) 'Genre: une catégorie utile d'analyse historique', *Les Cahiers du GRIF,* nn. 37–38, pp 125–53.

Scott, J.W. (1991) 'The Evidence of Experience', *Critical Inquiry*, 17(4), pp 773–97.

Scott, J.W. (2009) 'Fantasy Echo: History and The Construction of Identity', *Critical Inquiry*, 27(2), Winter, pp 284–304.

Segato, R. (2007) *La Nación y sus otros: Raza, etnicidad y diversidad religiosa en tiempos de políticas de la identidad.* Buenos Aires: Prometeo.

Scheper-Hughes, N. and Lock, M. (1987) 'The Mindful Body: A Prolegomenon to Future Work in Medical Anthropology', *Medical Anthropological Quarterly*, 1(1), pp 6–41.

Spivak, Ch. (2009) [1988] *Les subalternes peuvent-elles parler ?*. Paris: Éditions Amsterdam.

Staunæs, D. (2003) 'Where have all the subjects gone? Bringing together the concepts of intersectionality and subjectification', *NORA-Nordic Journal of Feminist and Gender Research*, 2(11), pp 101–10.

Stoetzler, M. and Yuval Davis, N. (2002) 'Standpoint Theory, Situated Knowledge and the Situated Imagination', *Feminist Theory*, 3, pp 315–33.

Valcarcel, M. (2014) 'Sierva de Allah: cuerpo, género e Islam', *Revista Cultura y Religión*, 8(2), pp 54–82.

Valcarcel, M. (2016a) 'Construcciones y trayectorias identitarias de mujeres que profesan el islam en Argentina', *Clivajes, Revista de Ciencias Sociales*, 3(6), pp 31–57.

Valcarcel, M. (2016b) 'Los hijos y la belleza del mundo: más allá de la moral sexual y familiar en el Islam', *Zona Franca*, 24, pp 74–99.

Voigt Espinola, C. (2013) 'El velo que (des)cubre a la comunidad árabe musulmana de Florianópolis', in S. Montenegro and F. Benlabbah (eds) *Musulmanes en Brasil. Comunidades, instituciones e identidades.* Rosario: UNR, pp 93–116.

Zine, J. (2006) 'Unveiled Sentiments: Gendered Islamophobia and Experiences of Veiling Among Muslim Girls in a Canadian Islamic School', *Equity and Excellence in Education*, 39(3), pp 239–52.

# EIGHT

# The impact of religious unorthodoxy on family choices and women's well-being in Turkey

*F. Kemal Kızılca*

## Introduction

Studies investigating the gendered effects of religion tend to conclude that women's workforce participation increases as societies become more secular (Hertel, 1988; Guetto et al, 2015). However, any proposition that connects secularity with women's empowerment remains incomplete as long as the link between secularity-led paid work and women's welfare is not clearly defined. Empowerment relates not only to employment, but also to the resulting changes in domestic work and time use patterns (Charusheela, 2003). This chapter provides evidence from Turkey, a Muslim-majority country, on how religious *un*orthodoxy is related to number of children and generations living in a household, both of which strongly link to women's time burden, and consequently, to their welfare.

The evidence provided in this chapter complements the findings of my recent contribution (Kızılca, 2016) in which I develop an empirical strategy which considers consumption of religiously forbidden (*haram*) or disliked (*makruh*) goods in Turkey as a signal of a household's unorthodox stance. There I show that consumption of products that contradict orthodox Sunni taboos exhibits a strong positive effect on women's labour force participation, and to some extent, educational participation. Unorthodoxy stimulates women's participation not only directly, but also through mediating factors, including lower numbers of children, and number of generations living in the same household. However, that study does not provide a detailed analysis of household structures and 'sinful' consumption. The current chapter establishes that missing link between religious unorthodoxy with women's agency, by showing that *haram* and *makruh* consumption associates with a significant decrease in both the number of children, and the probability of being a 'large' household. A number of previous works, mainly by feminist scholars, touch on the issue of gendered connotations of liquor consumption and regulations in Turkey.[1] This study contributes to the existing literature by providing novel statistical evidence on the link between 'sinful' consumption and household structures that exert an important influence on women's time use patterns.

Turkey constitutes a useful environment to investigate the effects of religion on gender indicators for multiple reasons. As the great majority of Turkish citizens declare themselves as Muslims (99% according to the World Values Survey), any study conducted in Turkey reflects results from a population that lives under the influence of Islam, which stands as the most controversial denomination with respect to its relations with fundamental freedoms, democratic values and women's rights. Moreover, despite the backward trend in the last decade, Turkey has a unique history of a laic state across Muslim-majority countries; and a non-negligible proportion of Turkish citizens have secular lifestyles. The relative freedom in (non)religious practices in Turkey allows researchers to observe the societal variations across secular/religious or orthodox/unorthodox lines and interpret them with respect to their gendered outcomes. Lastly, the drift towards Sunni authoritarianism in Turkey in the last decade makes an important case to observe how women's issues and body politics are instrumentalized in the process of a theocratic transformation.

Previous research on religion and fertility nexus suggests that fertility rates fall with secularization (Heaten and Cornwall, 1989; Newman and Hugo, 2006; Blume, 2009; Guetto et al, 2015). The effect of religion on household types (nuclear vs. large households), however, remains underexplored. This chapter investigates both issues by using the concept of unorthodoxy. The notions of secularization and unorthodoxy do not necessarily overlap, as followers of certain denominations and sects (for example *Alevi*s), differ substantially from orthodox Sunnis in their lifestyles and gender relations – even if they define themselves as religious. The use of 'unorthodoxy' is advantageous in the sense that it accounts for the behaviour of the members of heterodox sects or denominations, along with secular constituents of society.

This chapter starts with a literature review on the effects of religion on women's status, fertility rates and family types. Afterwards, the methodology as well as the dataset used in this study are explained. The following section provides the multivariate statistical estimates on family types and number of children within households. These results are discussed in the subsequent section. The final section provides the concluding remarks.

## Literature review

Turkey occupies an important position in the literature that explores interconnections between gender and secularization because of the revolutionary developments in the *laïcité* (secularity) principle and women's rights just after the foundation of the Turkish Republic in 1923, as well as the resurgence of Sunni Islam as an important element in the political arena in the last decade(s).

Kandiyoti (1987, 1991) demonstrates how the issue of women's rights was central to the definition and formation of *laïcité*[2] principle in Turkish history. First feminist organizations in Turkey appeared during the second constitutional era of the Ottoman Empire after 1908. This period also witnessed the rise of Turkish nationalism as a secular ideology against Islamism to which Ottoman rulers adhered as a panacea against the disintegration of the Empire. Women's status constituted a core topic in the debates among 'Turkists', Islamists, and the 'Westernists', while the leading voices of the nationalist movement (both women and men) were also outspoken supporters of feminist ideas. Consequently, the foundation of the Turkish nation state marked substantial improvements in *de jure* rights of women, which included provision of equal access to educational rights, abolishment of polygamy, equal rights in marriage, employment rights, suffrage, and so on.

Tekeli (1981) shows that as a reflection of the improvements in women's rights in the political sphere, the share of women representatives in the Turkish Parliament remained well above Western averages until the mid-1940s. She further asserts that in the 1930s, policies aiming at women's empowerment played a symbolic role in distinguishing the ideology of the newly founded Turkish state from the fascist states of the era that promoted secondary roles for women. Kandiyoti (1987) and Toprak (1981) suggest that the positive impact of these revolutionary steps in terms of women's rights remained limited in rural areas in the early republican period. Another limitation of these policies arose from the fact that they consisted of rights 'granted' by mostly male rulers at the cost of deterrence of further development of women's organizations (Tekeli, 2010).

While the Turkish Republic had long been considered the only secular country in the Muslim-majority world, anti-secularist movements always existed throughout its history. These movements became more visible in the political arena in 1970s, when the National Salvation Party, a Sunni Islamist organization, participated in three successive coalition governments (Toprak, 1981). Political Islamists gained momentum after the 1980 military coup (Şen, 2010), and eventually came to power when the Justice and Development Party (AKP) formed a single-party government after the 2002 elections. Consequently, in contrast to the establishment of the *laïcité* principle during the foundation of the Republic, the last decade witnessed the rise of Sunni Islam as the primary guide in state governance (Şen, 2010; Criss, 2010).

Sunni transformation of the Turkish state has important implications for the status and the freedoms of the secular and non-Sunni citizens of the society, who constitute the subject of this study. Membership of certain Sunni *tariqat*s (sects) remains essential in determining both individuals' and institutions' (for example firms' and NGOs') interactions with the state. Non-Sunnis – especially Alevis –, non-Muslims, atheists, seculars, or any group of people whose lifestyle does not comply with orthodox Sunni doctrine have been labelled as 'either privileged and exclusionary or as potentially treasonous' (Kandiyoti, 2016, p 105). At the institutional level, regulations and policies that discriminate against non-Sunni denominations are rather concrete. An ever-increasing proportion of government expenditure has been directed to the promotion of the Sunni creed through exponentially growing numbers of religious courses, preachers, publications, mosques and other buildings assigned to these activities. Unlike state-owned Sunni mosques, the government refuses to officially recognize Alevis' *cem evleri* (gathering houses) as places of worship and thus does not provide them with any kind of financial support. Similarly, state-determined curricula of the mandatory religious courses in primary and secondary education, or the publications of the Directorate of Religious Affairs, almost totally ignore the Alevi creed and other religions (Öktem, 2008; Toprak et al, 2009; Karakaya-Stump, 2017).

Strict limitations imposed on production, sales and promotion of alcoholic drinks, as well as the surge in the excise tax on alcohol remain among the religiously motivated interventions in unorthodox lifestyles. Serving of liquor is prevented in government premises, fewer pubs and restaurants are granted sales permits, and they are forced to move out of downtown areas in many cities. Alcoholic drinks are pushed out of the public sphere in effect (Arat, 2010; Evered and Evered, 2016a).

Sunnification policies have strong gendered implications. One of the important developments is the lifting of the notorious headscarf ban in 2008. Before then, veiled women were asked to take their headscarves off before entering certain state premises on secularism grounds. Lifting of the ban is particularly important for women who refused to take their headscarves off in the 'public sphere', thus were not allowed to attend universities or work in the public sector before the amendment to the legislation. Although research suggests a strong correlation between wearing headscarves and accepting more traditional roles against working (Konda, 2007), this amendment has the potential to stimulate educational and labour force participation of veiled women.

Body politics – by which I refer to a set of regulations, legislations and discourses that target women's realms – plays a central role in differentiation of political stances of government circles and the opposing unorthodox groups. One of the fault lines is the government's handling of rising violence against women and children as individual cases as opposed to their categorization as being political and systematic by dissent. Controversies heighten as the government prescribes more traditionalism and religion as cures against the 'disease', and rejects criticisms regarding the impunity of the perpetrators either in defence of patriarchal values or because of their institutional connections (Kandiyoti, 2016). Moreover, in line with the policy of considering women primarily as carers, the government initiated an 'at least three children' campaign and provided maternity benefits to stimulate fertility (Yilmaz, 2015). Legal limitations were put into force on abortion and Caesarean section operations in 2012. In defence of these pro-natalist and traditionalist policies, the government representatives outspokenly rejected the notion of gender equality and repeatedly condemned feminists on several occasions.

In Turkey, followers of the Alevi sect differ from Sunnis both in their unorthodox religious practices and in gender norms. For example, they do not necessarily abstain from alcoholic drinks, paintings or sculptures of human figures; and Alevi women do not use hijab – even including the devout ones. Alevis pray, women and men together, by performing their ritual dances (*semah*) in *cem evleri* (gathering houses); and women can lead these rituals.[3] Therefore, the umbrella term 'unorthodox' defined in this study refers to a combination of quite heterogeneous groups, including secular Sunnis, Alevis, non-Muslims and so on.

Previous works show that religiosity affects fertility rates positively, regardless of religious denominations, or geographies (Frejka and Westoff, 2008; Norris and Inglehart, 2011). However, mediating factors, including the efforts of religious institutions such as churches, may boost the magnitude of the effect (McQuillan, 2004). Policies to promote fertility are not gender neutral in nature; on the contrary, they propose traditional roles for women. These roles might comprise not only child rearing, but also eldercare activities. Few studies investigate the effect of existence of older family members on women's labour force participation. Living with elderly relatives may facilitate women's participation as long as the elderly relative contributes to child rearing (Maurer-Fazio et al, 2011), or may exert a negative effect by increasing the burden of caring responsibilities (Kotsadam, 2011; Dildar, 2015). The direction of the effect might also depend on the gender of the elderly relative. While the presence of an elderly female relative promotes women's employment, living with elderly male relatives may have a negative effect (Spierings, 2014). The following section provides statistical evidence on how religion is linked to number of children (which acts as a proxy for fertility) in households and family types in Turkey.

## Methodology

I draw the data used in this study from TURKSTAT's Household Budget Surveys from 2007 to 2013. TURKSTAT conducts these cross-sectional surveys on approximately 8,000 households each year; and they consist of three types of questionnaires that contain detailed information on households' characteristics, household level consumption statistics and data on individual characteristics. As these surveys do not have a panel dimension (the same households are not surveyed in consecutive years), and they do not include regional information, the data does not allow the researcher to control for time-invariant individual characteristics or cross-regional differences.

Borrowing the empirical strategy that I developed in Kızılca (2016), I define a household as 'unorthodox' if its members declare that they consume *any* amount of products that are considered *haram* (forbidden) or *makruh* (disliked) in the orthodox Sunni faith. In Islamic culture, *Haram* and *makruh* are not confined to consumption habits; in fact, they refer to sinful or discouraged behaviour in general. I limit the analysis to consumption because of its measurability and data availability.

Pork and alcohol are typical examples of *haram* consumption for orthodox Sunnis. As a reflection of religious doctrine in daily life, pork is hardly available for sale in Turkey and it is substituted with other kinds of meat. However, the same does not apply to liquor; its consumption is relatively common despite the strict limitations that have been put into force in the last decade.[4] The usual consumers of liquor in Turkey are the secular Muslims, non-Muslims, Alevis, tourists and some devout Muslims who interpret the religious norms more liberally. The list of *makruh* products or behaviour remains more uncertain, and varies substantially across sects. Dog feeding inside the home is usually considered *makruh*, while other pets are disputed. The 'safe' approach would be to avoid feeding any pets. There is also a disagreement on the categorization of shellfish consumption between Hanefi and Shafi branches of the Sunni sect. Hanefis, who consider eating shellfish as *makruh*, represent the majority sect of Sunni Islam in Turkey.

The Household Budget Surveys include information on purchases of alcoholic drinks (*haram*), shellfish, and pet products, which I use as an indicator of pet ownership (*makruh*). While I classify consumers of these products as 'unorthodox', I do not make any remarks regarding the remaining group of households. The 'other' cohort consists of all the remaining households that do not signal unorthodoxy through consumption. Not only devout Sunnis, but also unorthodox Muslims who do not prefer to use these products or households who do not report their real consumption of *haram* fall in this category.

Since this study is concerned with the gendered implications of household structures in the context of caring, I limit the analysis to married women's households. Table 8.1 shows that 2.5 million married women live in unorthodox households, while the number of married women living in the 'other' group was 16.5 million in 2013. The consumption-based definition of unorthodoxy would underestimate the 'true' figure of unorthodox households in Turkey because of a probable avoidance of declaring consumption of alcoholic drinks. This underreporting would imply a downward bias in the coefficient estimations reported in the next section, in which I document separate estimation results for two variables of interest, namely, number of children younger than 15 years of age in the household, and the probability of being a 'large' household. The bias would occur because of the imperfection in identifying the unorthodox households that remain in the 'other' cohort.

In the Household Budget Surveys, approximately 95% of the households have three or fewer children under 15. When a dependent variable accumulates on so few non–negative values, traditional statistical methods that impose no restriction on observed values – such as ordinary least squares (OLS) – produce biased results. This occurs because OLS might estimate negative values for, let us say, the number of doctor's visits of a patient, or the number of accidents that occur in a certain location, which are typical examples to 'count data'. In modelling count data, two other statistical methods, namely, Poisson and negative binomial regression (NBREG) are preferred over OLS as they are designed to address this issue. NBREG has the advantage of

**Table 8.1.** Summary statistics for individual characteristics of married women and their households

| | Unorthodox | | | Other | | |
|---|---|---|---|---|---|---|
| | 2007 | 2013 | All years (2007–13) | 2007 | 2013 | All years (2007–13) |
| In labour force† | 0.2104 | 0.3415 | 0.3073 | 0.1261 | 0.2013 | 0.1781 |
| Educ: primary or less | 0.6775 | 0.6249 | 0.6352 | 0.8521 | 0.7994 | 0.8256 |
| Educ: secondary | 0.2144 | 0.1683 | 0.1949 | 0.1107 | 0.1231 | 0.1168 |
| Educ: tertiary or more | 0.1082 | 0.2068 | 0.1699 | 0.0372 | 0.0775 | 0.0576 |
| Number of children under 15 | 0.9797 | 0.7703 | 0.8634 | 1.3128 | 1.1608 | 1.2355 |
| Hhtype: nuclear | 0.7934 | 0.8414 | 0.8013 | 0.6986 | 0.7515 | 0.7194 |
| Hhtype: large | 0.1995 | 0.1446 | 0.1860 | 0.2917 | 0.2294 | 0.2626 |
| Hhtype: other | 0.0071 | 0.0139 | 0.0127 | 0.0097 | 0.0191 | 0.0180 |
| Urban | 0.7894 | 0.7710 | 0.7721 | 0.6907 | 0.6670 | 0.6752 |
| Real HH income‡ | 1.1916 | 0.9631 | 1.0511 | 0.8078 | 0.6641 | 0.7102 |
| N | 692 | 1,202 | 7,120 | 7,897 | 8,097 | 57,335 |
| N_pop | 1,436,719 | 2,509,094 | 14,378,826 | 15,852,437 | 16,448,173 | 112,803,101 |

Notes: †Excludes unpaid workers in family enterprises.

‡ 0 000 TL in 2003 prices.

accounting for 'overdispersion', which refers to the common problem of excess variability in the data. Nevertheless, in the estimations, both the Poisson and NBREG regressions produced very similar results, as the next section documents.

The second dependent variable used in this study is a binary one, taking the value 1 if the type of the household is 'large', which means that more than one generation live in that household. I use unorthodoxy, woman's education level, household income, a dummy for urban areas as well as year dummies as explanatory variables in the estimations. Household income is certainly affected by the number of the adult members, thus, a bias in its coefficient estimate is expected. Nevertheless, its inclusion in the estimations is essential, as a decision to switch to a nuclear family might bring extra costs. Furthermore, the use of a consumption-based definition of unorthodoxy necessitates controlling for income.

## Results

As Table 8.1 shows, labour force participation for paid labour of married women remains rather low in Turkey compared to the OECD average (63%), but it has steadily increased since the 2008–9 recession. An 'added worker effect'[5] is the probable driving force behind this trend (Karaoglan and Okten, 2015); however, its discussion falls beyond the scope of this study. What is worth noting are the striking differences between the two cohorts in every indicator shown in Table 8.1. The share of women who have a university degree or more in unorthodox households is almost triple the corresponding share in other households. The average number of children under 15 was 0.77 vs. 1.16 in 2013 for unorthodox and other households, respectively. We also observe approximately a 9 percentage points' difference in the share of nuclear families between the two groups. Furthermore, unorthodox households are more concentrated in urban areas, and the total real income of them remains higher than the other cohort. The sizeable differences with regard to all variables referred to in Table 8.1 imply that higher labour force participation rates of women among the unorthodox households associates also with welfare improvements. In the following, I provide the tests for statistical significance of the differences between the two cohorts.

Estimations for the factors affecting the probability of living in a large household are presented in Table 8.2. The second and third columns of the table provide average marginal effects (A.M.E.)[6] of the explanatory variables after logit and probit regressions, respectively. The size of the coefficients does not change much depending on the estimation method; and they have expected signs: probability of multiple generations living in the same household decreases substantially with education and urbanization at a given income level. The coefficient of Unorthodox, the main variable of interest, implies that consumption of *haram* or *makruh* products associates with a reduction around 5.5 percentage points in the probability of a married woman living in a large household. The magnitude of its effect is not as high as a degree in education, or urbanization; nevertheless, it is highly significant and not negligible.

**Table 8.2.** Probability of living in a large household

|  | OLS | Logit (A.M.E.) | Probit (A.M.E.) |
|---|---|---|---|
| Unorthodox | −0.052‡ | −0.057** | −0.053‡ |
|  | (0.007) | (0.008) | (0.007) |
| Educ.: secondary | −0.107‡ | −0.115‡ | −0.111‡ |
|  | (0.006) | (0.006) | (0.006) |
| Educ.: tertiary or more | −0.229‡ | −0.226‡ | −0.220‡ |
|  | (0.007) | (0.005) | (0.005) |
| Urban | −0.144‡ | −0.140‡ | −0.140‡ |
|  | (0.006) | (0.005) | (0.005) |
| Real HH income† | 0.076‡ | 0.085‡ | 0.074‡ |
|  | (0.006) | (0.005) | (0.005) |
| N | 64,455 | 64,455 | 64,455 |

Notes: Standard errors in parentheses. Base education category is primary school and less. Estimations include year dummies.
† 0 000 TL in 2003 prices.
‡ $p < 0.001$

Table 8.3 provides the results of the estimations for the number of children. Not surprisingly, the number of children correlates negatively with women's education and urbanization. Household income also has a negative relationship with the number of children after controlling for household types. Most importantly, these results show that unorthodoxy associates with a reduction in the number of children of around 0.26, an effect that remains stronger than urbanization.

## Discussion

The statistical estimates provided above establish a significant relation between religion and household structures. Probability of living in a large household for married women decreases (around 5.5 percentage points) if the household signals religious unorthodoxy through consumption. In the same vein, households of married women have significantly lower number of children (−0.26) on average if anyone in the household consume 'sinful' products. These results are obtained after isolating the effects of education, urbanization and household income, thus they are expected to reflect cultural differences between the two cohorts. Switching to nuclear families and reductions in the average number of children associates with women's empowerment both through their positive effect on labour force participation (Kızılca,

2016) and through improvements in time use patterns (Kongar and Memiş, 2017).

**Table 8.3.** Number of children

|  | OLS | Poisson (A.M.E.) | NBREG (A.M.E.) |
|---|---|---|---|
| Unorthodox | −0.231*** | −0.263*** | −0.264*** |
|  | (0.013) | (0.015) | (0.015) |
| Educ.: secondary | −0.342*** | −0.299*** | −0.299*** |
|  | (0.013) | (0.012) | (0.012) |
| Educ.: tertiary or more | −0.484*** | −0.415*** | −0.413*** |
|  | (0.017) | (0.016) | (0.016) |
| Hhtype: large | 0.693*** | 0.695*** | 0.723*** |
|  | (0.019) | (0.020) | (0.024) |
| Hhtype: other | 0.138*** | 0.113** | 0.112** |
|  | (0.039) | (0.037) | (0.037) |
| Urban | −0.228*** | −0.208*** | −0.208*** |
|  | (0.015) | (0.015) | (0.015) |
| Real HH income¶ | −0.006 | −0.026* | −0.027* |
|  | (0.009) | (0.013) | (0.013) |
| N | 64,455 | 64,455 | 64,455 |

Notes: Standard errors in parentheses. Base education category is primary school and less. Base HH type is nuclear family. Estimations include dummies for years and age groups.

¶ 0 000 TL in 2003 prices.
* $p < 0.05$.
** $p < 0.01$.
*** $p < 0.001$.

This study measures religious unorthodoxy through a proxy variable, that is, 'sinful' consumption. Any conclusion that would be drawn from the estimations provided here, therefore, is bound by the representative power of this definition for the unorthodox members of the society. There is no doubt that consumption of alcoholic beverages constitutes a strong sign of religious unorthodoxy in Turkey. However, because of the excessive taxes levied on these drinks, they are no longer affordable for a large group of households. Similarly, pet products are also purchased by mostly higher–income circles. Consequently, the variable 'unorthodox' does not cover a sizeable share of potential consumers who cannot afford these products; and estimations provided here are probably too low to reflect the 'true' effect of detachment from religious taboos.

Another caveat that applies to any interpretation of the results of this study relates to the causality issue. This chapter establishes a link between religious unorthodoxy and household structures. Exploration of push and pull factors that influence a person's or a household's religious stance, however, remains beyond the scope of this study. If forces that drive a person, household or community towards secularity or unorthodoxy at the same time influence household structures, the findings reached in this study might be indicative of correlations, but not causations. According to Inglehart and Norris' (2003) secularization hypothesis, household types change from large to nuclear families, fertility rates drop and people become less religious as a result of industrialization. In other words, industrialization stands as the main determinant behind secularization trends and the change in household structures. In the same vein, experiencing 'existential insecurity', such as living in a life-threatening environment, suffering from large income fluctuations, or lacking healthcare, affects fertility and the probability of becoming more religious positively (Norris and Inglehart, 2011). Thus, one might suggest that the negative link observed between unorthodoxy and household structures in this study might be driven by the effect of industrialization, or insecurity that the people in the 'other' cohort experiences in excess of the unorthodox households. Such a suggestion would require further evidence that the unorthodox households are more exposed to the effects of industrialization, or more 'secure' than the 'other' cohort; however, investigation of this issue falls beyond the scope of the current work. In any case, the significant differences between unorthodox and other households with regard to number of children and household types that are observed in this study remain concrete.

## Conclusion

Household types constitute important determinants of time use patterns of their members. The expected direction of the effect of living with parents on women's workforce participation depends on a number of factors. In the absence of institutional childcare services or in the case of insufficient wage levels to afford them, elderly relatives may foster women's participation by providing those services. However, previous research shows that living with the elderly affects women's participation negatively in Turkey. This may be either due to traditional gender roles that the elderly people advocate within the households, or women's established roles as the main provider of unpaid eldercare activities (Dildar, 2015). It is therefore safe to assert that switching away from large to nuclear or other household types associates with an improvement in women's time constraints in the Turkish case. I would expect the same conclusion to apply to other countries where institutional caring services for elderly people are not widely available. A decrease in the number of children is also known to exert a positive effect on women's time use patterns for the same reasons (Kongar and Memiş, 2017). Consequently, one important conclusion that can be drawn from the results of this study is that increased labour force participation stimulated by religious unorthodoxy (as established in Kızılca, 2016) has a positive association with women's well-being in Turkey as it also encourages switching from large to nuclear families as well as lower fertility rates.

This study both contributes to and moves beyond the literature that establishes a link between secularization and women's agency. The evidence from the Turkish Household Budget Surveys strongly supports the idea that women who live in 'sinful' households, that is households that do not follow Sunni dogmas in their consumption patterns, are faced with lesser burdens of childcare and eldercare responsibilities. In the Turkish context, I would speculate that secularized Sunni households represent the majority of this 'sinful' cohort. I further suggest that the widely presumed religious vs. secular dichotomy in the previous literature misses the substantial dissimilarities among alternative worldviews within Islamic sects. In Turkey, most of these dissimilarities are embodied in Alevi and Sunni differentiation. Thus, the wider notion of 'unorthodoxy' serves better than 'secularization' as it accounts for the unique position of Alevis – including the devout ones – with regard to the linkages between religion and gender relations in Turkish society. Once the gendered implications of unorthodoxy are established, what follows is the importance of protection and promotion of negative freedom of religion, which refers to 'the right to be spared the religious practices of people of other faiths' (Habermas, 2008), on the path to women's empowerment.

## Notes

[1] See Secor (2001), Arat (2010), Evered and Evered (2016a and 2016b), and Kandiyoti (2016).

[2] The Turkish word for secularity, *laiklik*, originates from French. The second Constitution of 1924 defines Turkish state as a *laik* state.

[3] See Shankland (2003) for a detailed survey on Alevis in Turkey; and Karakaya-Stump (2017) for an account of their relations with the state after 2002.

[4] In the Budget Surveys, approximately 7% of households declare alcohol consumption. However, the 'real' figure might double the self-declared amount. See Kızılca (2016) for further details.

[5] 'Added worker effect' refers to a woman's decision to join the workforce to compensate for income loss after a male in the household becomes unemployed or his income decreases.

[6.] 'Marginal effect' is the response of a dependent variable (probability of a large HH, in this case) to a unit change in an explanatory variable.

## References

Abadan-Unat, N., Kandiyoti, D. and Kıray, M.B. (eds) (1981) *Women in Turkish society*, vol. 30, Leiden: Brill.

Arat, Y. (2010) 'Religion, Politics and Gender Equality in Turkey: Implications of a Democratic Paradox?', *Third World Quarterly*, 31(6), pp 869–84.

Blume, M. (2009) 'The Reproductive Benefits of Religious Affiliation', in E. Voland and W. Schiefenhövel (eds) *The Biological Evolution of Religious Mind and Behavior*, Berlin, Heidelberg: Springer, pp. 117–26.

Charusheela, S. (2003) 'Empowering Work? Bargaining Models Reconsidered', in D. Barker and E. Kuiper (eds) *Toward a Feminist Philosophy of Economics*, London: Routledge, pp 287–303.

Criss, N.B. (2010) 'Dismantling Turkey: The Will of the People?', *Turkish Studies*, 11(1), pp 45–58.

Dildar, Y. (2015) 'Patriarchal Norms, Religion, and Female Labor Supply: Evidence from Turkey', *World Development*, 76, pp 40–61.

Evered, E.Ö. and Evered, K.T. (2016a) 'From Rakı to Ayran: Regulating the Place and Practice of Drinking in Turkey', *Space and Polity*, 20(1), pp 39–58.

Evered, E.Ö. and Evered, K.T. (2016b) 'A Geopolitics of Drinking: Debating the Place of Alcohol in Early Republican Turkey', *Political Geography*, 50, pp 48–60.

Frejka, T. and Westoff, C.F. (2008) 'Religion, Religiousness and Fertility in the US and in Europe', *European Journal of Population/ Revue Européenne de Démographie*, 24(1), pp 5–31.

Guetto, R., Luijkx, R. and Scherer, S. (2015) 'Religiosity, Gender Attitudes and Women's Labour Market Participation and Fertility Decisions in Europe', *Acta Sociologica*, 58(2), pp 155–72.

Habermas, J. (2008) 'Notes on Postsecular Society', *New Perspectives Quarterly*, 25(4), pp 17–29.

Heaton, T.B. and Cornwall, M. (1989) 'Religious group variation in the socioeconomic status and family behavior of women', *Journal for the Scientific Study of Religion*, 28(3), pp 283-299.

Hertel, B.R. (1988) 'Gender, Religious Identity and Work Force Participation', *Journal for the Scientific Study of Religion*, 27(4), pp 574–92.

Inglehart, R. and Norris, P. (2003) *Rising Tide: Gender Equality and Cultural Change Around the World*, Cambridge: Cambridge University Press.

Kandiyoti, D. (1987) 'Emancipated but Unliberated? Reflections on the Turkish Case', *Feminist Studies*, 13(2), pp 317–38.

Kandiyoti, D. (1991) 'End of Empire: Islam, Nationalism and Women in Turkey', in D. Kandiyoti (ed) *Women, Islam and the State*, London: Palgrave Macmillan, pp 22–47.

Kandiyoti, D. (2016) 'Locating the Politics of Gender: Patriarchy, Neo-liberal Governance and Violence in Turkey', *Research and Policy on Turkey*, 1(2), pp 103–18.

Karaoglan, D. and Okten, C. (2015) 'Labor-Force Participation of Married Women in Turkey: A Study of the Added-Worker Effect and the Discouraged-Worker Effect', *Emerging Markets Finance and Trade*, 51(1), pp 274–90.

Kızılca, F.K. (2016) 'Breaking with Dogma: Unorthodox Consumption Patterns and Women's Labor Market Outcomes in Turkey', *Feminist Economics*, 22(4), pp 1–30.

Konda (2007) *Gündelik Yaşamda Din, Laiklik ve Türban Araştırması* [Survey on Religion, Laicism and Islamic Headscarf in Daily Life], Istanbul: Konda Araştırma ve Danışmanlık.

Kongar E. and Memiş E. (2017) 'Gendered Patterns of Time Use over the Life Cycle in Turkey', in R. Connelly and E. Kongar (eds) *Gender and Time Use in a Global Context*, New York: Palgrave Macmillan, pp 373–406.

Kotsadam, A. (2011) 'Does informal eldercare impede women's employment? The case of European welfare states', *Feminist Economics*, 17(2), 121–44.

Maurer-Fazio, M., Connelly, R., Chen, L. and Tang, L. (2011). 'Childcare, eldercare, and labor force participation of married women in urban China, 1982–2000,' *Journal of Human Resources*, 46(2), 261–294.

McQuillan, K. (2004) 'When Does Religion Influence Fertility?', *Population and Development Review*, 30(1), pp 25–56.

Newman, L.A. and Hugo, G.J. (2006) 'Women's Fertility, Religion and Education in a Low-fertility Population: Evidence from South Australia', *Journal of Population Research*, 23(1), pp 41–66.

Norris, P. and Inglehart, R. (2011) *Sacred and Secular: Religion and Politics Worldwide*, Cambridge: Cambridge University Press.

Öktem, K. (2008) *Being Muslim at the Margins: Alevis and the AKP*, Middle East Report 246, pp 5–7.

Şen, M. (2010) 'Transformation of Turkish Islamism and the Rise of the Justice and Development Party', *Turkish Studies*, 11(1), pp 59-84.

Shankland, D. (2003) *The Alevis in Turkey: The Emergence of a Secular Islamic Tradition*, London and New York: Routledge.

Spierings, N. (2014) 'The Influence of Patriarchal Norms, Institutions, and Household Composition on Women's Employment in Twenty-Eight Muslim-Majority Countries', *Feminist Economics*, 20(4), pp 87–112.

Tekeli, Ş. (1981) 'Women in Turkish politics' in Abadan-Unat et al (1981), pp 293–310.

Tekeli, Ş. (2010) 'The Turkish Women's Movement: A Brief History of Success', *Quaderns de la Mediterania*, 14, pp 119–23.

Toprak, B. (1981) 'Religion and Turkish Women', in Abadan-Unat et al (1981), pp 281–92.

Toprak, B., Bozan, I., Morgül, T. and Sener, N. (2009) *Being Different in Turkey. Religion, Conservatism and Otherization*, Bogaziçi University, Open Society Foundation (Turkey), Istanbul.

Yilmaz, Z. (2015) '"Strengthening the Family" Policies in Turkey: Managing the Social Question and Armoring Conservative–Neoliberal Populism', *Turkish Studies*, 16(3), pp 371–90.

# Part 3
# Contemporary women's religious experiences

# 'Between me and my God': a life story narrative of conciliating cultural discourses and personalization of Islam

*Ladan Rahbari and Chia Longman*

## Introduction

In the growing body of academic literature on gender, women and Islam, patriarchal and traditional interpretations of women's position in Islam are making place for an increased focus on the more agentic images and aspects of women's practices of religion or religiosity (Guta and Karolak, 2015; Joseph, 2006). This phenomenon reflects women's agency within and beyond the religious frameworks, but at the same time, it incorporates challenges of women in both traditional and modern contexts dealing with traditional interpretations of religion. While in states with traditionalist interpretations of Islam, such as Iran, women's deviance from cultural-religious norms might put their social image and well-being at risk, in Western liberal democracies with Muslim minorities, many religious women struggle with acceptance and inclusion (Yasmeen and Markovic, 2014).[1] This chapter aims to contribute to a better understanding of the relation between gender and Islam by portraying and exploring a subjective account of conciliating religiosity and modern individualism. The chapter thus explores a contemporary subject that affects Muslim's women's lives in the Global North.

The study is conducted based on a life story narrative of a Muslim migrant woman from Iran, now living in Belgium. Her life story and experiences prior to and after migration are analysed to reveal how she has built and made sense of her religiosity in the European context. Muslim migrants in Europe have faced challenges defining their identity and fighting against Islamophobia especially since 11 September 2001. While emancipating themselves from representations purely based on their religious affiliation, Muslim migrants in Europe have largely remained attached to their countries of origin (Amghar, Boubekeur and Emerson, 2007) and their religious and cultural background.

The interviewee's country of origin, Iran, is known for its religious social, legal and political system based on a specific interpretation of Shiite Islam (Darvishpour, 2003; Farazmand, 1995). The Islamic Republic was established after the Iranian revolution in 1979 and has ever since enforced a version of Sharia law as the official law of the land. Despite this traditional legal and social setting, women living under traditional laws have long challenged the patriarchal ideologies attributed to traditional Islamic faith and practice (Moghadam, 2002).

By adopting a life story method, this chapter aims to investigate dynamics of conciliating supposedly contradicting cultural and religious discourses, and to explore religious belonging and personalization of faith. This method is chosen because it provides the opportunity to collect data textured by the respondent from her own interpretation of social circumstances (Sosulski, 2010). Life stories have an arbitrary character; on the one hand, a life story can read as mostly the researcher's description of what was said, done or intimated. On the other hand, it can be a full first-person narrative in the words of the person interviewed (Atkinson, 2002, p 123). We tried to present a combination of both of these approaches.

By analysing this life story narrative, we look at the ways the traditional religious beliefs inherited from the respondent's context of origin are integrated and conciliated with European secular discourses encountered in the West. It is assumed that in the context of migration, a *personalization of faith* takes place, which is used to construct individual identity. Despite distancing herself from traditional interpretations of religion, this does not disrupt the interviewee's sense of belonging to the religious group, while enabling her to integrate in the host society. In the following section, we review some of the existing literature on the personalization of religion in the Iranian context, followed by the methods section, in which the research method and methodological rationale are discussed. Then, after a brief introduction to the interviewee's life story, we move on to discuss the concept of personalization of religion and its implication in a Muslim migrant woman's life.

# Literature review

## *Personalization of religion: the Iranian context*

Anthropologists of religion have long discussed how univocally named sets of religious beliefs, practices and attitudes differ between individuals within religious groups. Gellner's (1969) study of Islam in Morocco showed that in the rural and tribal areas, religion was typified by the *personalization of religion* and a tendency to individualization (Gellner, 1969, cited in David Eller, 2007, p 215). Personalization is not reported only in Islam. Gross's (2012) study in Israeli schools showed that a more differentiated definition of the terms 'religious' and 'secular' was required to reflect the diversity of beliefs formed through personalization of religion. Personalization of faith, and secular perceptions of religion are also discussed to be a trend in various Western contexts, in which there is a tendency to ethical and religious individualism (Iversen, 2006; Smith, 2003).

The secularization process in the West and debates about the relationship between the religious and the secular add a layer of complexity to the issue of personalization and individualization of religion. Some scholars have seen the study of religion as an individual matter, which is problematic since this 'secular' approach depicts religion as something beyond all social analysis, irrelevant to the formation of culture and the study of society (Neusner, 2011). This approach is also seen as problematic since it ignores the historically religious–moral basis of currently secular states (Bedggood and Whiu, 2006), while power attributed to the sacred is an integral factor to understanding the religious and the secular and how they create legitimate discourses to regulate subjects (Moallem, 2005) by justifying the power relations.

Regarding the Islamic faith, personalization trends have sometimes been linked to the incompatibility of religion with social and technical developments as well as Islam's encounter and confrontation with Western philosophy, science and commercial expansion (Nasr, 2010) and forms of discrimination prevalent in the West (Bozorgmehr, 2001). The supposed conflict between Islam and *modernity* has likewise been a matter of debate. Some Muslim intellectuals and modernists have found the solution in a personal Islam, and try to interpret Islam, like Christianity, in terms of an inner relationship between the *individual* and *God*. Proponents of a so-called 'liberal Islam' (Aras, 2004) either do not recognize a social role for religion and religious law, or they consider the full implementation of religious law to belong to a past era of Islamic tradition and non-applicable in the contemporary era

(Mir Hoseini, 2006, p 59). For many intellectuals in Iran today, notions such as modernity, the West, universalism, tradition, and nativism are accepted as given (Mirsepassi, 2010, p 67).

Gender is an important dimension of personal identity in both secular and Islamic discourses and is used by some Iranian diaspora scholars such as Moghissi (1993) and Shahidian (1994) to point out the inadequacy of traditional religion to produce emancipatory effects in women's lives from within religious frameworks, while others are more optimistic that Islam can be compatible with women's empowerment (Najmabadi, 1998). While patriarchal interpretations of Islam permeate both the legal rights of women and general cultural and social attitudes and values (Shahidian, 2002), in recent decades Iran has gone under great social change. This has especially taken place regarding women's position and status in society, ranging from an increase in women's level of education (Rahbari, 2016), to women's role in running campaigns for human and women's rights inside and outside the country (Fathi, 2015; Geneva Summit, 2016). Hence Iranian women have been active participants in creating social change in the country from within the existing cultural and religious limitations (Mir Hoseini, 2006a) and cultural mindsets (Ahmadi, 2006).

Almost 40 years after the Islamic Revolution, young Iranian generations who have undergone an extensive Islamic education are increasingly globalized due to their growing interaction with other contexts. This partially comes from the large number of migrants, many of whom stay in contact with their homeland and networks in Iran, but also thanks to the growing access to cyberspace and the internet.[2] These shifts have also had some modernizing consequences for the social/institutional construction of gender identities (Hegland, 2009), as well as for women's rights issues, which have become a prominent subject of criticism of the Islamic Republic, both inside Iran and among the large diaspora of an estimated four million Iranians.

The Iranian migrant population is extremely heterogeneous with respect to ethnicity, religion, social status, language, gender, political affiliation, education, legal status, and timing and motivation for departure (ranging from political to sociocultural and economic issues) (Hakimzade, 2006). Although the longing for *Iranian-ness* is a constant factor shaping the diaspora, forms and ideas about what constitutes Iranian identity are subject to negotiation (Mohabbat-Kar, 2016, p 11). In terms of religious beliefs and practices, the Iranian diaspora is characterized by irreligiousness, agnosticism and atheism as well as by practising and non-practising Muslim identification. There are also

Iranian Zoroastrian, Baha'i, Christian and Jewish minorities (Gholami, 2015; Bozorgmehr, 2001).

The Iranian diaspora is dispersed throughout the globe, yet predominantly resides in North America and West European countries, including Belgium. Iranians migrated to Belgium in two waves. The first wave of refugees arrived in Belgium after the Islamic Revolution in 1979, when the political situation in Iran with its social instability and precarious situation of religious minorities were sufficient ground for asylum seekers to be granted a residence permit. Since the 1990s, the recently arrived Iranians have mostly been seeking work or higher education in the receiving countries. Like other migrants from Muslim-majority societies, they have sometimes faced Islamophobia in the West, where the presupposed 'Muslim' and 'brown' populations are held responsible for global and local crises (Maly, 2016; Lootens, 2016). Revived by these debates, women's Islamic outfit and body management practices have repeatedly become the subject of political and public debate (Longman, 2003; Verbanck, 2015; Jabrane, 2016). These debates have potentially affected women's body management and daily choices of bodily practices.

## Methodology

Feminist researchers have been concerned with writing women's histories, alternative, small, forgotten and untold stories (Kouritzin, 2000; Hyvarinen, 2008). Examining women's life stories helps uncover these stories, and narratives, which are documented from women's own standpoints. They capture distinctive elements and help uncover resiliency at different stages across the life span. They also include and mirror events including both macro-history (historic events) and micro-history (individual-level events) to show how they converge and shape a person's development (Sosulski, 2010, pp 34–5).

The participant in this study (hereafter called by the pseudonym Maryam) was selected from among six respondents who shared their life stories with the first author, in the framework of a larger study on Iranian women's migration to Belgium. This specific life story is appealing for its depiction of the experience of the *personalization of religion*. Although the personalization of religion was the general trend in all six narratives, the five stories other than Maryam's included experiences of the individualization of religion and the inclination to accept the Western model of religiosity as the good or the superior model. Maryam's life story was different in that she managed to adapt to the dominant paradigm of the secular liberal State, where religion is a personal choice, and reconciled it with her religious beliefs; and in that she self-identified as a feminist, and was at the same time critical of Western feminism.

Two interviews took place in private spaces in Belgium in the spring of 2016. Maryam was informed about the research goal and plan, and for further transparency the list of questions was provided before the interview. She was also assured of confidentiality of the data and informed of her right to stop the interview process at any point. The first interview was an informal and introductory conversation, while the second interview was semi-structured and based on open questions. This interview was recorded and transcribed verbatim and then translated from Farsi to English by the first author. The provided quotes are literal extracts. Due to Maryam's preference, personal information has not been included in the discussions.

## Maryam's brief life story

Maryam was born to a traditional Muslim family in Iran. Being the only daughter of her parents, she grew up with older brothers. She spent most of her time with her mother who nurtured her to fully observe Islamic (Shiite) practices. The relation between mother and daughter was at times 'hard' as Maryam's mother had set strict rules for her to achieve educational success and to be raised as a proper Muslim girl. They sometimes had disputes, after which Maryam would "always listen to [her] mother's advice". These discussions almost always happened because of religious obligations as this was the most important thing that mattered to her mother. Maryam learned to be a virtuous woman, as a part of which, she explained, she learned to help with the house chores.

After Maryam graduated from university and started a part-time job, she often fantasized about living alone and breaking the rules of religious and gendered behaviour, including observing strict Islamic veiling and daily prayers. Shortly after graduation from university, she found an opportunity to pursue her studies in Belgium. This was a scary decision for her. She had never lived alone, nor had she any experience of staying out of the parental house, or "even sleeping over at friends' houses". In fact, she had never travelled without companions or guardians. Much to her surprise, her mother was the most supportive person in the family and played a significant role in convincing her father that this was the right decision for her future. Maryam moved to Belgium a few years before the time of her interview with the researcher and has been living in Belgium ever since. Like many other migrants from developing countries, Maryam has at times encountered social and financial difficulties. The migration experience, the experience of an independent life, and her sudden exposure of her body and her hijab as an 'alien', 'unfamiliar' object in the Western context changed her approach towards her understanding of morality and religion. She experienced hostility due to her religious body management choices and contrary to what she had once expected. She now observes Islamic practices and holds on to a new personalized understanding of Islamic traditions.

## Between me and my God: personalization of religion

Maryam's family, especially her mother, played an important role in her life. Before moving to Belgium, Maryam was a practising Muslim without feeling she ever had any choice in choosing her faith and whether she wanted to be a practising believer. As Maryam explained, "I did not have any other alternatives." Her family expected her to maintain her religiosity and a sense of obligation to guard the 'family honour'. The discourses built around family honour have been sources of debates on gendered control and women's agency in different contexts (Withaeckx and Coene, 2011; Fazio, 2007). But within the cultural and religious limitations enforced in the name of family honour ,which limit women's movement and freedom, Maryam could go beyond the conventional rules of conduct; as she related, "[in that context] whatever you do is your family's honour; you are carrying around the heavy weight of [their] honour. My parents were like weights I carried on me ... in my context, a father should always be around and control his daughter."Maryam recognized the effects of historical context and generational differences, especially in women's situation and marriage patterns, on her life. Studies in Iran have reported a change to modern marriage in urban areas (Azadarmaki, 2015), while traditional and early marriage trends continue to exist in rural areas.[3] Maryam acknowledged the significance of this historic shift in her life trajectory. "If it were twenty years ago, it would be impossible for me to do anything other than the traditional marriage."After parting from her family who reside in Iran, Maryam chose her own favourite Islamic practices; the practices that she has personally found most interesting and fulfilling: "I am [still] very dedicated, when it comes to fasting, but not in daily prayers. Because I think there is a certain education in the fasting, at least for me, which I cannot find in daily prayers ... [some] practices [are] closer to my heart."Before migrating to Belgium, Maryam had not imagined that had the 'obligations' been lifted, she would continue to observe Islamic practices. Thus, her continued interest in practising Islam after migrating to Belgium surprised her. However, she *personalized* her faith. She adopted a more critical approach towards faith and chose the practices she wanted to observe: "I had previously thought if I got away from family and had my own place [I would stop practising my religion] ... But I did not do it. I have [instead] totally personalized the religion in the way I want it."Maryam reflected on her actions, and on the reactions of people who found her too 'modern' to wear the hijab (a practice she has continuously observed). However, she continued to view religion as 'discursive' and textual. As such, she described religion as subject to individual interpretation:

> 'I know there are many who do not accept [the way I practise the religion]. They say you should be either 100% accepting it, or 100% rejecting it; I totally disagree with this ... others can interpret [the religion] for themselves ... [Religion] is just interpretation; it is a discourse that needs [personal] analysis.'

Maryam's viewpoint also revealed a conscious and explicit rejection of the patriarchal and male-centred views on the interpretation of religion by the 'religious reference'.[4] Instead, she referred to a more dynamic, individual and up-to-date conceptualization of Islamic belief as 'functional' in the contemporary period.

Maryam believed that her choice of wearing the hijab was not only perceived as a sign of oppression by some Europeans, but also questioned by Iranians living in the West; they viewed her as a person who submitted to the regulations of an oppressive regime. While she had struggled with the decision of wearing the hijab in a secular context, she saw her final choice as not only a religious decision, but as a kind of social statement not only targeting the host society, but also the society of origin:

> '[Hijab] is more a cultural and social symbol to me, rather than a religious one and from the other hand, it is related to Iran[5] ... I also think that by wearing the hijab, I can show that you can be born from Muslim parents in a religious, middle class family, keep your hijab, and go abroad alone.'

Maryam's story revealed the importance of migration and change in the social context in her life trajectory. Migration was a turning point in her religious and social experience. Despite having had a traditional upbringing, the modern context in the Iranian society that has emerged in the last century and gradually taken over society (Povey, 2015; Sustar and Sepehriwa, 2009) has made it possible for Iranian youth such as Maryam to conciliate the Islamic discourse with the secular approach to practise their individuality.

## Islam and feminism in the narrative

Maryam came across Western notions of women's rights, equality and feminism through extensive reading before migrating, but she has identified as 'feminist' only after migration. She did not affiliate her feminism to any of the existing currents of feminism in the interview (that is liberal, socialist, radical, and so on); instead, she described her feminism in terms that demonstrated similarities to what has been called *Islamic feminism*, as she explained:

> 'I see things from a religious viewpoint, but also from my being a feminist. Because I don't like that women become sexual commodities for men ... [this idea] is first religious ... feminism later came to me, so the base was religious and later social and feminist ideas were added to it.'

Islamic feminism has been widely discussed in the feminist literature of Muslim contexts such as Iran (Mir Hoseini, 2006; Moghissi, 2002). The concept of Islamic feminism arose from a shift in feminist theories to include all women by accepting the multiplicity of women's self-identification (Moghissi, 2002, p 125). Although hard to define because of the broad meanings the terms 'feminist' and 'Islamic' can entail, as Maryam explained, Islamic feminism refers to a feminism that is an extension of the faith position rather than the rejection of this position (Kynsilehto, 2008). Before moving to Europe, Maryam believed European women enjoyed more gender equality compared to women in Iran. She learned about the problems Western women struggled with, among which she referred to the hypersexualized representations of women and the gendered wage gap. She then concluded that social and economic differences between Eastern and Western societies made it impossible to do a comparison between them; "everything has its own context," she emphasized.

Maryam pointed out the human rights and women rights activism, which build their narratives on their perceptions of Islam, and how she found the Islamic portrayal of femininity more attractive: "The way [women are treated] in Islam is more emotion-based and beautiful. I might be a feminist, but I think the feminism that I see [in the West] questions the idea of femininity … That kind of equality is not attractive to me."

Maryam's perception of Islamic faith still connected her to the Muslim community. She recognized a certain responsibility towards that community; a weight that she felt even in everyday activities in a secular context: "When I [succeed in something] I am happy for having worn my veil … I feel as if with every choice I make, I can represent my religion." She has perceived that Muslim migrant women are sometimes viewed as oppressed and asocial – an image that she has tried to redefine. Explaining what she meant by 'the Muslim woman's image' in the West, Maryam showed her frustration at receiving negative comments after the Brussels terrorist attacks of March 2016.[6] She referred to the effects of mobility and migration in her own life and concluded: "I have always been aware that I should be extra well-behaved with Europeans … I am very conscious about this … I think Europeans don't have the chance to challenge themselves … They need opportunity of [more mobility to challenge their ideas]."

Maryam asserted that migration was a turning point in her life that led to her choice of being a 'religious' person, even when living in a 'secular' state such as Belgium. Maryam's story showed how life stories can elucidate the bridge between structures and the person. In her life, the personalized version of religious identity enabled Maryam to keep her bonds with her religious and national identification while portraying her also as a modern woman who could make life-changing decisions. Maryam also made the choice to embrace her 'difference' by choosing to practise Islam publicly, by wearing the hijab. Since her 'difference' was established even without the hijab, due to an intersection of socio-economic positions (her skin colour and ethnic background, language, gender and class related), her choice to wear the hijab was a statement of defiance to some existing prejudgments.

## Discussion and concluding remarks

This chapter considered the life story of a Muslim migrant woman in Belgium to investigate dynamics of conciliating supposedly contradicting cultural and religious discourses, and to explore how the migration experience from a traditional Muslim context to a modern Western context with regard to gendered religious beliefs and practices changed the life trajectory and her attitude and approach towards Islam. We have used the life story method to look deep into the supposedly conflicting aspects of identity-making processes in a young Iranian woman's life. The analysis illustrated how she reconciled traditional religious beliefs and gendered domestic and public roles with her identification as a Muslim feminist and a migrant in Belgium.

Despite being raised in a traditional context, Maryam broke out of the strict religious frameworks enforced in her society of origin, but she kept elements of the Muslim faith. This shift was made possible by the migration experience, which distanced her from her original context. Her journey to make a balance between her faith and the desire to integrate in the new context in Belgium has been challenging and has resulted in the personalization of religion. Maryam's 'religious becoming' has been a conscious process of reconciling her Islamic beliefs and living in a secular society in Europe. Maryam's life story narrative is also situated in an era in which a modern interpretation of religion has been embraced by the young generations of the Iranian population, born after the 1979 revolution (Shirazi, 2012). The title of this chapter 'Between me and my God' referred to a common phrase in Farsi expressing the general idea that religion is a personal matter that one can adopt by keeping an internal dialogue with God. This phrase reflects Maryam's attitude towards religion, as well as the views of many other young Iranians who see religion as a matter of personal choosing (Sadeghi, 2010). Maryam's idea, which viewed religion as subject to individual interpretation, reflected a widespread change in Iranian youth's idea about religiosity, which has been facilitated by great changes in women's participation in social life and education (Rahbari, 2016).

Maryam's narrative revealed that despite her initial enthusiasm to stop practising Islam after migration and her encounter with a Western secular liberal society, but also with experiences of exclusion and discrimination as a Muslim woman, she embraced her faith as a cultural, national and personal identity maker. She personalized the Islamic practices and held on to a new personalized version of Islamic traditions. Religion thus became an individually reconstructed notion rather than a hegemonic structure, which helped her maintain the bonds with cultural roots without hindering the integration process. Although Maryam conditioned her body and appearance to the general traditionalist religious expectations of her upbringing, in the host society she reinterpreted its rules and regulations on social conduct, gendered spatial settings and feminine virtues, as a form of social statement to defy prejudices towards Muslim practices of veiling. She also re-discussed these regulations and questioned them, and in the process produced a personal religious discourse that included gender equality as a main characteristic which is compatible with liberal notions of 'personal choice making', 'freedom of expression' and 'individualism'. Maryam became and identified as a Muslim feminist by finding similar elements between her faith and feminist principles of women's freedom and gender equality.

This chapter aimed to contribute to a better understanding of the changing face of Islam as a religion in a young Iranian woman's life, and thereby reveals the broader diversity and complexity in the relationship between women and religion through lived experience.

Besides the transformative impact of migration on the individual, local societal changes and challenges within both home and host contexts must be considered, which will affect the choices and negotiations that one might make. On the one hand, there is the generational shift in the Islamic Republic of Iran, where women are increasingly educated and moving more into the workplace than before. In an age of globalization, the youth are also increasingly exposed to alternative ways of life. On the other hand, besides the promise of freedom, in the West there is also the increase in discrimination against migrants and the rise in racism and Islamophobia. Maryam's life story cannot be representative of all Muslim women who migrate from gender-traditionalist religious contexts to Western liberal-secular societies. Her narrative provided an insight into certain 'clashes', but foremost it showed the potentialities for conciliating a religious identity with a feminist identity, through the process of the personalization of faith.

## Notes

[1] A manifestation of this struggle is the EU Court of Justice's ruling in 2017 that allowed companies to ban staff from wearing visible religious symbols such as the hijab (Rankin and Oltermann, 2017).

[2] The percentage of Iranians using internet from overall population has grown from less than 10% in 2006 to 48.9% in 2016 (See: http://www.internetlivestats.com/internet-users/iran/).

[3] It is estimated that approximately 17% of girls in Iran get married under the age of 18 (see: http://www.girlsnotbrides.org/child-marriage/iran).

[4] Religious references are mostly male clerics who have religious authority and are to be followed (see: http://www.oxfordislamicstudies.com/article/opr/t125/e1437).

[5] Maryam dons a Roosari or a shawl which is the predominant Iranian style of hijab. An Iranian Roosari is a piece of triangular colourful cloth tied under the chin, while an Iranian shawl is usually worn loosely around the head and neck.

[6] On 22 March 2016, three suicide bombings occurred in Belgium, at Brussels Airport, and Maalbeek metro station. Thirty-two civilians and three perpetrators were killed, and more than 300 people were injured. Another bomb was found during a search of the airport. Islamic State of Iraq and the Levant (ISIL) terrorist

group claimed responsibility for the attacks (see: https://en.wikipedia.org/wiki/2016_Brussels_bombings).

## References

Ahmadi, F. (2006) 'Islamic Feminism in Iran: Feminism in a New Islamic Context', *Journal of Feminist Studies in Religion*, 22(2), pp 33–53.

Amghar, S., Boubekeur, A. and Emerson, M. (2007) *European Islam: Challenges for Public Policy and Society*, Brussels: Centre for European Policy Studies.

Aras, B. (2004) 'The Future of Liberal Islam', *Futuers*, 36, pp 1025–48.

Atkinson, R. (2002) 'Life Story Interview', in J.F. Gubrium and J.A. Holstein (eds) *Handbook of Interview Research: Context and Method*, London and Delhi: Thousand Oaks, pp 121–40.

Azadarmaki, T. (2015) 'Family Change in Iran: Transition from Traditional Marriage to Modern One', *Journal of Socio-Cultural Change* [in Farsi], 1(3), pp 5–16.

Bedggood, M. and Whiu, L. (2006) 'Women, Religion, and the Law in Aotearoa/New Zealand: The Complexity of Accommodating Different Value Systems in Law', in A. Whiting and C. Evans (eds) *Mixed Blessings: Women, Laws & Religion*, Boston and Leiden: Martinus Nijhoff, pp 129–60

Bozorgmehr, M. (2001) *No Solidarity: Iranians in the US*. Available at: https://iranian.com/Opinion/2001/May/Iranians/index.html

Darvishpour, M. (2003) 'Islamic Feminism: Compromise or Challenge to Feminism?', *Iran Bulletin Middle East Forum*, summer issue, pp 55–8.

David Eller, J. (2007) *Introducing Anthropology of Religion: Culture to the Ultimate*, London and New York: Routledge.

Farazmand, A. (1995) 'Religion and Politics in Contemporary Iran', *International Journal on Group Rights*, 3(3), pp 227–57.

Fathi, N. (2015) *Meet the Iconoclast Inspiring Iranian Women to Remove Their Headscarves*. Available at: http://www.vogue.com/13255544/masih-alinejad-my-stealthy-freedom/

Fazio, I. (2007) 'The Family, Honour and Gender in Sicily: Models and New Research', *Modern Italy*, 9(2), pp 263–80.

Geneva Summit (2016) Darya Safai at Geneva Summit: Campaigner for Right of Iranian Women to Enter Sports Stadiums. Available at: http://www.genevasummit.org/darya-safai-at-the-geneva-summit/

Gholami, R. (2015) *Secularism and Identity: Non-Islamiosity in the Iranian Diaspora*, Burlington and Surrey: Ashgate.

Gross, Z. (2012) 'Multiple Religious and Secular Definitions of Secular Adolescents in Israel', *Journal of Empirical Theology*, 25, pp 1–21.

Guta, H. and Karolak, M. (2015) 'Veiling and Blogging', *Journal of International Women's Studies*, 16(2), pp 115–27

Hakimzade, S. (2006) *Iran: A Vast Diaspora Abroad and Millions of Refugees at Home*, Migration Policy Institute. Available at: http://www.migrationpolicy.org/article/iran-vast-diaspora-abroad-and-millions-refugees-home

Hegland, M.E. (2009) 'Educating Young Women', *Iranian Studies*, 42(1), pp 45–79.

Hyvarinen, M. (2008) 'Analyzing Narratives and Story-Telling', in P. Alasuutari, L. Bickman and J. Brannen (eds) *The Sage Handbook of Social Research Methods*, Los Angeles: Sage, pp 447–60.

Iversen, H.I. (2006) 'Secular Religion and Religious Secularism: A Profile of the Religious Development in Denmark Since 1968', *Nordic Journal of Religion and Society*, 19(2), pp 75–92.

Jabrane, E. (2016) *Flemish-Moroccan Politician Calls for Burkini Ban in Belgium*. Available at: https://www.moroccoworldnews.com/2016/08/194558/flemish-moroccan-politician-calls-burkini-ban-belgium/

Joseph, S. (2006) *Encyclopedia of Women & Islamic Cultures: Family, Body, Sexuality and Health*, Volume 3, Leiden and Boston: Brill.

Kouritzin, S.G. (2000) 'Bringing Life to Research: Life History Research and ESL', *TESL Canada Journal/Revue TESL du Canada*, 17(2), pp 1–35.

Kynsilehto, A. (2008) *Islamic Feminism: Current Perspectives, Tampere Peace Research Institute*, Occasional Paper No. 96, University of Tampere: Finland.

Longman, C. (2003) 'Over our Heads? Muslim Women as Symbols and Agents in the Headscarf Debate in Flanders, Belgium', *Social Justice. Anthropology, Peace and Human Rights*, 4(3–4), pp 300–32.

Lootens, D. (2016) *Aanslagen Brussel en Zaventem: Hoog Tijd om Prioriteiten te Stellen!*. Available at: https://www.vlaamsbelang.org/aanslagen-brussel-en-zaventem-hoog-tijd-om-prioriteiten-te-stellen/ (Retrieved 30 December 2016)

Maly, I. (2016) *Aanslagen in Brussel*. Available at: http://www.kifkif.be/actua/aanslagen-in-brussel

Mir Hoseini, Z. (2006) *Islam and Democracy in Iran: Eshkevari and the Quest for Reform*, London and New York: IB-Tauris.

Mir Hoseini, Z. (2006a) 'Muslim Women's Quest for Equality: Between Islamic Law and Feminism', *Critical Inquiry*, 32, pp 629–45.

Mirsepassi, A. (2010) *Political Islam, Iran, and the Enlightenment*, Cambridge: Cambridge University Press.

Moallem, M. (2005) *Between Warrior Brother and Veiled Sister*, Berkley, Los Angeles and London: University of California Press.

Moghissi, H. (2002) *Feminism and Islamic Fundamentalism: The Limits of Postmodern Analysis*, London: Zed Books.

Mohabbat-Kar, R. (2016) *Identity and Exile*, Volume 40 of the Publication Series on Democracy, edited by the Heinrich Böll Foundation in co-operation with Transparency for Iran. Available at: https://www.boell.de/sites/default/files/identity-a-exile_web.pdf

Najmabadi, A. (1998) 'Feminism in an Islamic Republic: 'Years of Hardship, Years of Growth', in Y. Yazbeck Haddad and J.L. Esposito (eds) *Gender, and Social Change in the Muslim World*, New York: Oxford University Press, pp 59–84.

Nasr, S.H. (2010) *Islam in the Modern World: Challenged by the West, Threatened by Fundamentalism, Keeping Faith with Tradition*. New York: HarperOne.

Neusner, J. (2011) 'The Theological Enemies of Religious Studies: Theology and Secularism in the Trivialization and Personalization of Religion in the West', *Religion*, 18(1), pp 21–5.

Povey, T. (2015) *Social Movements in Egypt and Iran*, London: Palgrave Macmillan.

Rahbari, L. (2016) 'Women in Higher Education and Academia in Iran', *Sociology and Anthropology*, 4(11), pp 1003–10.

Rankin, J. and Oltermann, P. (2017) *Europe's Right Hails EU Court's Workplace Headscarf Ban Ruling*. Available at: https://www.theguardian.com/law/2017/mar/14/employers-can-ban-staff-from-wearing-headscarves-european-court-rules

Sadeghi, F. (2010) 'Negotiating with Modernity: Young Women and Sexuality in Iran', in A. Herrera and A. Bayat (eds) *Being Young and Muslim*, Oxford: Oxford University Press, pp 273–90.

Shahidian, H. (2002) *Women in Iran: Emerging Voices in the Women's Movement*, Westport and London: Greenwood Press.

Shirazi, A. (2012) *A Look at Modern Spirituality and the Youth in Iran*. Available at: http://www.ihrr.org/ihrr_article/youth-en_a-look-at-modern-spirituality-and-the-youth-in-iran/

Smith, C. (2003*) The Secular Revolution: Power, Interest and Conflict in the Secularization of American Public Life*, Berkley, Los Angeles, London: University of California Press.

Sosulski, M. R. (2010) 'Life Story Narrative Analysis', *Journal of Sociology & Social Welfare*, 37(3), pp 29–57.

Sustar, L. and Sepehriwa, S. (2009) 'Iran: Rebellion and Reaction', *International Socialist Review (online)*, 67, September. Available at: http://isreview.org/issue/67/iran-rebellion-and-reaction.

Verbanck, I. (2015) *Boerkini: 'Om de vrouw haar vrijheid te garanderen, moeten we haar het kiezen verbieden'*. Available at: http://www.knack.be/nieuws/belgie/boerkini-om-de-vrouw-haar-vrijheid-te-garanderen-moeten-we-haar-het-kiezen-verbieden/article-opinion-613739.html

Withaeckx, S. and Coene, G. (2012) '"Glad to Have Honour": Continuity and Change in Minority Women's Lived Experience of Honour', *Journal of Gender Studies*, 23(4), pp 376–90.

Yasmeen, S. and Markovic, N. (2014) *Muslim Citizens in the West: Spaces and Agents of Inclusion and Exclusion*, London and New York: Routledge.

# TEN

# 'We are all Goddesses': female sacred paths in Italy

*Roberta Pibiri and Stefania Palmisano*

## Introduction[1]

The aim of this chapter is to reflect on the relations between women and religion, by analysing a new form of spirituality coming from the Anglophone world, Goddess Spirituality, which has arrived in Italy in the new millennium. The analysis moves from secondary data on alternative spiritualities in Italy and is based on ethnographic research carried out in 2013–14 by one of the authors[2] in the Turin Goddess Spirituality group. We chose this group because it was the first in Italy where the Avalon tradition developed in Glastonbury by Kathy Jones (founder of the earliest officially recognized Goddess temple) took root.

Goddess Spirituality is one of the most important – and in some ways challenging – forms where the movement of rediscovering paths of the sacred female are evident. Specifically, this movement grew out of both reinterpretation of monotheistic religions' sacred texts carried out by feminist scholars (Daly, 1973; Ruether, 1983; Schussler-Fiorenza, 2013) and archaeological, historical and mythographical studies witnessing the existence of Neolithic matrifocal societies in ancient Europe devoted to worshipping the Goddess or Great Mother (Stone, 1976; Gimbutas, 1989, 1991; Eisler, 1987), in synergy with the feminist movement and the first groups experimenting the practices and rituals on which this spirituality is based. Leading pioneers of the Goddess Spirituality movement were Starhawk and Vicki Noble in the United States and Kathy Jones in the United Kingdom.

The most recent surveys on Italians' religiosity in Italy (Garelli, 2014, 2016) contain no traces of feminine spirituality because it has no critical mass, that is to say a small number of people follow alternative spiritualities.[3] As some studies demonstrate (Crespi and Ruspini, 2014; Giorgi and Palmisano, 2016), while an ever-increasing proportion of women leave the Catholic Church, the majority do not redirect their spiritual seeking outside the Catholic milieu by approaching the world of so-called alternative spiritualities.

Italian alternative spirituality, on the other hand, has been studied in some qualitative research (Giordan, 2006) and, more recently, paying particular attention to proposals aimed mainly at women (Fedele and Knibbe, 2013; Berzano and Palmisano, 2014; Bernacchi, 2016; Pibiri, 2016). These studies suggest that Goddess Spirituality provides a unique laboratory for understanding women–religion relations. Many studies about women in both old and new religions understand gender as merely a biographical variable illustrating specific differences between how men and women approach religion. Goddess Spirituality study, however, calls into question basic assumptions of both old and new religions. Here, gender is not only a biographical variable: the female is the divine principle and basic organizer of the symbolic, spiritual/religious and axiological system of reference. In other words, Goddess Spirituality tends towards divine female energy – called the Great Mother – while elaborating its theology (Goldenberg, 1979). This is a daring feminist revolution, especially considering that the movement is by now widespread internationally, giving birth to a new awareness of the concept of gender in the spiritual sphere and its intertwining with demands of a secular nature – with pragmatic consequences for the social and political planes as well as the religious.

We claim that 'female spirituality', as proposed by Goddess Spirituality, is nothing less than a paradigm shift with regard to 'women's spirituality': the former (Goddess Spirituality) is an ontologically female spirituality interpreting gender as the divine principle and organizer of reality and placing it at the centre of theological reflection and spiritual practice (the female body itself is a vehicle connecting with the divine); and the latter (women's spirituality) sees gender study as a biographical variable with the intention of illuminating how men and women experience their religions.

This chapter considers the essential aims of this volume: if the female is the divine principle and organizer of reality, then how does this vision of the cosmology influence how religion, gender identity, the construction of the male and female and the relationship between the two are approached? Reference to the female as constituent characteristic will constrain us to examine aspects which are often neglected in the study of religion: the body, ritual and the centrality of lived religious experience.

This chapter is hereafter divided into the following sections. The next section reviews the theoretical debate and the empirical studies relevant to our case, starting from recent Italian studies (Palmisano, 2014, 2016) which reveal a process of female secularization unaccompanied by a spiritual revolution led by women. Differently from other European countries (Houtman and Mascini, 2002; Heelas and Woodhead, 2005), this female secularization/women's spiritual revolution binomial does not characterize female religiosity in Italy. We shall focus on these studies in order to assert that, while alternative (female) spiritualities in Italy are not revealed by statistical analysis, they are nevertheless growing, as some qualitative research (Pibiri, 2016; Fedele and Knibbe, 2016) testifies. The subsequent section describes Goddess Spirituality's beliefs and practices, followed by a section examining the ways in which Goddess Spirituality aims at deconstructing classical categories of studying traditional religion and how gender and religion are interpreted. The final section recapitulates the main findings.

## Literature review

Surveys of Italian religiosity since the 1970s have shown that women are more religious than their male peers. They display higher rates of Mass attendance, prayer, faith in God and volunteering work in the Church environment (Garelli, Guizzardi and Pace 2003; Cartocci, 2011; Garelli, 2014). In other words, women were the 'hardcore' faithful in practising religion – a datum in line with international tendencies in mainly Christian countries (Aune, Sharma and Vincent, 2008; Trzebiatowska and Bruce, 2012). The same surveys show that still today women are in the lead. Nevertheless, despite this persistence, a diachronic analysis of the European Values Study[4] data reveals that even Italian women's religiousness has undergone the progressive – albeit rather traumatic – secularization affecting Italian society (Giorgi and Palmisano, 2016). Furthermore, although Italian women continue to attend Mass more frequently, what is new – according to some authors basing their conclusions on the European Values Study data (Berzano and Palmisano, 2014; Crespi, 2014) – is that there has been a staggering drop in women's (compared with men's) feeling of affection towards religious practice. In other words, the decrease in women's attendance at Mass has been much more precipitate than men's. Some observers of the Italian situation (Segatti and Brunelli, 2010; Berzano and Palmisano, 2014) share this view that today women's religious practice is undergoing a slackening process, which makes it increasingly similar to men's. This exodus has been called 'the flight of women from the Church' (Matteo, 2012) or, more prosaically, female secularization (Crespi and Ruspini, 2014). The speed of this secularization process has caused a narrowing of the gender gap in Church religious practice over the past half century.

Millennials tend to follow the same trend (Garelli, 2016; Matteo 2012, 2014).[5] With regard to gender differences in religious behaviour, there is no doubt that we are witnessing a tapering off. Although the differences between boys and girls are fading, they have not disappeared: they are still present in some areas of religious life, particularly with regard to practice, where there is greater female presence in Mass attendance, in belonging to the Catholic Church and in prayer. This gender distinction in how religion is lived becomes more apparent in the field of spirituality (Palmisano, 2016). More girls than boys are interested in developing a spiritual life. Fewer girls than boys say they do not have a spiritual life. Surprisingly, however, in contrast with the past, gender no longer discriminates among those who develop their spiritual life according to the principles of their religion. One would have expected that more women than men would have chosen a spiritual path regulated by the principles of institutional religion (as is widespread in the Catholic Church), but one finds rather that this vision is shared almost equally by boys and girls. Nor does gender discriminate between conceptions of spirituality which do not refer explicitly to religion: about the same percentage of both sexes understand spirituality as seeking harmony and well-being.

Discontinuity with the past becomes even clearer when one takes into account another tendency, which, conversely, shows up an important gender difference: more girls than boys state that they experience religious and spiritual seeking in a personal way. Yet the Italian aptitude for personalized religious seeking stops short in the Catholic milieu – it does not extend to the world of alternative spiritualities or, as it has been defined, the holistic milieu (Heelas and Woodhead, 2005). Analysis of the uses made of alternative spiritualities' offer reveals that girls are not more present than boys in this field. More specifically, those data show that there are more young males than females at Oriental spirituality meetings, whereas attendance at New Age seminars and meditation groups is fairly equal (Palmisano, 2016). It is tempting to believe that the tenuous attraction of the holistic milieu is limited to young females because they cannot afford alternative spirituality's expensive goods and services, but it is not so; another study (Palmisano, 2014) confirms the same trend among adults. Examining the participation of adult Italians in the holistic milieu, this study found that in the 36–45 age group women are more numerous than men only in the Oriental spirituality meetings, but not in other New Age activities, where men take the lead. What is more, for all other age groups the difference disappears.

This finding merits attention because it calls into question the widespread perception (which one gathers in these contexts) that yoga, transcendental meditation, crystal healing and shiatsu, to give but some examples, are more attractive to a female public. Another reason to pay attention to this finding is that it emerges from Central and Northern European studies that the prevailing tendency is the opposite: women are more active and involved in the holistic milieu than men. Heelas and Woodhead's (2005) examination of holistic activities in Kendal, north-west England, shows that 80% of practitioners are women. In the Scottish Social Attitudes Survey (2001) analysing the gender gap in three specific activities – yoga and meditation; complementary medicines; and divination – reveal the same attraction for women. Based on World Value Survey data (1981, 1990, 2000) from 14 European countries, Houtman and Aupers (2008: 132) conclude that 'spirituality is more typically embraced by post-traditional women than by post-traditional men'.

How can the Italian counter-tendency be explained in the light of these studies, which support the idea that women take the lead in alternative spiritualities? We claim that findings negating the prevalence of women in the Italian holistic milieu correctly reflect the situation. Alternative spiritualities, with their mind-body-spirit mantra, encourage women to abandon the logic of 'sacrificing oneself' in favour of an 'expressive egoism' (Sointu and Woodhead, 2008), which legitimizes their dedicating time and attention to themselves. But this call is not very alluring to the majority of Italian women struggling with a cultural environment influenced by their tradition, permeated with Catholicism, which has praised the female virtues of sacrifice, renunciation and altruism, and has insisted on women's maternal vocation and wifely role (Donadi, 2014). Italian women must reckon with a society in which – compared with most European countries – gender inequality is greater (Plantenga et al, 2009), female employment is lower (Eurostat, 2015), housework is divided in the most traditional way (Carriero and Todesco, 2016), and such inequality is tolerated in society (Greenstein, 2009).

Nevertheless, even though female alternative spiritualities have not been captured by surveys, they are developing in Italy, as attested to by ethnographic research. In this context, Goddess Spirituality is the movement which has most attracted the attention of Italian scholars (Fedele and Knibbe 2013; Pibiri, 2016; Bernacchi, 2016). Thus we feel justified in believing that it would be heuristically useful to investigate 'female spirituality' qualitatively. In the following section analysing Goddess Spirituality's beliefs and practices, we reflect critically on women, religion and gender relations, and indicate the urgency of scholarly development of theories capable of rendering the gender dimension in the study of religious phenomena both reasonable and relevant.

## Goddess spirituality: methodology and analysis

In addition to the studies previously discussed in the literature review, this chapter is inspired by the findings of ethnographic research carried out in 2013–14 among one of the main Italian Goddess Spirituality groups. Headquartered in Turin, where the first experiments were carried out, it traces its heritage to the Avalon tradition transmitted by the Glastonbury Goddess Temple, the first officially recognized Goddess temple in the United Kingdom founded by Kathy Jones.[6] In particular, the Avalon tradition spiritual teachings, practices and seasonal ritual celebrations are based on the MotherWorld vision, a society model inspired by the Goddess and focused on motherly and care values. The spread of Goddess Spirituality in Italy was made possible by the pioneering work of the classical scholar Momolina Marconi (1937), by the feminist scholar Luciana Percovich,[7] and by the spiritual theory and practice aimed at reclaiming the path of the sacred female instituted by Sarah Perini, the Priestess of the Goddess of Avalon and founder of the first temple of the Goddess in Italy dedicated to the Lady of Avalon and to Diana.[8]

Goddess Spirituality is one of the main streams of contemporary Paganism (Harrington, 2007; Pizza and Lewis, 2009). It is a form of religiosity deriving from the process of 're-enchantment of the world' (Partridge, 2004; Lenoir, 2005) characterizing modern religiosity (Hervieu-Léger, 2003). Goddess Spirituality is seen as a source of empowerment for women (and for men who do not identify with traditional spiritual and masculine models) as to their role and gender identity, as well as their spiritual needs, which are not adequately addressed either by society as a whole or by traditional religions. It is transmitted by means of a specific female construction – reciprocally complemented by the male – making the most of the feminine by viewing it through a spiritual lens. This female construction can be defined according to two main interconnected principles operating on different levels: the 'cognitive/interpretative' and the 'expressive/ritual' (Pibiri, 2016). The varying modalities allow a process of awareness and promotion of the female quality of the sacred whose self-integration is a source of empowerment for members of both genders who follow this spiritual path (Pibiri, 2016).

Goddess Spirituality, then, is a form of religiosity deriving from a cosmological vision of the world and the sacred built on a the*a*logy (Goldenberg, 1979); a conception of the divine taking the form of feminine energy seen in nature, through its recurrence, and also in humankind, men and women whose body and individual self is considered an emanation and channel of its self-connection. This energy is symbolically represented by the Great Mother taking different shapes and appearances in accordance with historical eras and geographical and cultural contexts. Historically and culturally this spirituality originates from a process of reclamation and appreciation of female qualities and values, which, according to its advocates, had been hidden for centuries by patriarchal, monotheistic, traditional religions. By positioning itself as 'alternative' to traditional religious forms and models, and to their gender concepts, Goddess Spirituality is 'subversive' (as defined by Bromley, 1998), in total contradiction with dominant theologies – seen as authoritarian, exclusive, patriarchal and dogmatic – and the values they transmit. It presents a gender–religion relationship which may be defined as 'countercultural' (Woodhead, 2008): in presenting itself as 'alternative', it occupies a marginal position not only with respect to the broader social and religious context but also, by reason of its the*a*logy; it challenges traditional gender roles by critically opposing them, offering a more egalitarian gender-power distribution. Because of its the*a*logy's symbolic axiological cosmology and world vision, Goddess Spirituality proposes 'alternative' ways of (re)thinking the female and gender relationships marked by *partnership* (Eisler, 1987). Specifically, it is the founding principle of the social system which Eisler calls 'mutual', based on a balanced union between the female and male halves of humanity, whose relations aim at gender equality based on reciprocal valorization.

These elements make up the framework within which spiritual experience takes form and meaning for those who join Goddess Spirituality and whose definition originates from a process of rediscovery and reactualization of the ancient, pre-Christian female sacred paths as well as finding inspirations in indigenous religions throughout the world. The success of this 'alternative' framework has been facilitated by the reciprocal influence between the corpus of feminist study and research carried out in various disciplines, and social and political demands made by feminists and groups of women involved in the development of this spirituality's rituals. This exchange has allowed room for comparison and criticism among mainstream religious institutions and women, with their changing role in late modern society.

Goddess Spirituality in Italy has mainly meant – for women – a rejection of the dominant culture's patriarchal forms of religion in favour of a symbolic, axiological universe and an 'other' imaginary based on new practices and religious languages capable of adequately expressing their religious aspirations. This is a source of empowerment offering women – as a function of recognition of the divine's female qualities – a means of affirmation and claiming a more significant role in contemporary society. The same holds true for men who adhere to such a spiritual itinerary and no longer identify with traditional models of masculinity. Fieldwork carried out in the Turin Goddess Spirituality group in the Avalon tradition shows that the invitation to adhere to Goddess Spirituality implies an integration process between the material, practical and spiritual dimensions of existence, traversing recognition of its sacred value. It consists in maintaining constant connection with the sacrality of one's daily life as well as with the divine female energy present in nature and in every human being, honouring this energy and respecting its power and sacrality by means of actions, thoughts and feelings in tune with it. Fundamental to this process is an assumption of awareness of, and responsibility for, one's sphere in the world by means of recognition and integration of grey areas and healing of (mostly emotional) wounds caused by a patriarchal social, cultural and religious model.

Concretely, this reclamation of a female spirituality is defined in different ways: first, through the sacralization of the female body, which, by reason of its inherent periodicity – reflecting the Goddess's way of revealing herself in nature – and its power of giving life, is, along with its emotions and sexuality, a privileged channel of connection with the Goddess; second, by recalling spiritual roles central to ancient pre-Christian civilizations such as those of priestesses, oracles and connected practices (divination, carrying out initiations and celebrating ceremonies); third, by claiming the right to exercise professions which have always been considered female, for example healers, midwives and herbalists; and finally, by resurrecting the historical, cultural and spiritual inheritance of ancient matrifocal civilizations devoted to worshipping the female divine, honouring women who have contributed to its transmission from the past to the present.

Ritual practice occupies a central position in Goddess Spirituality's spiritual itinerary. This is based on spiritual experience gained through the body in seasonal ceremonial celebrations of the so-called Wheel of the Year. This specific symbol connects with various qualities of the Goddess's energy, encountering different phases of the Goddess through her various symbolic representations, in her periodicity connected with the passing of the seasons and the movement of the sun (solstices and equinoxes). More specifically, ritual performance (Turner, 1982, 1986) is a privileged place allowing the body to connect with its sacred self, which is a reflection and emanation of the female divine in a human being. This practice encourages the comprehension and construction of meaning based on an embodied form of learning and knowledge. This is to say that ritual practices define a protected space where, by means of meditation, visualization and symbolic acts, followers can deeply immerse themselves in their inner sacred space. It also enables a process of discovery, recognition and connection with what is considered the real self, or the sacred part of the self.

The distinguishing characteristics of an ontologically female spirituality may be understood better by focusing on the dynamics underlying the ritual performance. Connection with, and recognition of, the sacred part of the self are enhanced by the acceptance and integration of the parts in shadow and their associated emotions. This rests on the assumption that emotions constitute one of the main channels of communication with the divine and, consequently, the healing of one's emotional wounds. It also allows a rediscovery and reawakening of the female within oneself and the creation of a synthesis between the human being's two archetypical polarities – the female and the male.

## Women's spirituality versus female spirituality

Hitherto we have seen that Goddess Spirituality is an exemplary case for problematizing the question of female identity and traditional roles connected with it, both within traditional religions and in society at large, precisely because it is an ontologically female spirituality. It stimulates critical reflection on gender–religion relations, casting light on the substantial difference between 'feminization' involving traditional institutional religions and the specificity of a female religiosity in the strict sense. This specificity forces the shifting of the paradigm which has hitherto been employed in the study of women–religion relations, revealing a religiosity which has the gender question as its discriminating and fundamental characteristic, even to the heart of its theological reflections. This religiosity, in contrast with the patriarchal social and religious model, incorporates religious experience per se rather than norms and dogmas.

The interpretative key to the distinction between 'female spirituality' and 'women's spirituality' is the way in which Goddess Spirituality proposes the construction of the female, which is to say the interweaving between the complementary 'cognitive/interpretative' and the 'expressive/ritual' levels (Pibiri, 2016). If the construction of the female implies a cognitive dimension connected with the framework of meaning in which spiritual experience is structured and assumes meaning or the 'structure of plausibility' (Berger and Luckmann, 1966, p 132) of the tradition itself, at the same time it manifests itself through bodily and emotional expressiveness, and the physical and sensorial aspects of the ritual performance. In this sense, the ritual space is a physical, symbolic place where it is possible to contact and valorize the female aspects of the divine which are mirrored in the human being, asserting the otherness of which the Goddess Spirituality is a carrier.

Finally, in reclaiming and re-elaborating an ontologically female spirituality, the adherents of Goddess Spirituality have a marked tendency to become 'religious designers' (Rountree, 2004, p 121) in their way of being religious and relating to the sacred, the divine, emphasizing its creative dimension. This suggests three points worth reflecting on.

Although Goddess Spirituality in Italy is based on teachings transmitted by the Glastonbury Temple, it is still useful to explain how this spiritual path acquired a specific character from the national socio-cultural context. One important aspect of the formation of the group has been that of creating (on the pattern of Avalon Wheel) a specifically Italian Wheel of the Year dedicated to Diana, who is considered by adherents as the Proto-Italic goddess most representative of the country's pre-Christian spiritual heritage. The intention of this operation is to recover cultural and spiritual awareness of ancient Italian paths of the female sacred, reawakening and honouring the variegated manifestations of the female divine at local and regional levels.

A further aspect to be considered is the relationship between Goddess Spirituality and a socio-cultural environment – such as that of Italy – which has been greatly influenced by the Catholic tradition. Fieldwork (participant observation and interviews) reveals a shared critical attitude confirmed by Fedele and Knibbe (2016) – partly explaining their joining Goddess Spirituality – on the part of most adherents of the Catholic religion: dissatisfaction and disaffection with a religion considered patriarchal, which, in addition to negating the value of the female, negates the body and all its functions – and, therefore, its sacrality.

A final point concerns the relations between adherents from different generations. Fieldwork shows that older feminists, who created the conditions for the acceptance of Goddess Spirituality in Italy through their female emancipation movement, are handing over the torch to younger generations who emphasize the spiritual dimension of the feminist struggle.

## Conclusion

The arguments presented in this chapter have attempted to stimulate, and open new paths towards a reflection on women and religion (and by extension on gender–religion relations) based on a new form of spirituality from England – Goddess Spirituality – which has for some decades been taking root in Italy, too.

By reason of its theology considering the female as the divine principle and organizer of reality, Goddess Spirituality is a form of religiosity which may rightly be defined as ontologically female. This perspective problematizes the normal way of dealing with gender in research, which is to say as a mere biographical variable, on the same level as others, to which one has recourse in order to illuminate differences between men and women in religious life. Goddess Spirituality, however, considers gender as more than just a biographical variable.

Thus, the distinction between 'women's spirituality' and 'female spirituality' seems to be an approach leading to a better understanding of the relationship between gender and religion, and able to take into greater consideration the transformations affecting the religious phenomenon today. These transformations concern not only traditional religions, but also new forms of spirituality and religiosity which are capable of calling into question – and sometimes even subverting – the classical categories used in the study of the religious phenomena. The way in which gender is used and conceived in practising research is one of the elements supplying valuable analysis on this point.

Finally, it is worth emphasizing that the rebirth of the Goddess Spirituality movement in Italy is often linked with the re-emergence of awareness of the female principle – considered an archetype – both among men and women. Although the majority of its adherents are women, the gender issue should not be understood exclusively in its physical, biological manifestation, but the male and female, in their complementary relationship, should be considered as two integral aspects of the human being. To some extent, the valorization of the female principle focused on spiritual demands and directed by the partnership principle would also allow a reconsideration of accepted ways of conceiving and building the masculine in terms of cultural, symbolic and traditional religious systems.

Shifting the topic from the role played by women in traditional forms of religion to their active participation in discussing its basic assumptions and reclaiming specific female religiosity is the challenge facing religious scholars today. This aspect stimulates careful reflection on the possibility that an ever-increasing proportion of women reveal dissatisfaction with traditional religious models and values which neither concede space for femininity nor allow adequate expression of a spiritual need which manifests itself differently in men and women. Furthermore, we need to ask whether the personalization of religiosity – which in this context is to be considered a form of 'designer religion' – can be interpreted as confirmation of the existence of this intrinsic need.

These questions, albeit tortuous and little travelled, open up plausible research paths. It seems possible that these complementary ways of constructing the female, functioning creatively and in synergy, are capable of supplying appropriate discourse and symbols for both women's and men's religious/spiritual expression. Gender, considered as an integral part of Goddess Spirituality's symbolic, axiological universe based on the appreciation of the divine as being the female qualities in nature and humankind, generates personal empowerment, personal efficiency and a sense of responsibility. In this view, these are the preconditions essential for bringing about the social, cultural and spiritual change to which Goddess Spirituality tends and on which it is based in order to create a social model inspired by the partnership principle (Eisler, 1987). The 'mutual' social model (Eisler, 1987) emphasizes union between equals rather than patriarchal domination. Goddess Spirituality's contemporaneous spiritual/secular orientation is a source of empowerment for its adherents because it is capable of integrating into its symbolic, axiological universe a gender concept with a sacred dimension. This opens up the possibility of a radical change in the construction of male/female relationships according to the principles of Goddess Spirituality.

## Notes

[1] Whereas the chapter as a whole is the result of collaboration, the first two sections can be attributed to Stefania Palmisano and the third and fourth sections Roberta Pibiri. The conclusions are a joint effort.

[2] Roberta Pibiri carried out comparative ethnography about transformation processes of the self and the part played by emotions, which was published in her 2016 PhD thesis entitled '*Visita Interiora Terrae*. Religious Experience, Emotions and Transformation of the Self. Zen Sōto and Goddess Spirituality: a comparative ethnography'.

[3] Even though it seems that Italians are now more interested in spirituality than they were in the past, recent data (Palmisano 2014, 2016) do not lead to the conclusion that Italian Catholicism is giving way to unconventional spirituality.

Palmisano's statistical analysis details the percentages of Italians claiming to be 'religious' and/or 'spiritual' and confirms considerable overlapping between the two groups; this proves that in Italian popular consciousness, religion and spirituality are not two different, incompatible worlds. The data gleaned do not portray a spiritual revolution: in Italy, those who have taken part more or less regularly in non-mainstream religious activities (for example meditation, yoga or zen sessions, seminars on New Religious Movements or New Age) are a limited sector of the population.

4   The European Values Study is a survey programme on human values. It provides insights into the ideas, beliefs, preferences, attitudes, values and opinions of citizens all over Europe.

5   This reflection is based on the Italian Youth Religion Survey (Garelli, 2016), an analysis of young 'Millennials' (18–29-year-old youths) throughout the peninsula.

6   See www.goddesstemple.co.uk.

7   For a review of Luciana Percovich's influential works, see www.universitadelledonne.it

8   See tempiodelladea.org.

## References

Aune, K., Sharma, S. and Vincent G. (eds) (2008) *Women and Religion in the West: Challenging Secularization*, Aldershot: Ashgate.

Berger, P.L. and Luckmann, T. (1966) *The Social Construction of Reality*, New York: Doubleday and Co.

Bernacchi, E. (2016). 'Oltre al Dio Padre: la Spiritualità della Dea come nuova forma di empowerment delle donne?', *AG About Gender-Rivista Internazionale di Studi di Genere*, 5(10).

Berzano, L. and Palmisano, S. (2014) 'Prospettive di genere nella sociologia della religione italiana', in Consiglio Scientifico della Sezione AIS 'Studi di Genere' (eds) *Sotto la lente del Genere: la Sociologia Italiana si racconta*, Milan: FrancoAngeli, pp 119–29.

Bromley, D.G. (ed) (1998) *The Politics of Religious Apostasy. The Role of Apostates in the Transformation of Religious Movements*, Westport, London: Praeger.

Carriero, R. and Todesco, L. (2016) *Indaffarate e soddisfatte. Donne, uomini e lavoro familiare in Italia*, Rome: Carocci.

Cartocci, R. (2011) *Geografia dell'Italia cattolica*, Bologna: Il Mulino.

Crespi, I. (2014), 'Religiosità e differenze di genere in Italia: credenze, pratiche e cambiamenti generazionali', in I. Crespi and E. Ruspini (eds), *Genere e religioni in Italia: voci a confronto*, Milan, FrancoAngeli, pp 83–132.

Crespi, I. and Ruspini, E. (eds) (2014) *Genere e religioni in Italia. Voci a confronto*, Milan: FrancoAngeli.

Daly, M. (1973) *Beyond God the Father. Toward a Philosophy of Women's Liberation*, Boston: Beacon Press.

Donadi, P. (2014) 'Maternità e Virginità. Le due vocazioni femminili nella Mulieris Dignitatem', in I. Crespi and E. Ruspini (eds) *Generi e Religioni in Italia. Voci a confronto*, Milan: FrancoAngeli, pp 67−82.

Eisler, R. (1987) *The Chalice and the Blade: Our History, Our Future* (1st edn), San Francisco: HarperCollins Publishers.

Eurostat (2015) data. Available at: http://ec.europa.eu/eurostat.

Fedele, A. and Knibbe, K. (eds) (2013) *Gender and Power in Contemporary Spirituality: Ethnographic Approach*, New York and London: Routledge.

Fedele, A. and Knibbe, K. (2016) 'From Angel in the Home to Sacred Prostitute: Unconditional Love and Gendered Hierarchies in Contemporary Spirituality', in L. Gemzöe L., M-L. Keinänen and A. Maddrell (eds) *Contemporary Encounters in Gender and Religion: European Perspectives*, New York: Palgrave Macmillan, pp 195−216.

Garelli, F. (ed) (2014) *Religion Italian Style*, Aldershot: Ashgate.

Garelli, F. (2016) *Piccoli atei crescono. Davvero una generazione senza Dio?*, Bologna: Il Mulino.

Garelli, F., Guizzardi, G. and Pace, E. (2003) *Un singolare pluralismo*, Bologna: Il Mulino.

Gimbutas, M. (1989) *The Language of the Goddess*, San Francisco: Harper and Row.

Gimbutas, M. (1991) *The Civilisation of the Goddess*, San Francisco: Harper San Francisco.

Giordan, G. (2006) *Tra religione e spiritualità. Il rapporto con il sacro nell'epoca del pluralismo*, Milan: FrancoAngeli.

Giorgi, A. and Palmisano, S. (eds) (2016) *D come Donne, D come Dio*, Milan-Udine: Mimesis Edizioni.

Goldenberg, N. (1979) *Changing of the Gods: Feminism and the End of Traditional Religions*, Boston: Beacon Press.

Greenstein, T.N. (2009) 'National Context, Family Satisfaction, and Fairness in the Division of Household Labor', *Journal of Marriage and Family*, 71(4), pp 1039−51.

Harrington, M.J. (2007) 'Paganism and the New Age', in Kemp, D. and Lewis, J.R. (eds) *Handbook of New Age*, Boston: Brill.

Heelas, P. and Woodhead, L. (2005) *The Spiritual Revolution: Why Religion Is Giving Way to Spirituality*, Malden and Oxford: Blackwell Publishing.

Hervieu-Léger, D. (2003) *Il pellegrino e il convertito. La religione in movimento*, Bologna: Il Mulino.

Houtman, D. and Aupers, S. (2008) 'The Spiritual Revolution and the New Age Gender Puzzle: the Sacralization of the Self in the Late Modernity (1980–2000)', in K. Aune, S. Sharma and G. Vincent (eds) *Women and Religion in the West: Challenging Secularization*, Aldershot: Ashgate, pp 114–33.

Houtman, D. and Mascini, P. (2002) 'Why Do Churches Become Empty, while New Age Grows? Secularization and Religious Change in the Netherlands, *Journal for the Scientific Study of Religion*, 41(3), pp 455–73.

Lenoir, F. (2005) *Le metamorfosi di Dio. La nuova spiritualità occidentale*, Milan: Garzanti.

Marconi, M. (1939) *Riflessi mediterranei nella più antica religione laziale*, Milano: Giuseppe Principat.

Matteo, A. (2012) *La fuga delle quarantenni. Il difficile rapporto delle donne con la Chiesa*, Soveria Mannelli: Rubettino.

Matteo, A. (2014) 'Donne, giovani ed esperienze di fede', in I. Crespi and E. Ruspini (eds), *Genere e religioni in Italia: voci a confronto*, Milan, FrancoAngeli, pp 83–132.

Palmisano, S. (2014) 'The God of the Small Things: Between Catholicism and Alternative Spirituality', in F. Garelli (ed) *Religion Italian Style*, Aldershot: Ashgate, pp 115–39.

Palmisano, S. (2016) 'La spiritualità del dio personale', in F. Garelli (ed) *Piccoli atei crescono. Davvero una generazione senza Dio?*, Bologna: Il Mulino, pp 169–200.

Partridge, C. (2004) *The Re-enchantment of the West. Alternative Spiritualities, Sacralization, Popular Culture, and Occulture* (Vols 1–2), London: T&T Clark International.

Pibiri, R. (2016) 'Genere e religione: la costruzione del femminile nella Spiritualità della Dea in Italia', in A. Giorgi and S. Palmisano (eds) *D come Donne, D come Dio*, Milan-Udine: Mimesis Edizioni, pp 79–97.

Pizza, M. and Lewis, J.R. (eds) (2009) *Handbook of Contemporary Paganism*, Leiden-Boston: Brill.

Plantenga, J., Remery, C., Figuiredo, H. and Smith, M. (2009) 'Towards a European Union Gender Equality Index', *Journal of European Social Policy*, 19(1), pp 19–33.

Rountree, K. (2004) *Embracing the Witch and the Goddess. Feminist Ritual-Makers in New Zealand*, New York and London: Routledge.

Ruether, R.R. (1983) *Sexism and God-Talk: Toward a Feminist Theology*, Boston: Beacon Press.

Schussler-Fiorenza, E. (2013) *Changing Horizons: Explorations in Feminist Interpretation*, Minneapolis: Fortress Press.

Segatti, P. and Brunelli, G. (2010) 'L'Italia religiosa. Da cattolica a generalmente cristiana', *Il Regno*, 10, pp 337–51.

Sointu, E. and Woodhead, L. (2008) 'Spirituality, Gender, and Expressive Selfhood', *Journal for the Scientific Study of Religion*, 47(2), pp 259–76.

Stone, M. (1976) *When God Was a Woman*, New York: Dial Press.

Trzebiatowska, M. and Bruce, S. (2012) *Why Are Women More Religious than Men?*, Oxford: Oxford University Press.

Turner, V.W. (1982) *From Ritual to Theatre: The Human Seriousness of Play*, New York: PAJ Publications.

Turner, V.W. (1986) *The Anthropology of Performance*, New York: PAJ Publications.

Woodhead, L. (2007) 'Why so Many Women in Holistic Spirituality? A Puzzle Revisited', in K.Flanagan and J. Jupp (eds) *The Sociology of Spirituality*, Aldershot: Ashgate, pp 115–125.

Woodhead L. (2008) 'Gender Differences in Religious Practices and Significance', in J. Beckford and N.J. Demerath III (eds) *The SAGE Handbook of the Sociology of Religion*, Los Angeles: SAGE, pp 566–86.

# ELEVEN

# Explorations of spiritual embodiment in belly dance

*Angela M. Moe*

## Introduction

Belly dance[1] is a largely misunderstood form of movement, highly stereotyped as a derogatory and exploitive display of the female body. However, as a product of eclectic cultural histories, belly dance represents an amalgamation of dance genres that have been practised for millennia across the Middle East and North Africa. Its origins can be traced back several thousands of years, with contemporary iterations of the dance representing only a fraction of the means with which it has been utilized within public and private life. The global West, including various European nations and the US, has had a palpable influence on public perceptions of belly dance (Shay and Sellers-Young, 2005).

Interestingly, a vibrant subculture of belly dancers has developed in recent years, particularly in the US. This chapter examines how US belly dancers view the practice as a spiritual endeavour, particularly in light of the negative perceptions surrounding it. I discuss findings from a decade-long ethnographic study (2003–13) involving several data collection methods: observations, journal entries, online statements and qualitative interviews. The long-term and multi-method approach of this work was necessary due to the lack of research on this topic and the complexity involved in understanding it.

Findings suggest that belly dance holds much potential as an embodied spiritual practice, particularly when premised on holistic health (integration of body, mind and spirit). As such, the chapter contributes to this critical examination of women's spirituality within contemporary contexts. I take an interdisciplinary approach, bridging sociology of the body, religion, and holistic health, in examining how women construct their identities, carve out spiritual space, and reclaim their ability to control and cultivate spiritual practices through a dance form that remains adaptive and relatively uncodified. I begin with an introduction to belly dance, followed by a literature review on holistic health and spirituality. I then review the methods used in this research and discuss my findings along four themes: spiritual practice, creative connection, energy flow, and groundedness. I conclude with a summary of findings and contributions to existing scholarship on belly dance as spiritual embodiment.

## Literature review

Archaeological evidence from ancient Egypt and neighbouring lands along the eastern Mediterranean Sea suggest that components of what we know as belly dance today predate the Abrahamic religions, being central to many of the region's diverse cultures since at least 3400 BCE. Temple drawings, pottery, stone sculptures, bone carvings, and other artefacts found throughout the region suggest that a variety of belly dance movements played meaningful roles in ancient rituals, celebrations, and a variety of daily activities (Knapp, 1981). Specifically, forms of belly dance were likely to have been used by both women and men in tribal rituals aimed at creating good communal energy, as well as warding off or appeasing various spirits or deities. Dance may have been used in ceremonies designed to bring about ample rain and sun, eradicate plant-destroying insects and disease, and produce bountiful harvests. It likely also played important roles in holiday celebrations, courtship practices, marriage ceremonies, sex education, birthing support, and funeral rites (Dox, 2005; Knapp, 1981; Stewart, 2000).

While a rich and diverse history surrounds belly dance, it is viewed quite narrowly today due to misconceptions arising from a variety of sources related to colonial expansion, tourism and globalization. While space constraints prohibit a thorough review, suffice it to say these factors have developed over the last several hundred years and cumulatively represent gendered commodification and objectification of female performers in the Middle Eastern region, and elsewhere. Such influences have worked to place female performers under heavy scrutiny as well as legal and social ostracism (Dougherty, 2005; MacMaster and Lewis, 1998).

For example, women in orientalist writings and paintings were often depicted as voluptuous, semi-nude, and sexually inviting objects within harems or slave markets (Alloula, 1986). It is well known that Ottoman harems were highly secretive, with their members completely sequestered from public view, and that women were trafficked against their will from colonized outposts. Such sexualized imagery contributed to the exoticism associated with the Middle East, a region becoming increasingly controlled by European powers

(Carlton, 1994; MacMaster and Lewis, 1998). Indeed, throughout the colonial period of North Africa, female entertainers were paid quite modestly for their dancing. Many submitted to requests, or threats, to converse with patrons, perform striptease, dance nude, and prostitute (van Nieuwkerk, 1995). Such expectations were well entrenched in the minds of tourists, businessmen, and military personnel, due in part to orientalist travelogues produced by the likes of Gustave Flaubert (Carlton, 1994; MacMaster and Lewis, 1998).

Greater credence was given to these conceptions of women through various public spectacles in the late 1800s and early 1900s. As a marketing ploy, North African 'dancing girls' were brought to the 1893 World Columbian Exposition (Chicago World's Fair) to perform a 'hootchy kootchy' dance, which quickly became notorious and economically lucrative for the fair's promoters. During the same period, Oscar Wilde published *Salome*, which took much artistic liberty with the biblically documented seduction of King Herod by his step-daughter's 'dance of the seven veils'. The play was quickly adapted to opera by Richard Strauss and reached European audiences with actresses such as Maud Allan playing the seductress turned *femme fatale* (Carlton, 1994). Belly dancing soon spread to various amusement parks such as New York's Coney Island, as well as burlesque theatres, travelling circuses, and vaudeville shows (Carlton, 1994). The fascination with the Middle East, its women and their dancing infiltrated the emerging cinematic industry as well, with over 200 films being shot on location in North Africa in the early 1900s. Scenes portraying music and dance were commonplace, with performers often playing the roles of seductresses, home wreckers, tricksters, villains, prostitutes or harem slaves (Dougherty, 2005; MacMaster and Lewis, 1998). It is not surprising then that belly dance is negatively viewed as an erotic and subjugating form of entertainment – certainly not a medium for spiritual expression.

Involvement by Western, particularly US, women began in earnest within urban centres in the 1960s and 1970s, following significant Middle Eastern immigration, which included a market for live Arabic music and evening entertainment. With few skilled dancers available for these venues, women artists from other genres infiltrated the scene. Demand and popularity grew, eventually giving rise to an industry of music and dance instruction to the lay public. Belly dancing has been on the rise since (Amaya Productions, 2010). Despite such popularity, however, academic studies of belly dance have been relatively scant until the last decade. Research indicates that women find myriad benefits to belly dancing, including greater confidence, body acceptance, physical fitness, and spirituality (Jorgensen, 2012; Kraus, 2014; Bock and Borland, 2011; Moe, 2012). Belly dance is also viewed as an outlet for social support and community building (Moe, 2014). These benefits are often associated directly with the level of freedom and autonomy allowed within the genre (Bock and Borland, 2011) and hold regardless of one's background, experience, skill level or health status (Moe, 2012).

As such there is much to explore regarding the physical, mental and spiritual benefits of belly dance. An appropriate lens through which to do so involves holistic health, which refers to an integrated paradigm for wellness, conceptualized broadly to include all forms of physical, mental and spiritual well-being. Holism dictates that good health is maintained through a balanced and integrated self, and dance is well established as a conduit for fusing body, mind and spirit (Halprin, 2000; Robison and Carrier, 2004). A broad conceptualization of spirituality is helpful when framing belly dance as a holistic practice, given the possibility that spiritual experiences may occur within activities that do not appear to be spiritual on their surface (McGuire, 2007). Thus, spirituality is defined broadly as any means in which 'individuals seek and express meaning and purpose and the way they experience their connectedness to the moment, to self, to others, to nature, and to the significant or sacred' (Puchalski et al, 2009, p 887).

## Methodology

I began belly dancing in 2003 as a hobby, but as a sociologist specializing in gender, it quickly became clear that this dance appealed to an array of women, regardless of age, ability, ethnicity, vocation, religion and so on. Indeed, there appeared to be much more to the genre than stereotypes allowed. Thus, following Sklar's (1991, p 6) guidelines for conducting dance ethnography, I relied on several data collection efforts so as to examine belly dance within its 'contextual web of social relationships, environment, religion, aesthetics, politics, economics, and history' (p 6). This methodological approach allowed me not only to position belly dance within a larger cultural context, but also to broaden the lens through which the experiences of contemporary belly dancers may be examined.

I began recording my observations within the local belly dance community within a few months of starting classes. These observations expanded to national and international educational lectures, technique and choreography workshops, as well as live performances (as both audience member and performer). I documented over 1,000 hours; the first 300 hours were analysed via an 'open' (unstructured) format, followed by code condensing and thematic identification. These early thematic patterns formed the basis of additional data collection, informing my decisions on what types of data to collect, when and from whom. Subsequent observations were used more contextually throughout the study, by providing additional explanation to experiences and perceptions shared by participants.

A second stage of data collection occurred between 2006 and 2007, when I recruited women to journal about why they belly dance. Recruitment occurred in person through verbal and written announcements at various belly dance events primarily through the Midwestern US. Approximately 500 belly dancers were reached through these efforts, 150 showed interest in participating, and 18 eventually did participate. They were given little direction about when, how often and in what format they could journal. I simply asked them to spend some time over the course of a few weeks recording their responses to the question 'Why do you belly dance?' The intent was to allow them flexibility in describing and interpreting their experiences. Fifty-four journal entries were submitted through electronic word processing documents, hand written notes and audio-recordings, ranging in length from a few sentences to 10 pages of transcribed text. These were coded through an 'open' (unstructured) format, followed by a condensing of codes and thematic identification. Through continued analysis of these journals, along with the observations, four themes emerged that have shown to be consistent throughout the ethnography: healing, sisterhood, empowerment and spirituality.

During the same period of time, 160 online statements were collected from women on two popular US-based discussion boards offered through bellydance.tribe.net (a popular social networking venue for dancers prior to Facebook). I focused these efforts on long discussion threads related to why women belly dance. These included 'What's your interest?' (bellydance.tribe.net), 'Why do you dance?' (yogaandtheindigo.tribe.net), and 'Body image in bellydance' (bellydance.tribe.net). The above referenced themes were used as a loose guide in analysing these posts. While I have remained open to additional or different thematic categories, they remained the best means of making sense of the data. Such confirmation of the main thematic categories provided an element of methodological and analytical triangulation.

The final stage of data collection involved 67 qualitative, semi-structured interviews with US belly dancers from 2009 to 2011. Recruitment occurred through snowball and convenience sampling, beginning with informants known to me, and aided by electronic postings advertising the research over listservs, Facebook pages and websites. I reached a fairly diverse sample representing all regions of the US. Seventeen were in their 20s, 13 were in their 30s, 21 in their 40s, 11 in their 50s, and 5 were over 60. They were mostly white, with 3 identifying as Latina, 3 as Native American, 2 as black, and 2 as Asian. Six identified as also having Middle Eastern ancestry. The majority were also married or otherwise in committed relationships, and all but two indicated being heterosexual.

The interviews occurred in person and by phone, depending on the preferences and location of participants. Phone interviews were most common, as they provided greater convenience for the participants. They were also more cost-effective, enabling me to generate a more diverse sample from around the country than would otherwise have been possible. They lasted 60–90 minutes and were guided by a list of questions focused on each participant's introduction, background and current status in belly dancing; observed changes (physically, mentally, emotionally, spiritually) that may be credited to belly dancing; and perspectives on the current state of belly dancing. Every participant either self-selected or was assigned a pseudonym. The interview transcripts were analysed similarly to the previous data. The four primary themes were again used as a backdrop, with an open mind towards new ones. These interviews were helpful in confirming and fleshing out the nuances within these overarching themes, such that each now contains several subthemes that have given rise to a variety of additional, more focused, analyses. The following sections represent the subthemes for spirituality.

## Spiritual practice

The women represented an array of religious and spiritual identifications, including major monotheistic and polytheistic world religions as well as pagan, earth-based and unlabelled spiritualities. The ways in which these identifiers are reconciled with, enhanced by, and/or incorporated into creative movement, as well as into larger conceptions of health, provide insight into the various meanings women place on belly dance. Some, for instance, viewed belly dance as an extension of their spiritual expression. This was most salient for those who adhered to an established faith or religious institution. As Emma described, "Belly dancing is very spiritual. It's like moving meditation. There's a certain type of wholeness that I don't get anywhere else except for in Mosque, or during the mid-summer festival." While Emma identified as Muslim as well as pagan and a practitioner of Eastern meditation, these distinct belief systems worked together for her. They, along with belly dancing, encompassed an integrated and embodied sense of spirituality.

Others found that belly dance was in and of itself a spiritual practice. These women did not subscribe to a specific spiritual identity. For them, belly dance just felt good, and such feelings were associated with spiritual expression. Alisha explained, "I don't consider myself to be or want to be connected to organized religion and so I didn't really know how else to be spiritual, but dance helps me connect spiritually." For many of these women, belly dancing filled a void, particularly when they had not felt comfortable with established religious practices. Samantha noted, "Religious or spiritual communities where you're supposed to get that satisfaction or happiness, or whatever, that people seek … I feel like I have that with belly dancing."

Women also described the feminine nature of belly dance as facilitative of spiritual practice. There is a common saying among belly dancers, which Zaheen shared, that "This dance was created by women for women." The belief that belly dance is, at its core, woman based is very important to many practitioners. It connotes greater authenticity, ownership and pride in the dance form. Jeela explained, "I am rooting myself back to something that women have done for hundreds of years, something that has felt wonderful to their bodies, looks wonderful, shares the joy with their friends, family, husbands and lovers." Subsequently, it was not surprising to see amorphous references to goddesses. These were stated as reverence to Mother Earth, specific deities or the divine feminine in all women. For example, Emily stated, "I dance in homage to the Dakinis, goddess mothers and grandmothers who have danced before."

The theme of spiritual practice, then, concerns the means through which women find deeper, enhanced or newly found spirituality through belly dance. In some scenarios, belly dance complements and reinforces spiritual identities; in others, it supplants or replaces them. The specific feminine history surrounding the dance was central to these feelings. Regardless of how the women fit the spiritual component of belly dance into their belief systems, the common thread for all was that belly dance felt nourishing, supportive and right. In this way, belly dance supports a self-defined and holistic sense of spiritual practice.

## Creative connection

Many women described belly dance as a means through which to experience a deeper spiritual connection to others around them. There is a strong sense of community among belly dancers. Since the majority of belly dance classes and workshops are made up exclusively of women, this is often referenced as a 'sisterhood' (Moe, 2014). As Aoise noted, "Belly dancing is one of the few places I go that is all women. Even though I don't know anyone as an individual, it makes me feel as if I belong." Dancing before and with one another facilitated a social and emotional connection based on mutual understanding and appreciation. Abby described, "There's this connection to the other women that I really enjoy. I have met so many good friends. We support one another."

This sense of community was directly related to spirituality. As Caroline put it, "Just the quality of our emotional life ... what we can do for others and ways that we can improve our own lives and those of our neighbors. To lift us up to new levels. If that's spirituality, I'm totally into it." Many distinctly remembered moments when they felt they made meaningful connections to others. While many of these connections were to other dancers, some women felt like they had connected to spectators as well. Elissa explained, "There have been a few times when I've felt like all of a sudden it just connected. Like a few of those watching and I have just shared little bits of ourselves without having to say anything."

Some participants noted particular genres of belly dance where community identification, with other dancers as well as audience members, is more salient. ATS (American Tribal Style), an eclectic form of belly dance created specifically within the US, is based on group improvisation. A silent movement-based ritual, involving hand-arm gestures toward the heavens, one another, the earth, and oneself, precedes all performances. As Piper described it "ATS gives me the feeling of being almost ethereally different when I perform." Though ATS has evolved, it is common to see elements of this ritual included in classes and performances. Such practices seem to serve symbolically, if not literally, as a way of recognizing community. As Alisha stated, "I'm connecting with myself and connecting with other people. Finding the unique parts of myself through dance, but also finding how I'm the same as other women, past, present and future ... uniqueness but also sameness."

In short, creative connection refers to women feeling supported in their spiritual practices vis-à-vis other belly dancers, as well as spectators in some circumstances. Feeling supported and accepted meant a great deal to the women in that they did not always have places or people with whom they could spend time doing something that felt good, positive and affirming. Belly dance held an important quality in their lives, instilling a sense of connection and camaraderie with others. Such social support is a well-accepted precept of holistic health (Robison and Carrier, 2004).

## Energy flow

Spirituality was also found on more of an individual basis, with women feeling a sense of inner peace and joy through belly dance. Such feelings can also be known as 'flow' or a 'high'. The sensation is usually described as a form of euphoria or transcendence of the physical state (Halprin, 2000). As Fiona explained, "We're always connected to our physical world, but even if you're dancing in a room full of people, you can lose yourself in it." Belly dancing can allow a person to move past awareness of her physical self, as well as anyone who may have been watching her. The sense is that one is transcending external awareness, experiencing the event in the most personally gratifying way. Alexandria described this sensation well: "I enter a state of forgetfulness and intensification ... getting to a point where you're not thinking about what you're doing but you're still very much experiencing what you're doing."

Moreover, the benefits of this transcendent state often lasted beyond the physical period of dancing. Otter explained, "That light headed connectivity to another greater consciousness than yours, I feel that for a few days afterwards." As such, the women in this study seemed to link an effervescent quality of belly dancing to spirituality. The more routine and integrated such feelings became, the more easily they seemed to be able to enter the flow state. Such is arguably one of the objectives of spiritual practice – to focus elsewhere than on daily routines and societal norms. Subsequently, this energy flow facilitated personal joy and emotional well-being, and in terms of holistic health, an integration of physical movement with cognitive release, emotional buoyancy and spiritual awareness.

Relatedly, using the energy flow derived through belly dancing was particularly powerful in transcending concern over the (potentially scrutinizing) gaze of observers (Moe, 2015). For example, Martie described spiritual experiences with the dance that helped her to pay less attention to audience members' perceptions and more to her own internal awareness. She explained, "At first I hated the men who'd get all slobbery about it. After some time, something came over me ... I was able to stop time and only hear music as it flowed in and out of me ... then I felt what it's like to be really awake." Given the prevalence of negative stereotypes surrounding belly dance, such internalized awareness was extremely helpful for staying in the moment and appreciative of the range of benefits it offers. As Casmir elaborated, "It's a complete transformation. Your mind is at work on the dance. Your body is at work performing the dance. Your emotions, your soul, and your personality are set free in the dance. You are truly 'you' in that moment."

Thus, energy flow represents the perception of letting go of various expectations and inhibitions, in ways that often foster a transcendent state while dancing. Such experiences are often characterized by joy, bliss and a general happy state. Such positive and self-affirming states of consciousness are also facilitative of holistic wellness.

## Grounding

Grounding, or the process of centring oneself, is a common component of holistic based practices. In order to be fully well, one must feel fully stable – physically, mentally and emotionally (Robison and Carrier, 2004). As such, groundedness provides a sense of security, or a foundation, for one's spirituality. As Tina explained, "The first thing that comes to mind is that it calms me when nothing else can." Lola elaborated, "I don't have a very traditional view of anything spiritual, but if I have one at all it's just that being calmer and at peace is the way to be. It's nice to have something that can take you there, almost on command."

Such positive feelings were even more salient for women who were consciously dealing with 'dis-ease' (Robison and Carrier, 2004), such as illness, injury, personal strife or trauma. Once grounded, the women who embodied spirituality within their dancing were quick to acknowledge holistic integration. Maury stated, "It just makes me feel more grounded. It all works together. Dance takes care of me physically and mentally, and then my spiritual life does better." A particularly salient aspect of groundedness is trauma recovery, particularly due to interpersonal victimization. As Mandy noted: "It is very healing and is helping me deal with past issues. I was molested when I was young and when I dance I connect with something older and motherly, and it feels like I'm getting the biggest hug from all mothers past."

Thus belly dance facilitated a transformative process that was holistic in nature and spiritually relevant in terms of self-awareness and heightened confidence. Further, true embodiment of this integration allowed the spiritual benefits to become omnipresent in the lives of practitioners, like Lisa: "It's a part of who and what I am. I quit dance for a while and I didn't feel right. It's my heart. I can't live without it." Spiritual embodiment in this regard yields general peacefulness and contentment with one's place in the world. This can be especially salient after trauma or other disruptions to the body, mind and spirit.

## Conclusion

This chapter examined the spiritual component of belly dancing, as seen through the perspectives of women in the US who practise it. This work was based on a decade-long mixed-method ethnography, involving observation, online post content analysis, personal journalling and semi-structured interviews. Framed within theoretical constructs of holistic health, I examined how women construct their identities, carve out spiritual space and reclaim their ability to control and cultivate spiritual practices through belly dancing. Findings were presented along four themes: spiritual practice – finding deeper, enhanced, or newly found spirituality; creative connection – feeling supported by others; energy flow – releasing social expectations and inhibitions; and groundedness – finding balance, peacefulness and contentment.

At first glance there may be little about belly dance that could be construed as spiritual, particularly in light of stereotypes of the dance being singularly erotic and sexually demoralizing. However, as discussed, belly dance is heavily steeped in eclectic historical, cultural and spiritual connotations. It makes sense then that on closer examination and in accordance to those who practise it, belly dance holds much potential as an embodied spiritual practice that is premised on holistic integration. While contemporary iterations of belly dance are obviously distinct from its historical lineage, it is possible to connect it to the ways in which women have been able to honour their bodies and express spirituality through movement in various contexts throughout history. Of particular note is that these benefits seem to be related specifically to the level of freedom and creativity allowed in belly dance, as compared to more codified or regulated genres of movement (Bock and Borland, 2011). Indeed, individuals may find spiritual experiences in myriad outlets and contexts when the parameters of what is defined as religious or spiritual are loosened. Thus, practices that do not overtly appear to be spiritual on their surface become so (Stewart, 2000; McGuire, 2007).

This analysis corroborates and expands on findings of previous studies, with concerted attention to the various ways in which belly dancers define, interpret, express and embody their spirituality. Additionally, this chapter adds to a growing body of research on alternative spiritual practices – that is, finding spiritual salience in social contexts that are not traditionally viewed as spiritual in nature. It also suggests that interfaith dialogue and synthesis may occur in ways that strengthen women's spiritual resolve. As such, much can be learned from this work in terms of spiritual growth, and empowerment more generally, for women in the US. Specifically, this work builds on that of Kraus (2014) and Jorgensen (2012) in terms of documenting the various ways spirituality may be conceived through belly dance. Such past work has laid a solid framework for examining belly dance as a means of embodied spirituality, and I have extended this research by drawing specifically from the tenets of holistic health. As an art form that has appealed to women's embodied spirituality for millennia, belly dance is an area ripe for faith-focused analysis. Relying on a holistic health framework is helpful for making sense of how using one's body in a creative process can hold spiritual meaning.

## Note

[1]  This dance has many names depending on the context – 'Middle Eastern', 'Arabic' and 'Oriental' dance are common. Others are regionally and stylistically specific. Despite the misnomer of labelling a dance after a body part, 'belly' dance remains the most common term in the West and is subsequently used throughout this chapter.

## References

Alloula, M. (1986) *The colonial harem*. Minneapolis, MN: University of Minnesota Press.

Amaya, M. (2010) *American belly dance legends* (film), Albuquerque, NM: Amaya Productions.

Bock, S. and Borland, K. (2011) 'Exotic identities', *Journal of Folklore Research*, vol 48, no 1, pp 1–36.

Carlton, D. (1994) *Looking for Little Egypt*. Bloomington, IN: IDD Books.

Crosby, J. (2000) 'The goddess dances', in W. Griffin (ed) *Daughters of the goddess*, Walnut Creek, CA: AltaMira Press, pp 166–82.

Dox, D. (2005) 'Spirit from the body', in A. Shay and B. Sellers-Young (eds) *Belly dance*, Costa Mesa, CA: Mazda, pp 303–40.

Dougherty, R.L. (2005) 'Dance and the dancer in Egyptian film', in A. Shay and B. Sellers-Young (eds) *Belly dance*, Costa Mesa, CA: Mazda, pp 145–71.

Halprin, A. (2000) *Dance as a healing art*, Mendocino, CA: LifeRhythm Books.

Jorgensen, J. (2012) 'Dancing the numinous', *Journal of Ethnology & Folkloristics*, vol 6, no 2, pp 3–28.

Knapp, B.L. (1981) 'Egyptian feasts and dances of earliest times', *Arabesque*, vol 7, no 1, pp 12–14.

Kraus, R. (2014) 'Transforming spirituality in artistic leisure: How the spiritual meaning of belly dance changes over time', *Journal for the Scientific Study of Religion*, vol 53, issue 3, pp 459–78. Available at: http://onlinelibrary.wiley.com/doi/10.1111/jssr.12136/full.

MacMaster, N. and Lewis, T. (1998) 'Orientalism: from unveiling to hyperveiling', *Journal of European Studies*, vol 28, issue 1, pp 121–36.

McGuire, M.G. (2007) 'Embodied practices', in N. Tatom (ed) *Everyday religion*, New York: Oxford University Press, pp 187–200.

Moe, A.M. (2012) 'Beyond the belly: an appraisal of Middle Eastern dance (aka belly dance) as leisure', *Journal of Leisure Research*, vol 44, no 2, pp 201–33.

Moe, A.M. (2014) 'Sequins, sass and sisterhood', *Journal of Women & Aging*, vol 26, issue 1, pp 39–65.

Moe, A.M. (2015) 'Unveiling the gaze', in A. Trier-Bieniek (ed) *Feminist theory and pop culture*. Rotterdam, Netherlands: Sense, pp 1–17.

Puchalski, C.M., Ferrell, B., Virani, R., Otis-Green, S., Baird, P., Bull, J., Chochinov, H., Handzo, G., Nelson-Becker, H., Prince-Paul, M., Pugliese, K. and Sulmasy, D. (2009) 'Improving the quality of spiritual care as a dimension of palliative care', *Journal of Palliative Medicine*, vol 12, no 10, pp 885–904.

Robison, J. and Carrier, K. (2004) *The spirit and science of holistic health*, Bloomington, IN: AuthorHouse.

Shay, A. and Sellers-Young, B. (2005) *Belly dance*, Costa Mesa, CA: Mazda.

Sklar, D. (1991) 'On dance ethnography', *Dance Research Journal*, vol 23, no 1, pp 6–10.

Stewart, I.J. (2000) *Sacred woman, sacred dance*, Rochester, VT: Inner Traditions.

van Nieuwkerk, K. (1995) *A trade like any other*, Austin, TX: University of Texas Press.

# TWELVE

# From exclusion to inclusion: women and interfaith dialogue in the Mediterranean area

*Francesco Antonelli and Elisabetta Ruspini\**

## Introduction: the Mediterranean mosaic

The purpose of this chapter is to discuss women's contribution to interfaith dialogue in the Mediterranean area. The Mediterranean region – usually depicted as both a uniform region and a highly problematic area, where conflicts and migration flows pose considerable risks to the security of the entire region – is a challenge to policy makers and institutions. This can be explained by a combination of *causes discussed in this chapter.*

Even if access to a common sea has led to numerous historical and cultural connections between ancient and contemporary societies around the Mediterranean (we speak of a 'historical region', engaging in trade and sharing in common historical experiences (Giordano, 2012)), the Mediterranean is not a single society. Instead it is a multipolar world; the Mediterranean basin offers a mosaic of societies and cultures that have influenced (and are still influencing) one another (see, for example, Davis, 1977). Today, the Mediterranean region includes millions of people from a number of different cultures who are living in more than 20 different nations (some of which originated very recently) on three continents: Africa, Asia and Europe. The Mediterranean area is thus a complex system.

The Mediterranean area is subject to considerable uncertainties on its future. On the one hand, population growth, combined with the growth of coastal urban centres and the development of tourism, often concentrated in Mediterranean coastal areas, generates multiple environmental pressures (European Environment Agency, 2015).

---

\*    The introduction was written by Elisabetta Ruspini; the second and third sections by Francesco Antonelli; and the fourth section by Elisabetta Ruspini.

The total population of the Mediterranean countries (with coastlines along the Mediterranean sea) grew from 276 million in 1970 to 412 million in 2000 (a 1.35% increase per year) and to 466 million in 2010. The population is predicted to reach 529 million by 2025 (GRID-Arendal, 2013). On the other hand, Mediterranean countries face a long-standing economic, political and social crisis. The region has remarkable dissymmetry in demographic trends as well as in its economic and political development. Even if the area has an abundant concentration of natural resources, Mediterranean economies do not create enough jobs (Jolly, 2011), and the global economic crisis has resulted in high unemployment, particularly for young people and women. Other key challenges the region is facing are conflicts in the Middle East, terrorist threats and unresolved humanitarian and refugee crises. The Mediterranean is located at the heart of a main migration route. Migrants leave Sub-Saharan Africa (Cameroon, Eritrea, Ethiopia, Gambia, Guinea, Ivory Coast, Mali, Nigeria, Senegal, Somalia, Sudan (UNHCR, 2016)) and head to North African ports on the Mediterranean. These challenges, along with other complex factors, have pushed some young people in the region, particularly young men, towards radicalization.[1]

However, the Mediterranean region is not only an area of crisis and conflict, but also a space for opportunities and dialogue. The Mediterranean, a crossroads of peoples and cultures, is characterized by an invaluable natural and human capital. Overcoming pessimism and developing a positive agenda for the region is today a priority (Istituto per gli Studi di Politica Internazionale, 2016); a different future could exist for the Mediterranean. Interreligious dialogue is a powerful tool for achieving peace and stability at a time of increasing geopolitical tension. The Mediterranean region needs intercultural and interfaith institutions and actors to confront growing challenges. Indeed, institutions for intercultural dialogue and cooperation, religious representatives and interfaith organizations are today working together to build mutual understanding in the region. What is the role played by Mediterranean women in this process? Even if women have been objects more often than subjects of interfaith dialogue, they have nevertheless contributed in significant ways to the dialogue, just as dialogue has also contributed to their own self-understanding and empowerment (Cornille and Maxey, 2016), As shown by the findings from the 'Regional Dialogue on Women's Empowerment', launched by the Union for the Mediterranean (UfM)[2] Secretariat in 2015 and 2016, there is an urgent need to invest in the essential contribution of women as a response to the current challenges in the Mediterranean, including inclusive growth, extremism and radicalization, and migration. There is also an urgent need to invest in the contribution that young people can make to the future of the Mediterranean region: in January 2017, the UfM Member States adopted an action-oriented roadmap centred on Mediterranean youth's potential for promoting stability and development.

Starting from this premise, the chapter reviews some aspects of the past and current situation on interreligious dialogue in the Mediterranean area, and tries to identify how women can successfully support this process. Through an exploration of the relevant literature and online documents produced by interfaith meetings, the chapter shows that, today, interreligious dialogue has been changing its nature through a two-fold enlargement centred on the gender dimension, both *vertical* and *horizontal*. On the one hand, this dialogue is characterized by a growing involvement of intellectual women belonging to Christianity, Islam and Judaism; on the other hand, Millennial women (and men) are playing a key role in advancing intercultural and interfaith dialogue. The global, multi-ethnic and interconnected Millennial generation can shape social, economic, political and cultural life, especially with regard to intercultural understanding. Even if, both in the northern and southern Mediterranean, young men and women are often the primary victims of fundamentalism, social instability and extremism, they are also key protagonists in terms of promoting intercultural and interreligious dialogue.

## Interreligious dialogue

One can define interreligious dialogue as a process aiming to make the most intensive communicative relationships between personalities from different religious groups. In addition, people involved in interreligious dialogue refuse both fundamentalism and syncretism. So defined, interreligious dialogue seems to be a *procedural structure* based on an institutional secular framework that safeguards religious freedom without which dialogue would not be possible. Interfaith dialogue development can be divided into distinct stages. During the rise and emergence of industrial society, up to its crisis and its transition to a post-industrial configuration (from the late 19th century up to the 1980s), the main actors of interreligious dialogue were religious actors. This first period of development is composed of two phases (Fitzgerald, 2007; Bertoni, 2009; Pacini, 2011; Swidler, 2013):

1. *The pioneering phase of interreligious congresses.* This phase started in the US from the World's Parliament of Religions (Chicago 1893), the largest among many other congresses in the World's Columbian Exposition (the organizing committee consisted of 16 people from different religious backgrounds), up to the foundation of the 'Compassion Temple' in Washington in 1960. This period was characterized by a weak involvement of institutional religious elites and strong opposition to secularism.

2. *The Vatican Council II* (1962–65). This period was recognized by many non-Christian observers – Jewish groups in particular (Skorka and Stofenmacher, 2000; Alberigo, 2005; Giffin, 2014) – as the official starting point of interreligious dialogue, particularly through declarations on religious freedom (*Dignitas humanae*, 1965) and on dialogue with non-Christian religions, Muslims and Jews (*Nostra aetate*, 1965). Nevertheless these important statements implied quite an openness to modern values (such as tolerance and religious freedom) and during Paul VI's Pontificate (1963–78), interreligious dialogue continued on behalf of the original opposition to modern materialism and secularism (Versace, 2007).

So, the first period in the development of interreligious dialogue is driven by three main orientations: (a) religious mobilization (particularly by Christian churches) as a cultural and social alternative to a secularized world; (b) a feasible reaction against materialist culture; and (c) bolstering solidarity among different religions, against their common 'enemies': materialism and secularism (Antonelli, 2015). Eventually, the main paradox of this first phase of interreligious dialogue is the following: *it is only possible in a secularist frame but it is ultimately aimed against secularism*. This paradox is particularly serious when religious and intellectual elites are the only figures involved. On the one hand, the process was too hierarchical and limited, and one wonders whether it had a real impact on society, due to the exclusion of non-elites. On the other hand, men were traditionally the only participants in dialogue: women were excluded from the discussion. This double form of exclusion – people and women – ignored two key values of modernity (strongly linked with secularism): democracy and gender equality. Against this background, the first phase of interreligious dialogue was a contradiction in terms and it led to a change neither in religious institutions nor in their relationship with the modern social world.

Starting in the early 1970s, interreligious and interfaith dialogue changes its orientation (Bertoni, 2009; Fitzgerald, 2007). The second period of development is characterized by the search for common ground between different religions. Interreligious dialogue becomes *post-secular*[3] through the involvement of new actors and new issues: the legitimization of religions within the public sphere increases, while new interreligious dialogue focuses on peace building and religious freedom – two values completely compatible with the modernity project. This second period is marked by three distinctive changes.

First, the foundation of the NGO 'Religions for Peace' (1970) based in New York, the largest international coalition of representatives from the world's religions, dedicated to promoting peace and advancing effective multi-religious cooperation at global, regional, national and local levels. This NGO serves all continents, representing 90 countries; it networks with the World Council of senior religious leaders while respecting religious differences, common humanity and the influence of peace within every religion. Religions for Peace has created interreligious partnerships to discuss some important issues, such as stopping war, ending poverty and protecting the planet, convening nine World Conferences: Kyoto (1970), Lovanio (1974), Princeton (1979), Nairobi (1984), Melbourne (1989), Riva del Garda (1994), Amman (1999), Kyoto (2006) and Vienna (2013).

Second, the re-organization of the old 'Secretariat for Non-Christians' (launched by Pope Paul VI in 1964) into the 'Pontifical Council for Interreligious Dialogue (PCID)' by Pope John Paul II in 1988, as a dicastery of the Roman Curia and the centre of a wide network. It aims to promote interreligious dialogue with the following responsibilities: (1) to promote mutual understanding, respect and collaboration between Catholics and followers of others religious traditions; (2) to encourage the study of religions; and (3) to promote the formation of groups dedicated to dialogue. However, dialogue is often carried out at local level by individual churches, many of which are supported by regional or national dialogue commissions. The PCID works closely to support these commissions and encourages their formation in areas where they do not yet exist.

Third, the involvement and mobilization of political elites and civil institutions, developing a parallel and sometimes convergent interreligious dialogue through dedicated institutions, such as:

1. *The European Union (EU)*. Within the Treaty of Lisbon (article 17) – aimed at reforming the functioning of the EU following the two waves of enlargement which have taken place since 2004 – the EU introduced, for the first time, a legal basis for regular, open and transparent dialogue between EU institutions and churches, religious associations, and philosophical and non-confessional organizations.

The EU institutions have implemented dialogue sessions with representatives of religious organizations, notably COMECE (the EU Catholic bishops' conference), the Council of European Churches (CEC – including Protestant, Anglican, Orthodox and Old Catholic Churches), Muslim communities, the European Jewish Congress and also Hindu, Sikh and Mormon associations. Philosophical and non-confessional organizations participating in the process include Humanist organizations based on the secular neutrality of the public sphere, Freemasons, and free thought, ethical or adogmatic organizations.

2. *The already cited UfM, an intergovernmental organization bringing together all 28 EU Member States and 15 countries from the southern and eastern shores of the Mediterranean.* It provides a unique forum to enhance regional cooperation and dialogue in the Euro-Mediterranean region. In this context, UfM arranged an important international conference in Barcelona in 2015, with 80 representatives from institutions for intercultural dialogue and cooperation, interfaith organizations, religious authorities and prominent public personalities.

3. *The International Dialogue Center KAICIID (King Abdullah Bin Abdulaziz International Centre for Interreligious and Intercultural Dialogue).* It is an intergovernmental organization that promotes interreligious dialogue to prevent and resolve conflict. KAICIID was founded in 2012 by the Kingdom of Saudi Arabia, the Republic of Austria and the Kingdom of Spain. Its mission is to promote peace, tolerance and understanding among people of different faiths and cultures. KAICIID's work includes using dialogue to support peace building and social cohesion efforts in conflict areas. Crucially, KAICIID seeks to promote human rights, justice, peace and reconciliation, as well as curbing the abuse of religion as a means of justifying oppression, violence and conflict. It promotes the preservation and sacredness of holy sites, as well as respect for religious symbols, and focuses on issues pertaining to the dignity of human life and religious education.

The complex system of the post-secularist interreligious dialogue is the background for *women's involvement.*

## Women and contemporary interreligious dialogue

If Religions for Peace has recognized the fundamental role of women for a successful interreligious dialogue since 1970, it is only since the

1990s that women have increasingly and actively been engaged in interreligious dialogue groups of all kinds and in different places: this trend is linked to the emergence of new institutions of post-secular dialogue, such as the UfM and KAICIID. This renewed role is primarily based on two elements: first, new religious citizenship claims coming from some churches – particularly the Catholic Church – influenced by modern secular culture but, at the same time, with an institutional structure based on the exclusion of women (Berzano, Naso and Nuevo, 2016); and second, the fact that Middle Eastern and/or North African women's issues have gained greater visibility, especially since 11 September 2001. A number of issues included in contemporary interreligious dialogue focus on women's roles, women's rights and on the contribution and the integration of women in religious discourse and practices in different cultural contexts. As Ilaria Morali, consultant to the PCID-Pontifical Council for Interreligious Dialogue, has written:

> 'One time, during an interreligious meeting, I pointed out to the people who were present – all belonging to different religious élites – that religious leaders were all men and the conflicts among religions are very often caused by men ... They fell silent. In compensation I saw my Muslim colleague sitting in front of me, sending me a hug with an extraordinary smile and a thumbs up.'[4]

Women's contribution to interreligious dialogue is a multidimensional process that should not be limited to 'feminine' issues. Two key points emerged from our analysis based on a literature review (Taricone, 1998; Allievi, 2002; Sogni, 2009; Canta, 2014) and on a document analysis:[5]

1. *Female social actors.* Intellectual women – particularly Catholic and Muslim women – are the main social actors within the process of interreligious dialogue, an element connected to the historical exclusion of women from clerical roles within these religions. Using Enrica Tedeschi's (2014) typology in order to distinguish different female religious involvement, we can argue that *religious feminists* are actually the main promoters of interreligious dialogue among women. According to Tedeschi's typology we can define religious feminists as 'religious women who go against chauvinist power in traditional religions. They think women must gain increased recognition within religious institutions through an autonomous and very frequently gender oriented hermeneutic on the holy books'

(Tedeschi, 2014, p 92). However, their common aim is combined with different positions, such as the distance between religious feminists relating to different religions, particularly on issues related to female sexuality or the body. Issues link not only to different religious identities, but also to their social and cultural background. In the West, there are no doubts about the tension between secular feminists and religious feminists, as well as a stronger process that has happened in North African or contemporary Arabic societies characterized now by the re-traditionalization and re-Islamization of culture.

2. *Subjective orientations.* Post-secularism is the background of contemporary interreligious dialogue among women. This kind of dialogue does not just have a political external goal like the 'old' interreligious dialogue used to have. It aims to mobilize *critical resources* between and within traditional religions.

As Chiara Canta argues: 'The role of women within religion is a problem for many religions. Twenty years ago, during a UN Conference in Beijing in 1995, many people underlined a widespread presence of prejudice within all religious cultures. We often talk about Islamic fundamentalism but it appears in all countries' (Canta, 2014, p 231). According to this point of view, traditional theory on the complementarity between men and women in society – one of the most popular doctrines within traditional monotheistic religions – tends to be criticized on the basis of solidarity among women claiming substantial and symbolic equality. The focus is on women, on their role and 'natural' attitudes. Therefore, the inclusion of gender within interreligious dialogue mobilizes both cohesive and opposing dynamics. Women belonging to different religions share opposition to patriarchal power within religious institutions, but at the same time, positions about 'what to do' and 'how to do' are, in general, very different.

Nevertheless, this elitist dialogue involving intellectual women does not exhaust the whole field of interreligious dialogue in a post-secular frame, between gender and generation. In fact, if we see interreligious dialogue in a wider perspective, it re-mobilizes the public and social potential of religious issues among social actors. An intrinsic tension between a traditional authority value – coextensive at every traditional religious institution – and a disintermediation of the faith appears, involving civil society. When issues linked to religious identity as public identity, in a multi-ethnic society, are subject to public discourse, commented on on social networks, and lived in everyday life, are we not witnessing widespread interreligious dialogue?

Among several xenophobic discourses and much prejudice, interreligious questions in civil society do not open space for a new knowledge of the Other. In this framework, the woman's body is often the battlefield between opposing tendencies: on one side a normalization tendency, on the other the claim of subjectivity. Opposing views on the *affaire burkini* are a clear example of this. The *affaire* exploded in France during summer 2016: it is based on the ban of particular swimwear for Islamic women. The first city to announce such a prohibition was Cannes, where mayor David Lisnard said he wanted to prohibit 'beachwear ostentatiously showing a religious affiliation while France and places of religious significance are the target of terror attacks' to avoid 'trouble to public order'.[6] Several French cities – such as Villeneuve-Loubet, Lyon, Nice – followed the example of Cannes.

Within the debate on the *affaire*, two processes were at work. On the one hand, a normalization process based on a traditional Islamic background, with the prohibition of showing female nudity. On the other hand, a secularist normalization process grounded on Western common sense: it forbids religious normativity on behalf of the contemporary body aesthetic, with the aim of safeguarding women's interests, through a top-down approach. Both of these perspectives relegate women's subjectivities, their freedom to choose whether or not to wear the burkini (self-normativity). The public debate following this issue – vehiculated by both social networks and not only by mass media across Europe – raised two questions by Alain Touraine, put at the core of his reflection on Islam and emancipation:

> Muslim women living in a Western society like France, are a resistance nucleus against feminist achievements or, on the contrary, are they involving themselves within the same general emancipation movement? Maybe these women also represent a complex matching between different and opposing attitudes, a thing that could pull them to show a double ambivalence, on the one side towards their native culture and, on the other, to the society where they live? (Touraine, 2009, p 159)

The rise of these questions within a European public sphere produces a widespread dialogic potential. When one takes a position pro or against, arguing about it with another person, a wider reflexivity is active. As we will shortly see, new technologies, social networks and Web 2.0 offer a platform for confrontation.

## Millennials and interfaith dialogue

Alternative spaces in which women can be agents of peacemaking and peacebuilding are growing. Media technology has had a great impact on how to promote interreligious dialogue and Millennial women (and men) are, for various reasons, key participants in this process.

The term 'Millennials' defines people that reached adulthood at around the turn of the twenty-first century, women and men born in the 1980s and 1990s. The Millennial generation is not only large (around 1.8 billion young people across the globe); Millennials are also different in many ways from earlier generations. Even if it is not easy to define a whole generation, previous research highlights interesting trends (see, for example, Howe and Strauss, 2000; Greenberg and Weber, 2008; Taylor and Keeter, 2010; Rainer and Rainer, 2011).

Globally, the Millennial generation is the most educated, informed, and interconnected generation to date (see, for example, Weinbaum, Girven and Oberholtzer, 2016). Millennials are skilled in technology (they grew up with Web 2.0 technologies) and are able to multi-task. Learning online is 'natural' to them – as much as retrieving and resourcefully creating information on the Internet, blogging, communicating on cell phones, downloading files to iPods and instant messaging. Social networks are an extraordinarily important part of Millennials' lives. Millennials are also the most culturally, ethnically and racially diverse generation in history. They are more tolerant than other generations and much more open to change: the technology of this generation sustains friendship with people of other cultures and traditions. Millennials are more accepting than older generations of new family arrangements and care about gender equality. Unlike the generation before them, a large number of Millennials have had working mothers as well as fathers who helped at home, and even those in more traditional families get the message that equality is possible and important. The aspirations of Millennial-generation women are upsetting traditional gender roles, not only in the workplace, but at home as well. Millennial men and fathers are also more involved and egalitarian than men/fathers of previous generations. They are a highly social generation: most Millennials like working in groups and prefer a sense of unity and collaboration over division and competition. The economic and financial crisis of the last decade has deeply affected this generation and its lifestyle: Millennials prefer to make sustainable choices, to support socially responsible brands, to live experiences instead of materiality, and are attentive to shared-economy activities (Ruspini and Bernardi, 2018). As far as religion is concerned,

Millennials are much less likely to affiliate with any religious tradition (Pew Research Center, 2010). Millennials are less attached to organized religion than their parents or grandparents were at the same age. The Millennial approach to spirituality seems to be about choosing different 'religious experiences' – for example, meditation, yoga – rather than belonging to an organized congregation. Millennials are not as trusting as older adults when it comes to institutions like the government and Churches.

Multifaceted and multitasking, this generation easily joins social justice causes, and interfaith coalitions that pursue them, through shared online spaces (Stanton, 2013). The Internet has facilitated the creation of transnational, multicultural and multi-religious networks. Following Messina-Dysert and Radford Ruether (2014), in the religious sphere, where women's participation in religious traditions has generally been suppressed because of patriarchy, the digital world has offered tools of liberation, solidarity and empowerment (see also Llewellyn, 2015). The Internet phenomenon of the 'fourth wave' of feminism has provided women (and men) an unprecedented opportunity to communicate their personal viewpoints, to share their stories, to raise issues, to express opinions, to organize and find a platform on a day-to-day basis – regardless of ethnicity, sex, gender, age, disability, national origin, location or religion. As Chittal (2015) notes:

> Social media democratized feminist activism, opening up participation to anyone with a Twitter account and a desire to fight the patriarchy. By removing the barriers of distance and geography, sites like Facebook, Twitter, Tumblr, and Instagram have made activism easier than ever, facilitating public dialogues and creating a platform for awareness and change.

The use of the virtual space has changed significantly in comparison with the way it was used by the 'third-wave' feminism. The boundaries between online and offline have become blurred, creating a continuous stream of information and action (Magaraggia and Ruspini, 2017). The Internet is simultaneously a ground for education, activism and empowerment. As Hinsey states (2013, p 31) it is crucial to "recognize and critically interact with the ways technology is not only enhancing but shaping feminism as we move farther into a new digital age".[7] In an area such as the Mediterranean basin, there is a strong need not only to transmit interfaith knowledge, but also to teach interfaith education both through face-to-face lessons and online spaces as well (Gross,

2010). Some youth platforms and networks have demonstrated positive results in fostering interfaith dialogue, especially among women. A first example is the Euro-Med Youth Platform, which aims to bring NGOs from the European and Mediterranean regions together by assisting them in networking and capacity building, and exchanging best practices. The Euro-Med Youth Platform launched a call in May 2012 for a study on the role of young people in intercultural and interfaith dialogue in the Euro-Mediterranean region. This study stresses the need, from an institutional point of view, to further enhance the role of young people in the promotion of interreligious dialogue in the region (Magkou, 2012). A second example is the Networks of Mediterranean Youth (NET-MED Youth) project, a three-year project (2014–17) implemented by UNESCO and funded by the EU, aimed at providing young women and men (in Israel, Jordan, Lebanon, Libya, Morocco, Palestine and Tunisia) with the necessary skills, tools and capacities to share experiences and knowledge, to create youth networks, to take part in decision making and to develop youth policies that are inclusive, proactive and gender and disability sensitive (NET-MED Youth, 2014–15). The networking capacities of young people and youth organisations will be strengthened, particularly by increasing their interaction with the media and their use of ICTs-based platforms.

## Conclusion

The Mediterranean region is facing growing challenges, including inclusive growth, migration, extremism and radicalization. There is an urgent need to invest in the essential contribution of women belonging to different generations as a response to these current challenges. Interfaith dialogue – as a way to reach stability, to foster collaboration and constructive interactions, to deconstruct gender stereotypes and to support the ability of women from different religious traditions to bond and develop interfaith understanding through their relationships with other women – is creating opportunities and new fields of study. This chapter shows that, today, interreligious dialogue is deeply changing through a two-fold enlargement centred on the gender dimension: *vertical*, by women belonging to intellectual elites; *horizontal*, boosted by the generational shift. It also shows that women can greatly contribute to the expansion and consolidation of this dialogue. The examples discussed are not only significant, but also contribute to the deconstruction of the common assumption that feminism can only emerge and flourish when religion is removed from the public space.

## Notes

[1] Expert Meeting: 'Role of Women and Young People in Promoting Peace and Preventing Violent Extremism in the Euro-Mediterranean Region', organized by the Secretariat of UfM, UNDP and UN Women, Concept Note, 18–19 July 2017, Barcelona: http://rbas-knowledgeplatform.org/Docs/10186/Doc10348.pdf.

[2] UfM is an intergovernmental organization that provides a unique forum to enhance regional cooperation and dialogue in the Euro-Mediterranean region. The UfM Regional Forum is bringing together 500 Mediterranean key stakeholders, including Ministers, official delegations, civil society and private sector representatives, regional stakeholders, international financial institutions and socioeconomic project promoters (http://ufmsecretariat.org/who-we-are/).

[3] Post-secularism can be defined as a sociocultural and institutional configuration where a laic state and an official secularized civil society combine with a religious revival within political and public spheres. In addition, the sacred is more and more individualized (Casanova, 1994; Ferrara, 2009; Habermas, 2015; Berzano, Naso and Nuevo, 2016). If we focus on Europe, as Habermas asserts, there are three main factors at the base of the post-secularist rise: (1) wars and conflicts religiously defined beyond Europe – these events point out both the relativity of secularism in a global world and the need of a laic state as a guarantee for all people (religious and non-religious) that they will not be persecuted because of their faith; (2) political de-ideologization – traditional secular politics cannot guide sociocultural and personal sense, so religious re-ideologization gains ground within public life; and (3) immigration: 'of who, finding a job or asylum, comes from countries with pre-modern cultures' (Habermas, 2015, p 4).

[4] www.theologhia.com/2014/05/punti-fermi-per-il-dialogo.html.

[5] Workshops by the Center for Religious Studies 'Fondazione Collegio San Carlo' (Modena): *Male and Female He Created Them: Religious Elaboration on Gender Differences* (2003–04); the three Conferences 'Women and Monotheistic Religions', Rome 2011 and 2013; the Interreligious Symposium in Rabat 2014.

[6.] http://www.independent.co.uk/news/world/europe/burkini-ban-why-is-france-arresting-muslim-women-for-wearing-full-body-swimwear-and-why-are-people-a7207971.html.

[7] The transformative effectiveness of contemporary forms of activism is highly debated: on the one hand, while social media campaigns have been effective at raising awareness around the issues they are tackling, not all of them have created significant change; offline action is still very important (for example, peaceful protests, demonstrations, rallies and marches). On the other hand, social media can give a voice to those who are otherwise voiceless and people agree on the web's refreshing effect on feminism (see, for example, Hinsey, 2013; Schuster, 2013; Messina-Dysert and Radford Ruether, 2014; Chittal, 2015; Magaraggia and Ruspini, 2017).

## References

Alberigo, G. (2005) *Breve storia del Concilio Vaticano II*, Bologna: Il Mulino.

Allievi, S. (2002) *Donne e religioni. Il valore delle differenze*, Bologna: EMI.

Antonelli, F. (2015) 'Il dialogo interreligioso in un'ottica di genere: primi spunti di riflessione', in M. Miccio (ed) *Le identità affievolite*, Milan: FrancoAngeli.

Bertoni, E. (2009) *Il dialogo interreligioso come fondamento della civiltà*, Turin: Marietti.

Berzano, L., Naso, P. and Nuevo, J.A. (2016) *Futuro e religione*, in F. Corbisiero and E. Ruspini (eds) *Sociologia del Futuro. Studiare la Società del XXI Secolo*, Padua: CEDAM, pp 155–75.

Canta, C.C. (2014) 'Postfazione. Il genere nelle culture religiose' in I. Crespi and E. Ruspini (eds) *Genere e religioni in Italia. Voci a confronto*, Milan: FrancoAngeli, pp 231–36.

Casanova, J. (1994) *Public Religions in the Modern World*, Chicago: University of Chicago Press.

Chittal, N. (2015) *How Social Media is Changing the Feminist Movement*. MSNBC.com, NBCNews Digital. Available at: http://www.msnbc.com/msnbc/how-social-media-changing-the-feminist-movement.

Cornille, C. and Maxey, J. (eds) (2013) *Women and Interreligious Dialogue*, Eugene: Wipf and Stock.

Davis, J. (1977) *People of the Mediterranean: An Essay in Comparative Social Anthropology*, London: Routledge and Kegan Paul.

European Environment Agency (2015) *Mediterranean Sea Region*. Available at: https://www.eea.europa.eu/soer-2015/countries/mediterranean.

Ferrara, A. (ed) (2009) *Religione e politica nella società post-secolare*, Rome: Meltemi.

Fitzgerald, M.L. (2007) *Dialogo interreligioso. Il punto di vista cattolico*, Alba: Edizioni San Paolo.

Giffin, M. (2014) *Christian and Jewish Relations: A Progress Report*, Createspace Independent Pub.

Giordano, C. (2012) 'The Anthropology of Mediterranean Societies', in U. Kockel, M. Nic Craith and J. Frykman (eds) *A Companion to the Anthropology of Europe*, chapter 2, pp 13–31.

Greenberg, E.H. and Weber, K. (2008) *Generation We: How Millennial Youth are Taking over America and Changing our World Forever*, Pachatusan: LLC.

GRID-Arendal (2013) *Population Density and Urban Centres in the Mediterranean Basin*. Available at: https://www.grida.no/resources/5900. Accessed on September 2017.

Gross. Z. (2010) 'Promoting Interfaith Education Through ICT – A Case Study', in K. Engebretson, M. de Souza, G. Durka and L. Gearon (eds) *International Handbook of Inter-religious Education. International Handbooks of Religion and Education*, vol 4, Dordrecht: Springer, pp 377–388.

Habermas, J. (2015) *Verbalizzare il sacro. Sul lascito religioso della filosofia*, Roma-Bari: Laterza.

Hinsey, V. (2013) 'Girls Get Digital: A Critical View of Cyberfeminism', in *On Our Terms*, vol 1, no 1, pp 1–13.

Howe, N. and Strauss, W. (2000) *Millennials Rising: The Next Great Generation,* New York: Vintage Books.

Istituto per gli Studi di Politica Internazionale [ISPI] (2016) *Leaving the Storm Behind: Ideas for a New Mediterranean*, December. Available at: http://www.ispionline.it/node/16023.

Jolly, C, (ed) (2011) *Tomorrow, the Mediterranean. Scenarios and Projections for 2030*, 'Mediterranean 2030' Consortium. Available at: http://www.ipemed.coop/adminIpemed/media/fich_article/1323859454_Tomorrow_the-Mediterranean-2030_eng.pdf.

Llewellyn, D. (2015) *Reading, Feminism, and Spirituality. Troubling the Waves*, Basingstoke/New York: Palgrave Macmillan.

Magaraggia, S. and Ruspini, E. (2017) 'Contemporary Net-Activism: Beyond Gender Dichotomies?' in F. Antonelli (ed) *Net-Activism. How Digital Technologies Have Changed Social Actions*, Rome: RomaTre Press, pp 61–7. Available at: http://www.google.it/url?sa=t&rct=j&q=&esrc=s&source=web&cd=1&ved=0ahUKEwi_9Nvisb LYAhVDyaQKHayDBpoQFggoMAA&url=http%3A%2F%2Fromatrepress.uniroma3.it%2Fojs%2Findex.php%2Fnet%2Farticle%2Fdownload%2F688%2F684&usg=AOvVaw3AcaOEURPoDckhNRVUnsAk.

Magkou, M. (2012) *'Can we talk about this?' Young people Passing from Monologues to Dialogues for the Promotion of Intercultural and Interfaith Dialogue in the Mediterranean, Euro-Med Youth Platform*, Brussels: European Union Programmes Agency. Available at: http://euromedp.eupa.org.mt/wp-content/uploads/sites/4/2014/01/Can_We_Talk_About_This.pdf.

Messina-Dysert, G. and Radford Ruether, R. (2014) *Feminism and Religion in the 21st Century: Technology, Dialogue, and Expanding Borders*, 1st edition, London: Routledge.

NET-MED Youth (2014–15) *Report Summary – Year 1 Achievement*, UNESCO and European Union. Available at: http://www.netmedyouth.org/sites/default/files/upload/files/NET-MED%20Youth_Year%201%20Report%20Summary_0.pdf.

Pacini, A. (2011) *Oltre la divisione. L'intuizione ecumenica e il dialogo interreligioso*, Rome: Edizioni Paoline.

Pew Research Center (2010) *Religion among the Millennials*, 17 February: http://www.pewforum.org/2017/04/05/the-changing-global-religious-landscape/.

Rainer, T. and Rainer, J. (2011) *The Millennials: Connecting to America's Largest Generation*, Nashville: B&H Publishing Group.

Ruspini, E. and Bernardi, M. (forthcoming, 2018) 'Sharing economy e turismo. Il contributo delle nuove generazioni', in G. Nuvolati (ed) *Sviluppo urbano e politiche per la qualità della vita*, Florence: FUP Editore.

Schuster, J. (2013) 'Invisible Feminists? Social Media and Young Women's Political Participation', *Political Science*, vol 65, no 1, pp 8–24.

Sogni, G. (2009) *Donne delle religioni. La scoperta del femminile nelle religioni monoteiste*, Naples: Scritture.

Stanton, J. (2013) 'Boomers and Millennials Compare Interfaith Action', *The Interfaith Observer*, 15 March. Available at: http://www.theinterfaithobserver.org/journal-articles/2013/3/15/boomers-millennials-compare-interfaith-action.html.

Taylor, P. and Keeter, S. (eds) (2010) *Millennials: A Portrait of Generation Next. Confident, Connected, Open to Change*, Washington DC: Pew Research Center.

Taricone, F. (ed) (1998) *Maschio e femmina li creò. L'immagine femminile nelle religioni e nelle scritture*, Rome: Gabrielli Editore.

Tedeschi, E. (2014) *Tra una cultura e l'altra. Lo stato dell'arte nella sociologia interculturale*, Padua: Cleup.

Touraine, A. (2009) *Il mondo è delle donne*, Milan: Il Saggiatore.

Swidler, L. (2013) 'The History of Inter-religious Dialogue', in C. Cornille (ed) *The Wiley-Blackwell Companion to Interreligious Dialogue*, Oxford: John Wiley & Sons, pp 3–19.

UNHCR (2016) *Refugees and Migrants Sea Arrivals in Europe*, Monthly Data Update: December 2016. Available at: https://data2.unhcr.org/ar/documents/download/53447.

Versace, E. (2007) *Montini e l'apertura a sinistra. Il falso mito del Vescovo progressista*, Milan: Guerini e Associati.

Weinbaum, C., Girven, R. and Oberholtzer, J. (2016) The Millennial Generation. Implications for the Intellingence and Policy Communities, Santa Monica: RAND Corporation. Available at: https://www.rand.org/content/dam/rand/pubs/research_reports/RR1300/RR1306/RAND_RR1306.pdf.

# Index

References to figures and tables are in *italics*; references to footnotes have the page number followed by the note number (eg 36n3)